IMAGES
of America

MADAM WALKER THEATRE CENTER

AN INDIANAPOLIS TREASURE

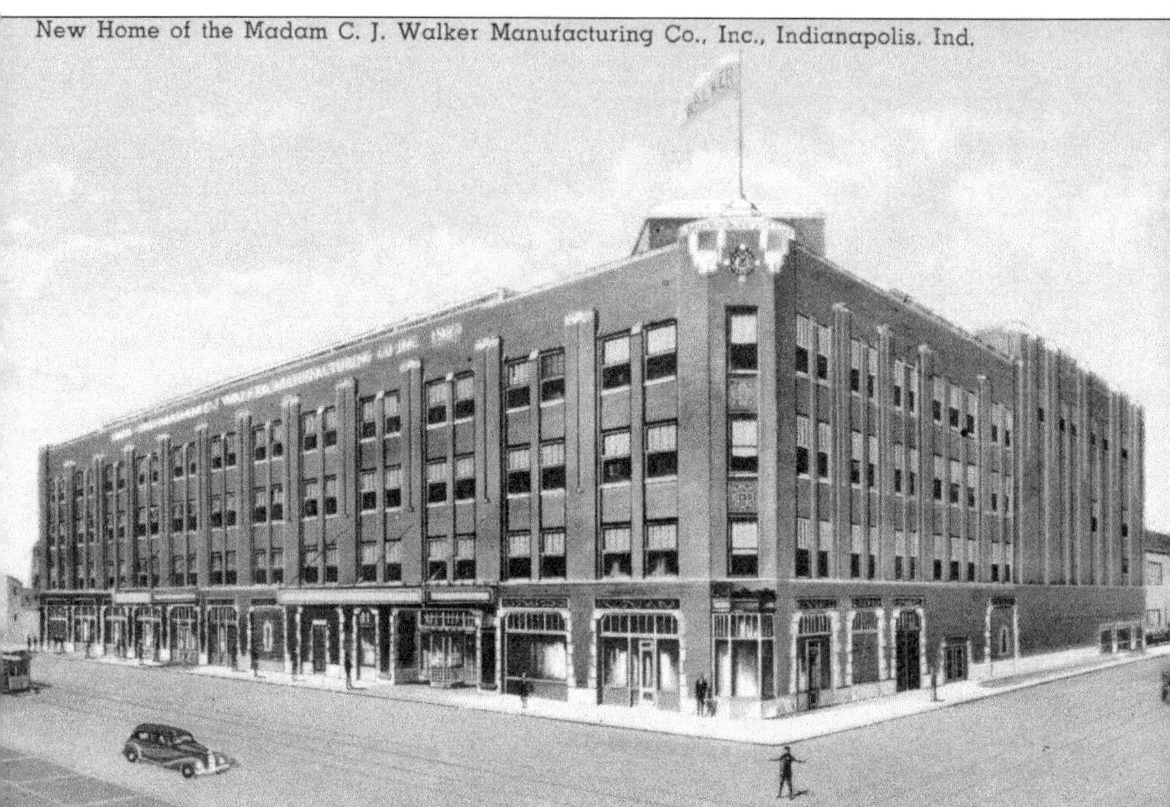

Promoting a New Headquarters, 1927. During the yearlong construction of its headquarters, the Madam C.J. Walker Manufacturing Company began distributing postcards with an architect's colorful pastel version of the building to publicize the expansion. (Courtesy of Madam Walker Family Archives.)

On the Cover: The Bohemian Club of Indianapolis. The Bohemian Club of Indianapolis, known for its elegant annual dinner dances, hosts one of the first events in the newly opened Madam Walker Building's Grand Casino Ballroom in February 1928. To ensure nonstop live music, the organization usually hired two orchestras. See page 38. (Courtesy of Madam Walker Theatre Center.)

IMAGES
of America

Madam Walker Theatre Center

An Indianapolis Treasure

A'Lelia Bundles

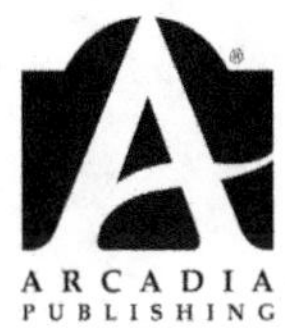

ISBN 9781531668594

Published by Arcadia Publishing
Charleston, South Carolina

Library of Congress Control Number: 2013937113

For all general information, please contact Arcadia Publishing:
Telephone 843-853-2070
Fax 843-853-0044
E-mail sales@arcadiapublishing.com
For customer service and orders:
Toll-Free 1-888-313-2665

Visit us on the Internet at www.arcadiapublishing.com

This book is dedicated in memory of my grandfather Marion R. Perry Jr. and my mother, A'Lelia Mae Perry Bundles, with thanks to my father, S. Henry Bundles, who still knows the stories.

Contents

Acknowledgments 6
Introduction 7
1. Madam Walker: Pioneer of Beauty 9
2. Anchoring the Avenue: Walker Headquarters 27
3. Beauty to Ballroom: A City within a City 37
4. Road to Success: A Career in Beauty Culture 47
5. Good Times: The 1950s and 1960s 75
6. Crowning Glory: Vintage Walker 87
7. Decline and Renewal: Making a Comeback 101
8. Capturing the Future: Jazz on the Avenue 117
Bibliography 126
About the Madam Walker Theatre Center 127

Acknowledgments

The sheer joy of perusing hundreds of photographs reminds me of the incredible accomplishments not only of my great-great-grandmother Madam C.J. Walker but also of the founding generation of Madam C.J. Walker Manufacturing Company employees. Without Madam Walker, her daughter A'Lelia Walker, attorneys F.B. Ransom and Robert L. Brokenburr, factory manager Alice Kelly, secretary Violet Reynolds, Walker Beauty School national supervisor Dr. Marjorie Stewart Joyner, and bookkeeper Marie Brooks Overstreet, there would be no story to tell.

I am fortunate that my grandfather Marion R. Perry preserved most of the photographs that now comprise the Madam Walker Family Archives and that Violet Reynolds lived long enough to shepherd the donation of a trove of materials from the Walker Estate trustees to the Indiana Historical Society.

I thank my late mother, A'Lelia Mae Perry Bundles, for encouraging me to tell the Walker story, and my father, S. Henry Bundles, for continuing to provide historical tidbits that otherwise would be lost.

Judith Ransom, Jill Nelson, Stanley Nelson, and Robert Ransom—descendants of Walker general manager F.B. Ransom—each play a critical role in keeping the legacy alive. Special thanks also go to Wilma Moore, senior archivist of African American history at the Indiana Historical Society, for her intimate knowledge of the Walker papers, and to Thomas Ridley, the Walker Theatre's much-loved resident docent.

Many foundations, corporations, and individuals have supported the Madam Walker Theatre Center (MWTC) in its present incarnation as a performing arts center. The Lilly Endowment of Indianapolis deserves special gratitude as do members of the MWTC board and staff who have worked so diligently through the years.

For photographs not in my personal collection, I thank the Museum of the City of New York; Malina Jeffers of Mosaic City; Jimmy Beard; Alan Ray; Charlene Cox; Tony and Lucy Reynolds; Cordelia Wills; Alpha Blackburn; Gina Woods; Richard McCoy; Walt Thomas; Paul Mullins and Lewis Jones of Indiana University-Purdue University, Indianapolis (IUPUI); and Susan Sutton and John Herbst of the Indiana Historical Society. This book benefits greatly from the photographs of Carl Black, William Rasdell, and John Hurst, who continue to chronicle MWTC events.

INTRODUCTION

Step inside the historic Madam Walker Theatre and savor the magic. Nearly nine decades of African American entertainers—from blues queen Mamie Smith to Motown legend Smokey Robinson—have performed on its stage.

Designed in 1927 as the new headquarters of the Madam C.J. Walker Manufacturing Company, the Walker Building is one of the few remaining Indiana Avenue structures from the days when the area vied with Memphis's Beale Street and Chicago's Bronzeville as well-known hubs of African American business and entertainment. Both a National Historic Landmark and an Indiana State Historic Landmark, it serves as a reminder of the Walker Company's place as one of the most successful black-owned American businesses of the first half of the 20th century.

Its founder, Madam Walker, was born Sarah Breedlove in 1867 on the same Delta, Louisiana, cotton plantation where her parents had been enslaved until the end of the Civil War. Orphaned at seven and widowed at twenty, she spent much of her adult life as a laundress in St. Louis. After concocting formulas for a shampoo and ointment that healed scalp disease when she was in her late thirties, she founded a company that eventually would train and employ thousands of women. By the time she died in 1919, she had parlayed her hair care products enterprise and savvy New York real estate investments into a million dollars' worth of assets. *The Guinness Book of World Records* has cited her as the first self-made American woman millionaire.

Drawn to Indianapolis—known as the "Crossroads of American"—by its relatively prosperous black business community and its well-connected transportation network, Madam Walker moved her company headquarters there from Pittsburgh in 1910. Quickly involving herself in the city's civic, business, and religious life, she joined Bethel AME Church, donated $1,000 to the new Senate Avenue YMCA, and became a member of the local National Negro Business League chapter.

In 1914, just as she had done on many occasions, Walker visited the Isis Theatre in downtown Indianapolis. To her surprise, the young white ticket booth operator informed her that admission for "colored people" had increased to 25¢, though it remained 15¢ for white customers. Refusing to pay the escalated price, Walker returned to her office and instructed her attorney to sue the Isis. Legend has it that she also vowed that day to build her own movie theater.

Although the Walker Building was completed eight years after her death, Walker had purchased the triangular-shaped lot not long after the Isis Theatre incident. The four-story, block-long flatiron building, located at 617 Indiana Avenue, originally was planned to house her corporate headquarters and factory. By the time the doors opened in December 1927, it had become much more. It was a forerunner of today's shopping malls with a drugstore, a beauty salon, a beauty school, a restaurant, professional offices, a ballroom, and a 1,500-seat theater.

Added to the National Register of Historic Places in 1991, the Walker Building makes Indianapolis one of the few American cities able to claim such tangible evidence of its African American cultural and entrepreneurial history. Chicago's original Regal Theatre, built in 1928, was razed in 1973. Tom "Honest John" Turpin opened St. Louis's Booker Washington Theatre in 1913, but it closed in 1930. Like the Walker, the Lincoln Theatre in Washington, DC, which opened in 1922, has been restored. Harlem's Apollo, which maintained a whites-only policy until 1934, has been a premier venue for black artists for eight decades. But the Walker stands alone among these three remaining theaters because an African American company originally built it.

As the Walker Theatre doors opened for the first time on the day after Christmas in 1927, blue-and-gold-uniformed ushers escorted guests to their seats for the afternoon matinee. After a screening of *The Magic Flame*—an Oscar-nominated silent film starring actors Ronald Colman and Vilma Bánky—the vaudeville dance team Lovey and Shorty thrilled theatergoers with their high-energy, fast-stepping routine.

As the lights came up, the audience was entranced by what it saw. Elaborate terra-cotta sculptures of Egyptian sphinxes, brightly painted friezes, decorative 20-foot bamboo spears, and life-sized chimpanzee statues posted as sentinels above the stage. No dance hall, movie theater, nor meeting place for African Americans in the city could even come close. Designed by Rubush and Hunter, the local architectural firm that had created some of the city's most distinctive downtown buildings—including the Circle Theatre, the Columbia Club, the Murat Temple, the Indiana Theatre, and the Indiana Roof Ballroom—the Walker Building today remains one of the nation's most notable surviving examples of African-inspired Art Deco.

Ironically, the late-1920s construction boom that added the Walker Building, Crispus Attucks High School, and the Phyllis Wheatley YWCA to the cluster of existing buildings that served African Americans was in part a by-product of racist policies that intensified from 1921 to 1928 when the Ku Klux Klan controlled Indianapolis city politics. The black community—hovering at 10 percent of the population and out-maneuvered by an at-large system for selecting elected officials—could not counter the political interests who wanted to segregate public facilities. The Walker Building, at least, served as some small consolation. For African Americans, it was a place where they could see first-run movies without the insult of rear entrances and dirty balconies, where they could enjoy Sunday dinner in the Coffee Pot restaurant, where they could host formal dances, and where they could shop at the Walker Drugstore with its promise that "positively no stale seconds, inferior or refuse merchandise will be used, stocked or sold."

By 1950, Indiana Avenue—like the main arteries of inner-city black communities across the nation—had begun a gradual decline. As integration opened previously off-limits housing and schools to African Americans, longtime residents and businesses migrated to other parts of town. As the city of Indianapolis targeted the district for interstate construction and rezoned the neighborhood for commercial enterprises and the expansion of the Indiana University-Purdue University, Indianapolis, campus, others were pushed out.

By the late 1970s, the Walker Building had lost most of its tenants and seemed destined for demolition. But a group of committed African American citizens mounted a campaign to preserve the building. After becoming incorporated as the Madam Walker Urban Life Center in 1979, they arranged for the purchase from the Walker Manufacturing Company and began planning its restoration.

After extensive renovations—supported by the Lilly Endowment, US Commerce Department funding, and other generous donors—the Walker Theatre reopened in October 1988. Today, the building serves as a center for arts education and a performance venue where audiences enjoy a diverse array of artists, from tap dancer Savion Glover and jazz trumpeter Wynton Marsalis to dramatic opera soprano Angela Brown and singer Patti LaBelle.

Walker Company general manager F.B. Ransom's greeting from the 1927 grand opening still applies today: "To those who toil, to those who think . . . to those who love good music, good pictures, high class entertainment amidst magnificent surroundings; to those who believe that our boys and girls are entitled to the best there is . . . to all classes; to all races, this house is dedicated."

One

Madam Walker
Pioneer of Beauty

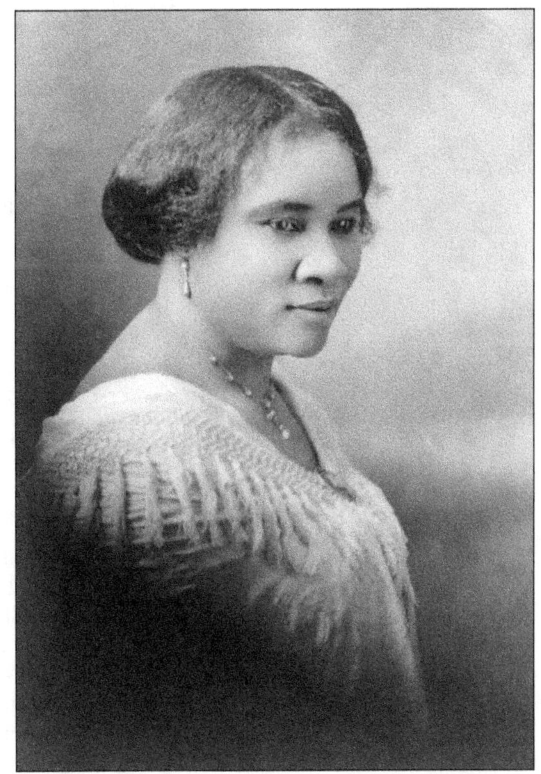

Madam Walker, Pioneer of Beauty. When Madam C.J. Walker posed for this portrait in Addison Scurlock's renowned Washington, DC, studio, she was well on her way to becoming one of the most successful African American entrepreneurs of her time. A pioneer of today's multibillion-dollar hair care industry, Madam Walker, born Sarah Breedlove, was a philanthropist, arts patron, and antilynching activist who used this image to promote her products. (Courtesy of Madam Walker Family Archives.)

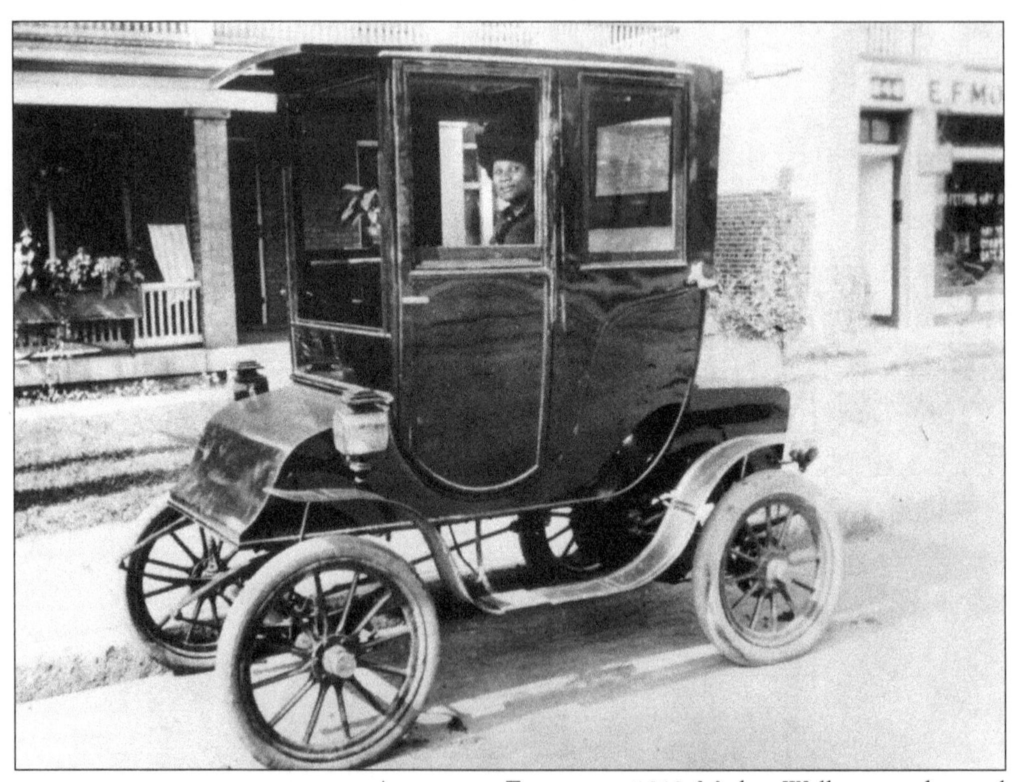

Afternoon Excursion, 1913. Madam Walker owned several cars and employed a full-time chauffeur, but for trips to the movies and for shopping, she preferred her Waverly Electric. Manufactured in Indianapolis at a plant not far from her home, these electric cars were marketed to women—especially wealthy women—as a more elegant alternative to noisier, gasoline-powered automobiles. (Courtesy of Madam Walker Family Archives.)

Path to Prosperity. Madam Walker enjoyed the trappings of wealth, including furs and diamonds, but she never forgot how poor she had been. She said, "Now my object in life is not simply to make money for myself in dressing or running around in an automobile, but I love to use a part of what I make to help others." (Courtesy of Madam Walker Family Archives.)

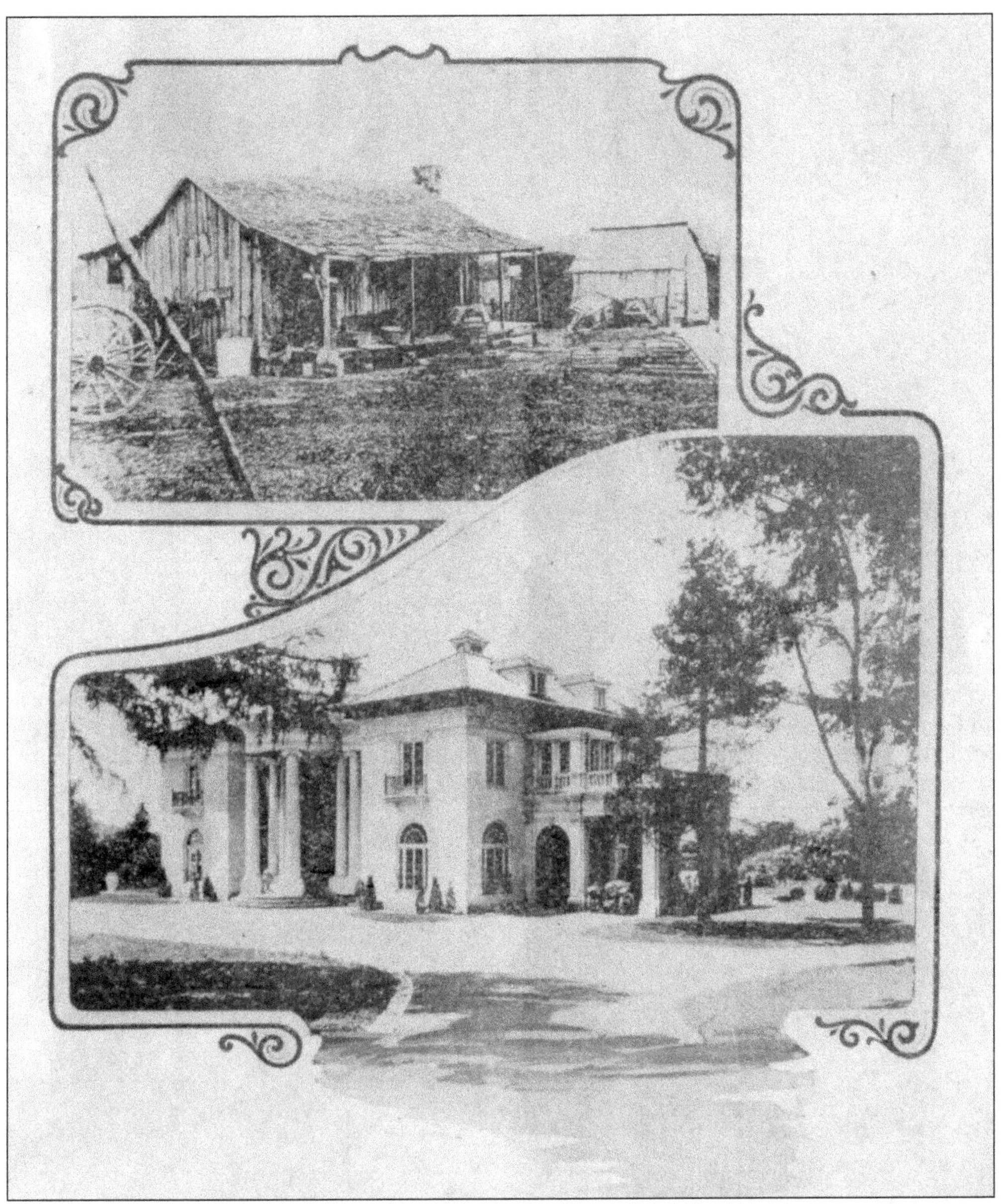

Cabin to Castle. Madam Walker's rise from a Delta, Louisiana, cotton plantation cabin to her Irvington-on-Hudson, New York, mansion just a few miles from John D. Rockefeller's estate added to her rags-to-riches mystique. Her official company biography emphasized her humble beginnings as a St. Louis washerwoman named Sarah Breedlove McWilliams, who had made as little as $1.50 a day before discovering the secret hair care formula. Orphaned at 7, married at 14, and widowed with a small child at 20, she left Vicksburg, Mississippi, in 1888 for Missouri where her brothers worked as barbers. In 1905, she moved to Denver, where St. Louis newspaper salesman Charles Joseph Walker joined her. They married in early 1906. Together they hit the road selling Walker's Wonderful Hair Grower. In 1910, after a brief stay in Pittsburgh, they moved to Indianapolis and divorced two years later. In 1916, Madam Walker established her personal residence in Harlem and then built Villa Lewaro, her Westchester County home, in 1918. (Courtesy of Madam Walker Family Archives.)

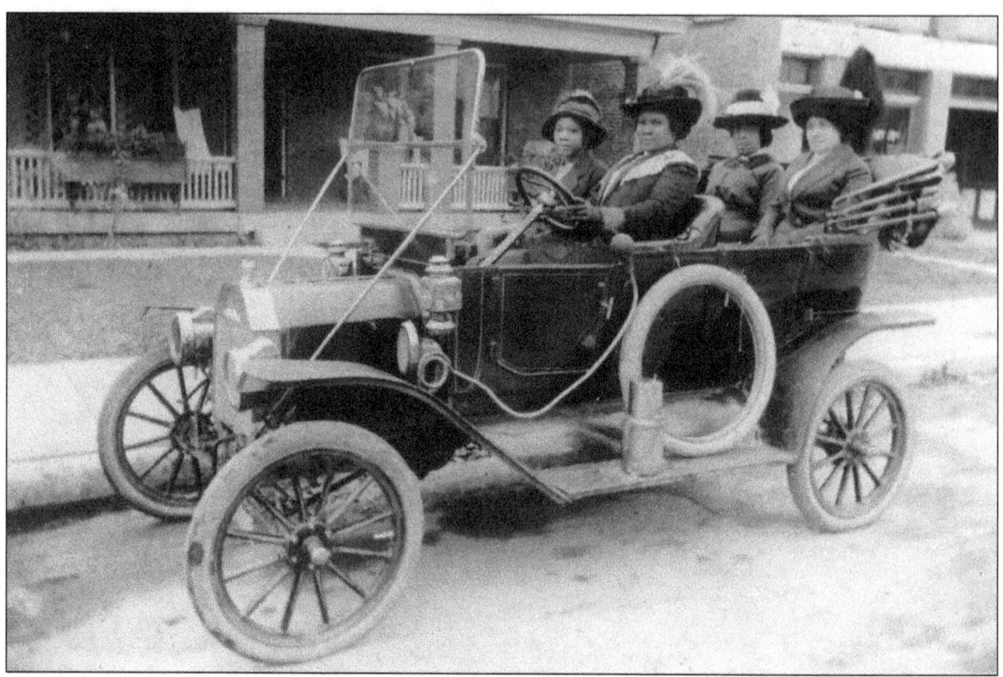

At the Wheel, 1912. Madam Walker spent much of each year on the road promoting her products and training sales agents in the Walker System of Beauty Culture. At the wheel of her Model T Ford, she appears with, from left to right, her niece Anjetta Breedlove, her bookkeeper Lucy Flint, and her factory forelady Alice Kelly. (Courtesy of Madam Walker Family Archives.)

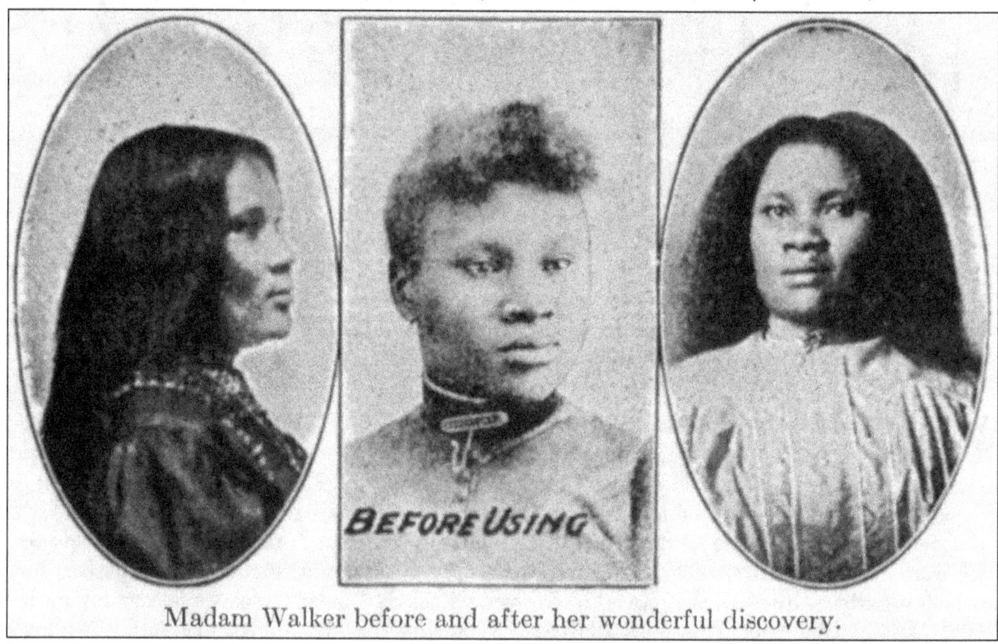

Before and After. The earliest known photograph of Madam Walker was taken probably during the 1890s when she suffered from the severe scalp disease that was causing her to go bald. In this early advertisement—with "after" images shot around 1906—she proudly displays the effects of her Wonderful Hair Grower. (Courtesy of Madam Walker Family Archives.)

Hope in a Jar. In 1906, around the time cosmetics mavens Helena Rubinstein and Elizabeth Arden were creating their creams and unguents for a mostly white clientele, Madam Walker was developing ointments and salves for black women. Walker's Wonderful Hair Grower—with its healing sulfur-based formula—was her first and most enduringly popular item, selling hundreds of thousands of tins each year. (Courtesy of Madam Walker Family Archives.)

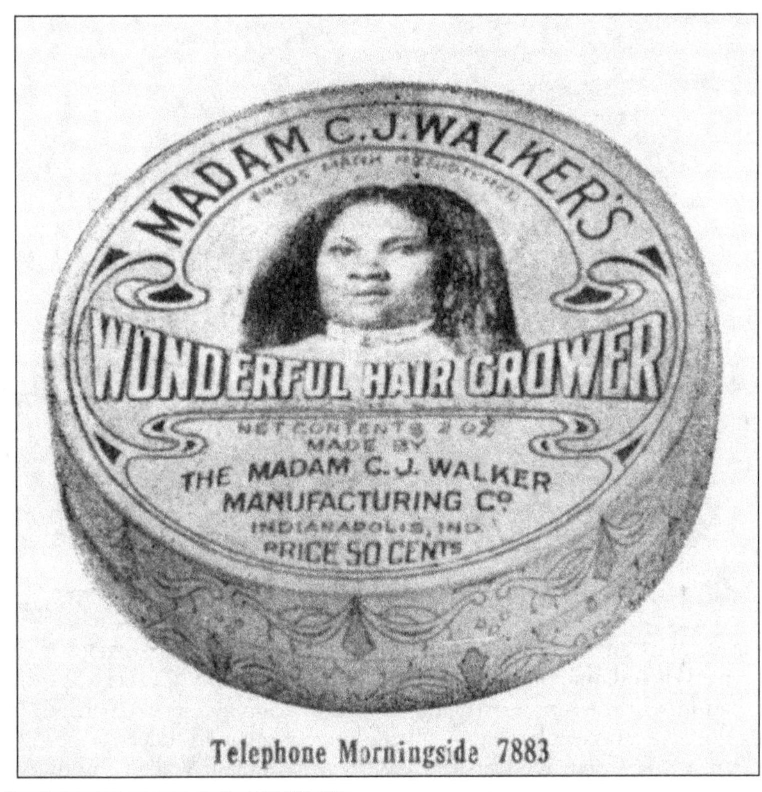

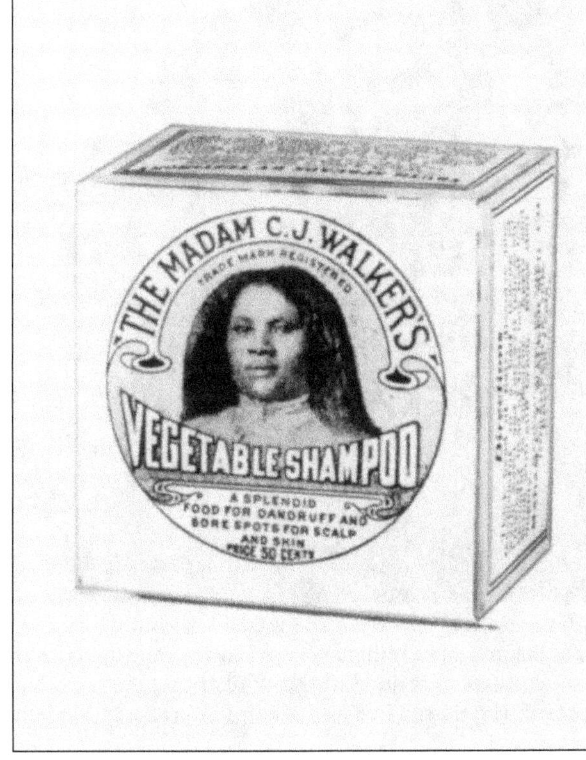

The Walker System. Essential to healthy hair was a clean scalp. At a time when most Americans lived in homes without indoor plumbing and electricity, Walker encouraged her customers to improve their hygiene regimen by washing their hair more frequently than they had been accustomed to doing. Her Vegetable Shampoo worked with her Wonderful Hair Grower to remedy dandruff and soothe scalp sores. (Courtesy of Madam Walker Family Archives.)

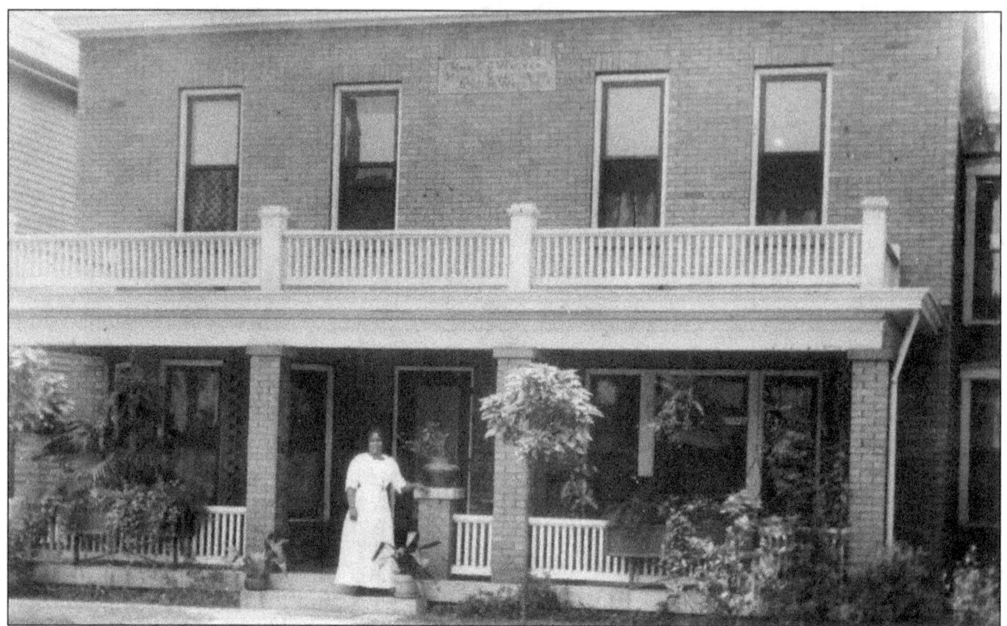

Crossroads of America. Madam Walker and her third husband, Charles Joseph "C.J." Walker, arrived in Indianapolis in February 1910. Called the "Crossroads of America" because of its location near the center of the nation's population and its extensive train and road network, the city offered a perfect base for Walker's burgeoning mail-order business. She soon purchased this home at 640 North West Street. (Courtesy of Madam Walker Family Archives.)

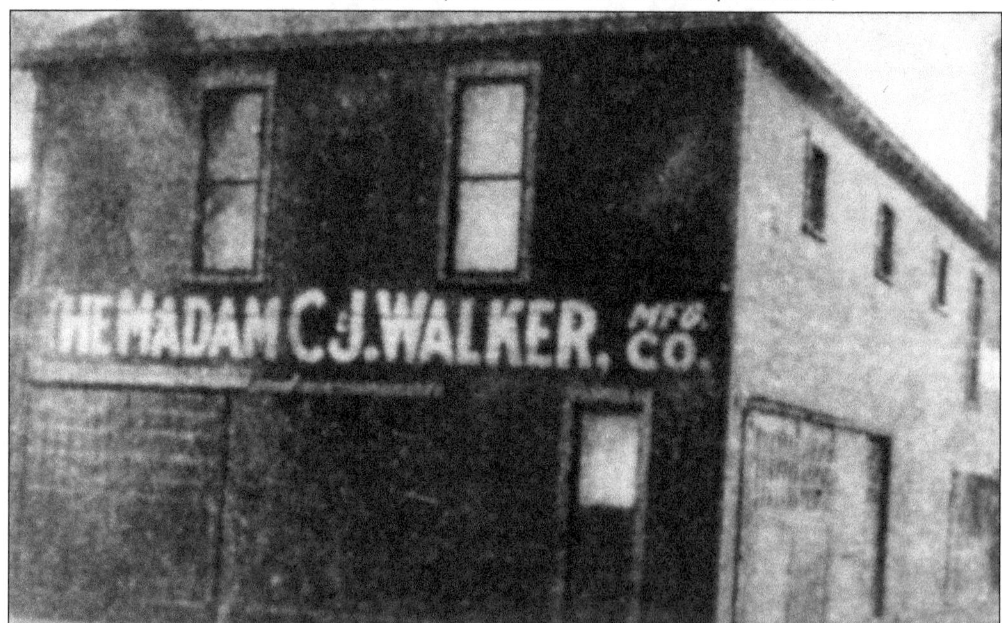

First Factory, 1911. Madam Walker's sales grew so quickly that she was able to build a factory behind her West Street home within a year of her arrival in Indianapolis. Products were mixed and packaged on the first floor. She and "beauty culturists," trained in the Walker System, provided scalp treatments, hairstyling, and manicures in the upstairs beauty salon. (Courtesy of Madam Walker Family Archives.)

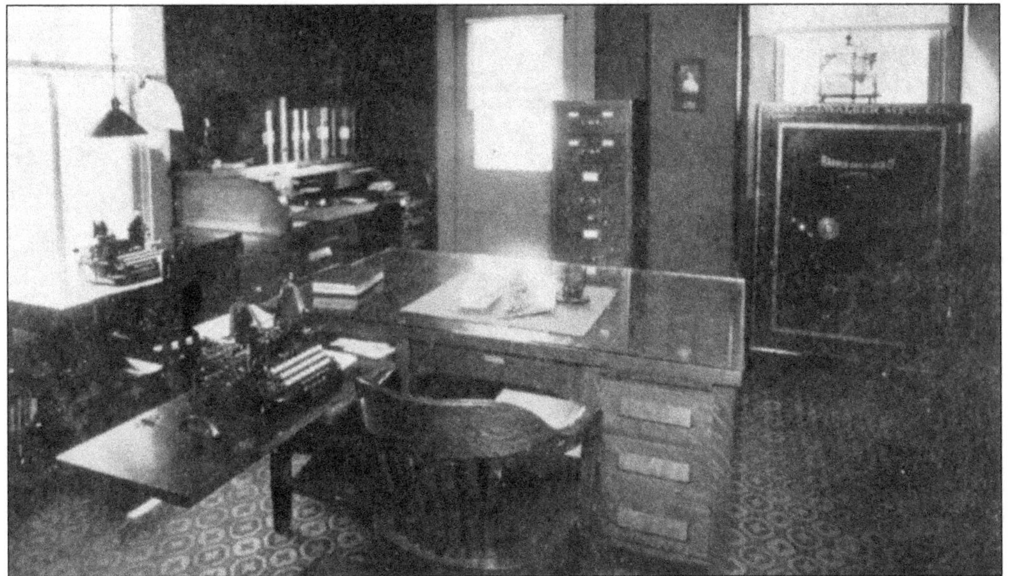

Soaring Sales. By April 1913, Madam Walker was selling $3,000 worth of goods each month at a time when mid-level corporate managers—almost all of whom were white men—were making about $1,200 a month. By 1918, her annual earnings reached $276,000, more than $3 million in today's dollars. That sum combined with her real estate investments and company valuation made her a millionaire. (Courtesy of Madam Walker Family Archives.)

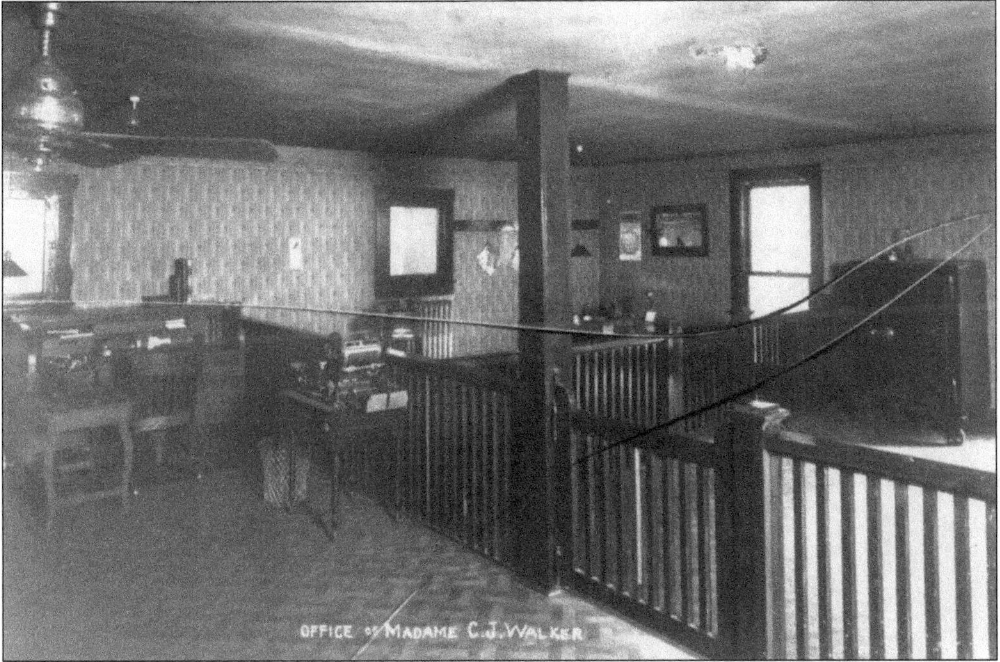

Each One, Teach One. The Walker Company office staff always looked forward to Madam Walker's visits. As one who had had little formal schooling as a child, she valued education. Each morning, she assembled her employees to read the morning newspaper aloud. "If one of us didn't understand a word, we all looked it up together in the dictionary," remembered a longtime secretary. (Courtesy of Madam Walker Family Archives.)

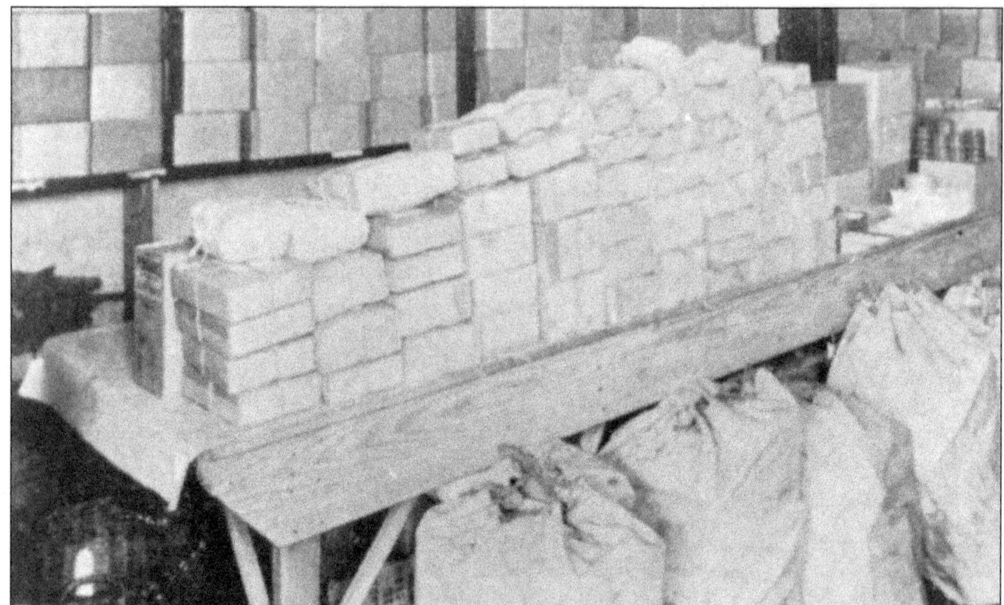

A Day's Work. The factory staff packaged and shipped hundreds of parcels each day to agents and individual customers throughout the United States, Central America, and the Caribbean. In addition to Walker's Wonderful Hair Grower and Vegetable Shampoo, the company manufactured Tetter Salve, Temple Salve, and Glossine. (Courtesy of Madam Walker Family Archives.)

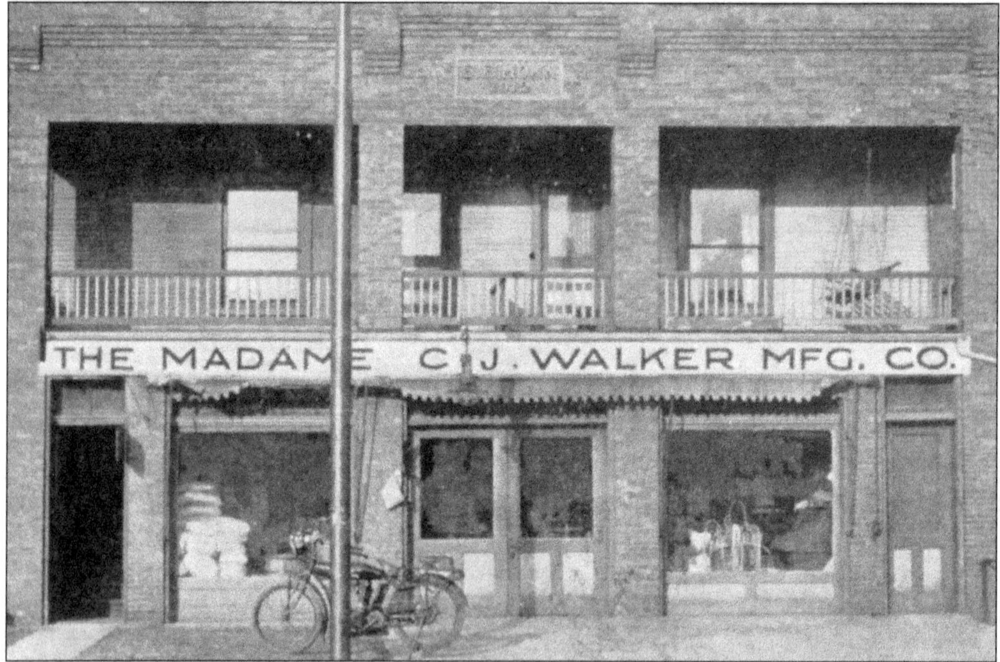

Rapid Growth. In just a few years, the Walker Company had outgrown its factory. To create additional storage for the drums of petrolatum, beeswax, coconut oil, and perfumes, Madam Walker purchased Edward F. Monn's feed supply company at 644 North West Street. As more people drove cars and fewer people needed oats for their horses, Monn became a coal dealer. (Courtesy of Madam Walker Family Archives.)

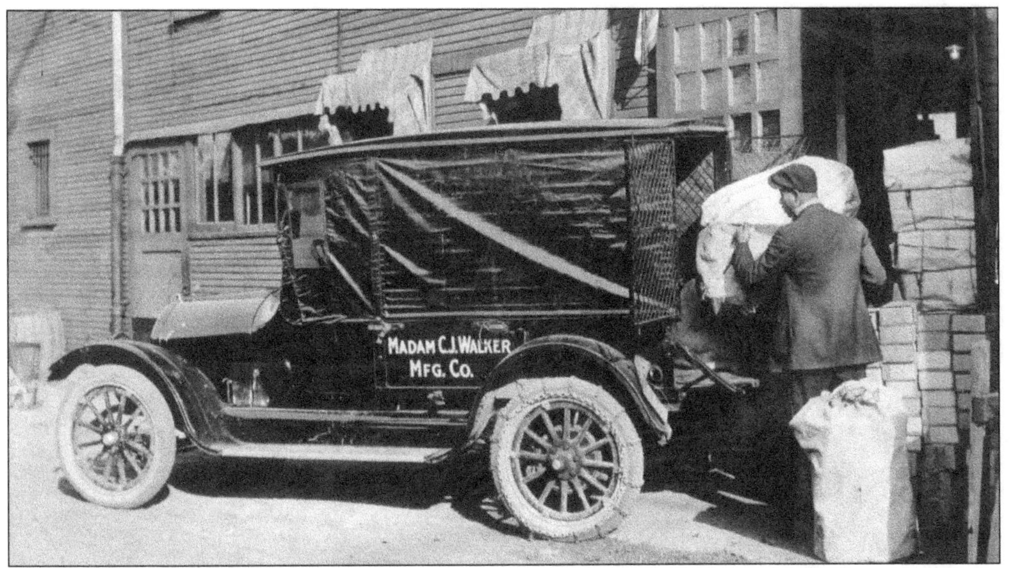

LOADING UP. Each afternoon, Walker products were delivered by truck to Indianapolis's busy Union Station, which serviced more than 200 trains a day. While the Walker Company was smaller than local manufacturers like Eli Lilly's pharmaceutical company and Carl Fisher's Prest-O-Light headlamp plant, it shipped an impressive volume of packages each week. (Courtesy of Madam Walker Family Archives.)

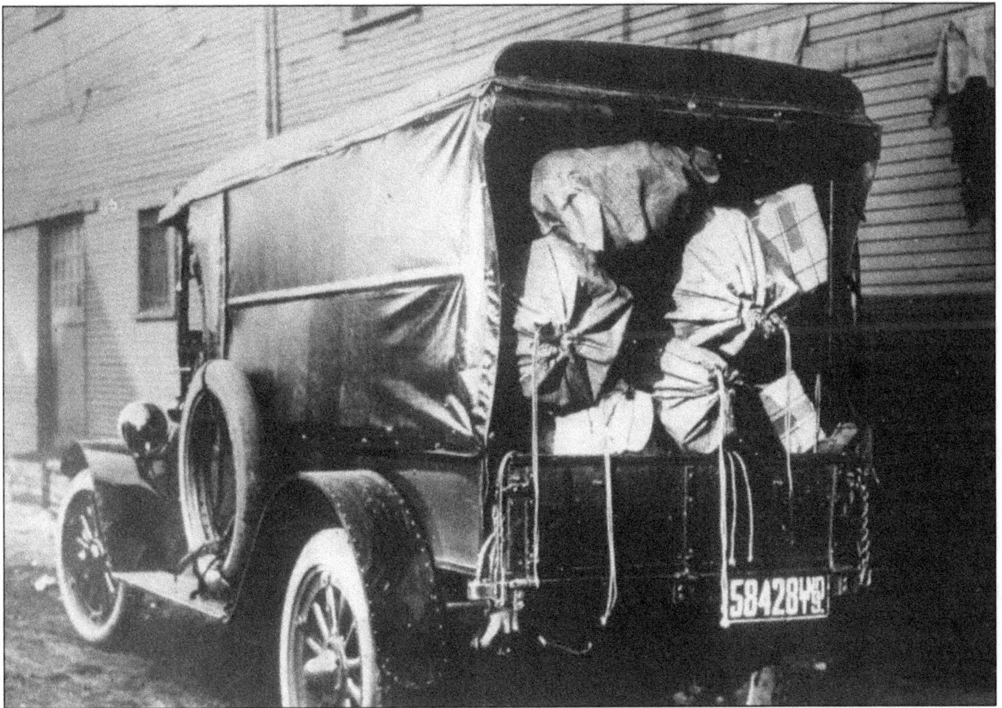

MAIL-ORDER DEMAND. Strongest mail-order sales for Walker's Wonderful Hair Grower were in the Central, Southern, and Southwestern United States where Madam Walker and her instructors had trained thousands of women by 1919. These agents purchased products at wholesale prices. (Courtesy of Madam Walker Family Archives.)

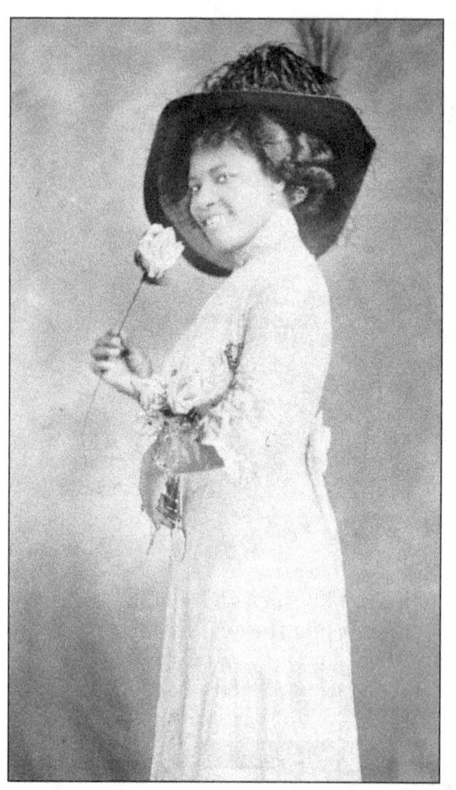

Apple of Her Eye. Born Lelia McWilliams—and later known as A'Lelia Walker—she provided much of the motivation for her mother's early success. A'Lelia's father and Walker's first husband, Moses McWilliams, had died when she was only two years old. During the 1890s, Sarah Breedlove McWilliams—who was to become Madam Walker—often went hungry as she struggled to provide for her daughter. (Courtesy of Madam Walker Family Archives.)

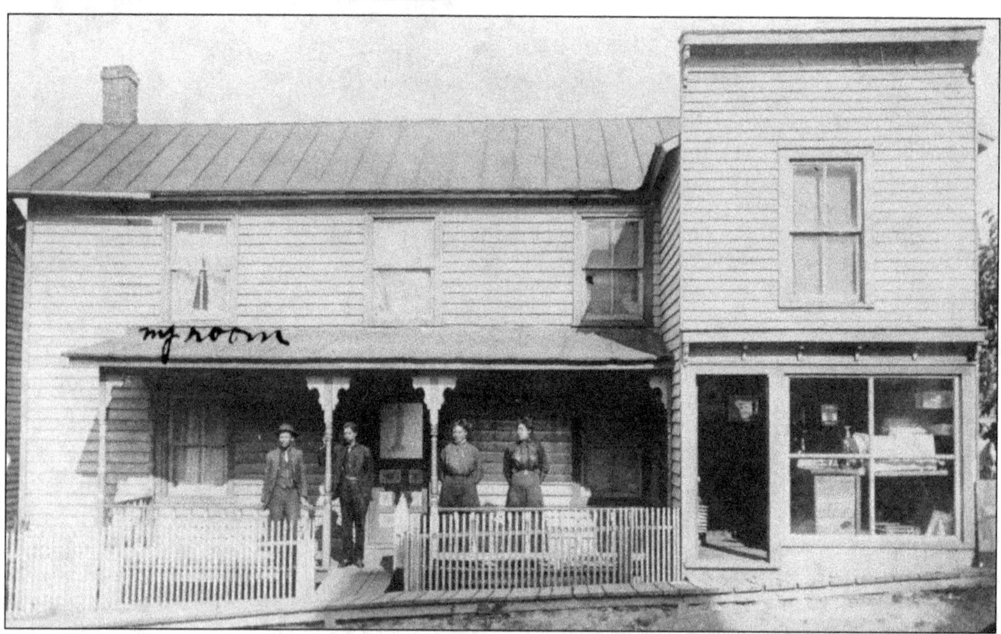

Bluefield, West Virginia. In 1906, when Madam Walker left Denver to expand her business in the South, A'Lelia managed the mail-order operation. In 1908, she joined her mother and stepfather in Pittsburgh's Hill District, where she ran the supply station and made sales and training calls along the East Coast. On the porch of this Bluefield, West Virginia, boardinghouse, she is third from left. (Courtesy of Madam Walker Family Archives.)

Following Her Mother's Footsteps. When Madam Walker moved her headquarters to Indianapolis in 1910, A'Lelia took charge of the Pittsburgh branch of Lelia College. While Madam focused on the Midwest and the South, she focused on the eastern seaboard. With an interest in expanding sales in the Caribbean and Central America, she visited Havana, Cuba, in 1914. (Courtesy of Madam Walker Family Archives.)

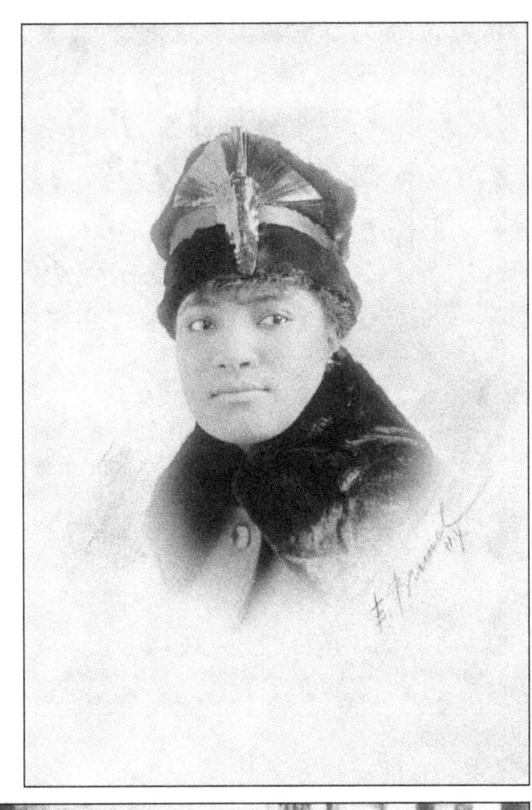

Spring Musicale. The Walkers shared a love of music, having heard ragtime, opera, classical, and sacred music during their St. Louis years. In April 1914, Madam honored A'Lelia with a spring dance and concert. Among the talented young local performers was Noble Sissle, who later collaborated with Eubie Blake on several successful musicals. During A'Lelia's Indianapolis visit, the Walkers enjoy a ride with their chauffeur. (Courtesy of Madam Walker Family Archives.)

Madam C J Walker and daughter on a sight—seeing tour

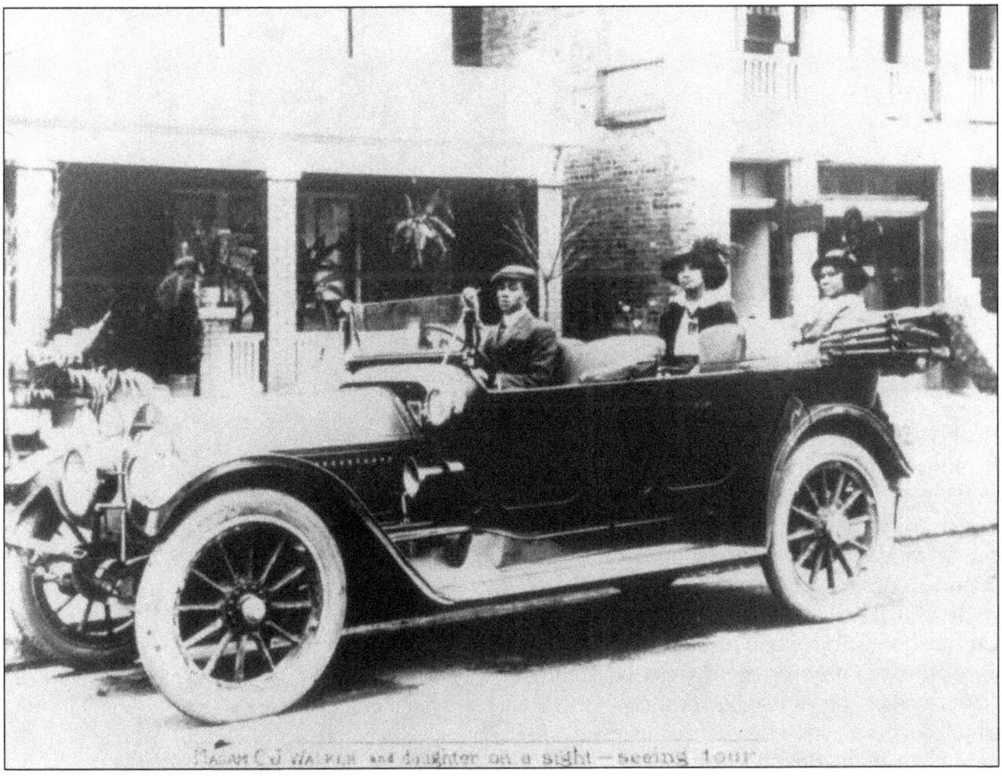

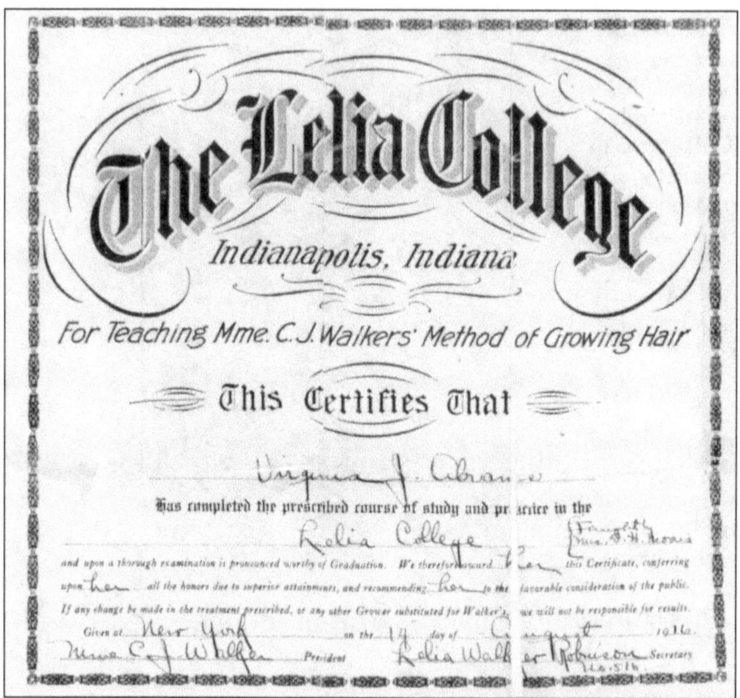

The Lelia College
Indianapolis, Indiana
For Teaching Mme. C.J. Walkers' Method of Growing Hair
This Certifies That
Virginia J. Abrams
Has completed the prescribed course of study and practice in the
Lelia College
and upon a thorough examination is pronounced worthy of Graduation. We therefore award her this Certificate, conferring upon her all the honors due to superior attainments, and recommending her to the favorable consideration of the public.
If any change be made in the treatment prescribed, or any other Grower substituted for Walker's, we will not be responsible for results.
Given at New York on the 19 day of August 1916
Mme C.J. Walker President Lelia Walker Robinson Secretary

Prized Possession. When Madam Walker opened her first training school in Pittsburgh, she selected the name Lelia College of Beauty Culture in honor of her daughter. Virginia Abrams received this certificate after completing a six-week course at the New York branch of Lelia College. Like others trained in the Walker System, she proudly displayed her diploma in her beauty salon. (Courtesy of Madam Walker Family Archives.)

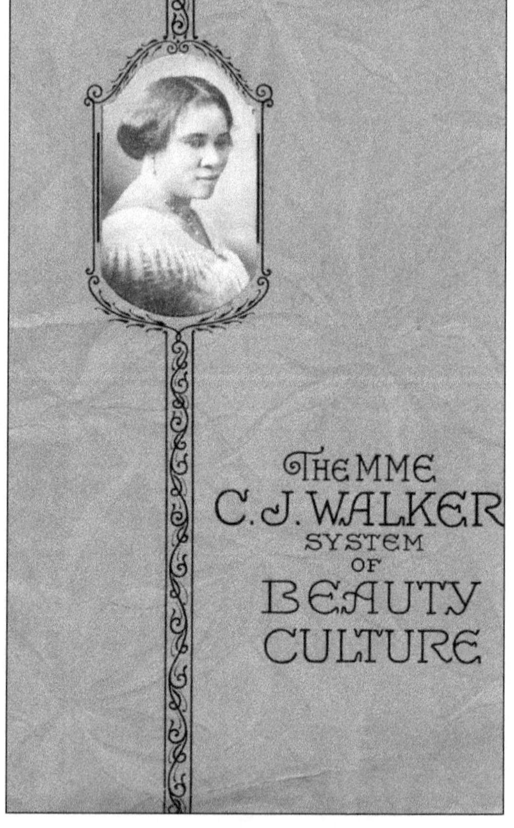

Business Opportunities. Madam Walker's rigorous beauty culture curriculum required students to learn anatomy, physiology, and hygiene as well as hairstyling. This 1928 course catalog emphasizes the business opportunities that awaited those who studied the Walker System of Beauty Culture. At a time when most professions were closed to women, the booklet boasted, "It is the most profitable business in which a woman can engage." (Courtesy of Madam Walker Family Archives.)

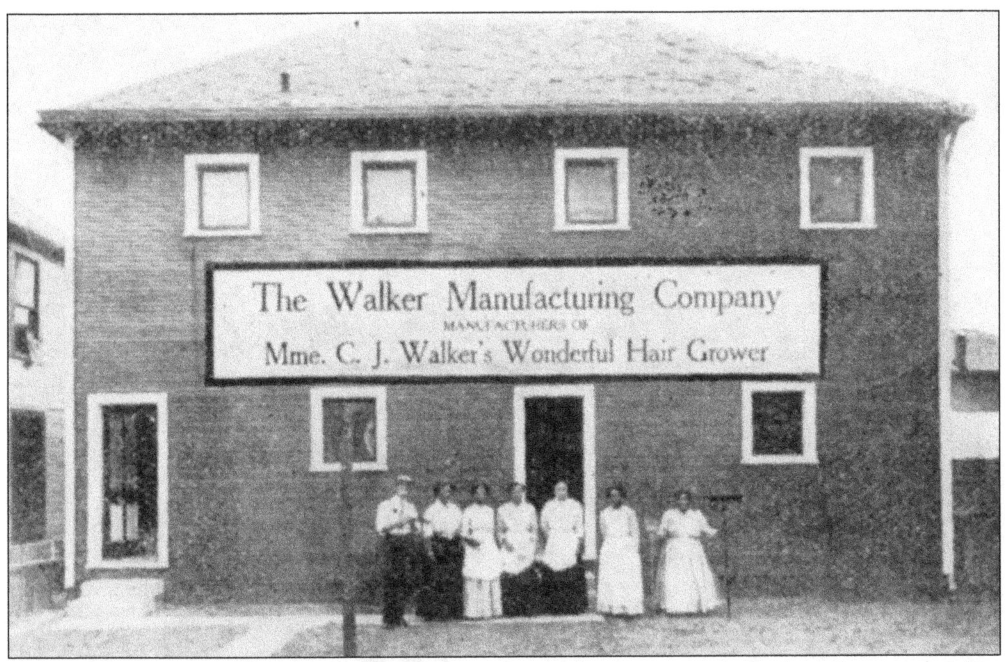

Best and Brightest. Madam Walker strategically sought the most-talented employees available, often hiring accomplished young African Americans who were shut out of jobs with other Indianapolis companies because of their race. Walker employees received paid vacation days, retirement pensions, and Christmas bonuses. (Courtesy of Madam Walker Family Archives.)

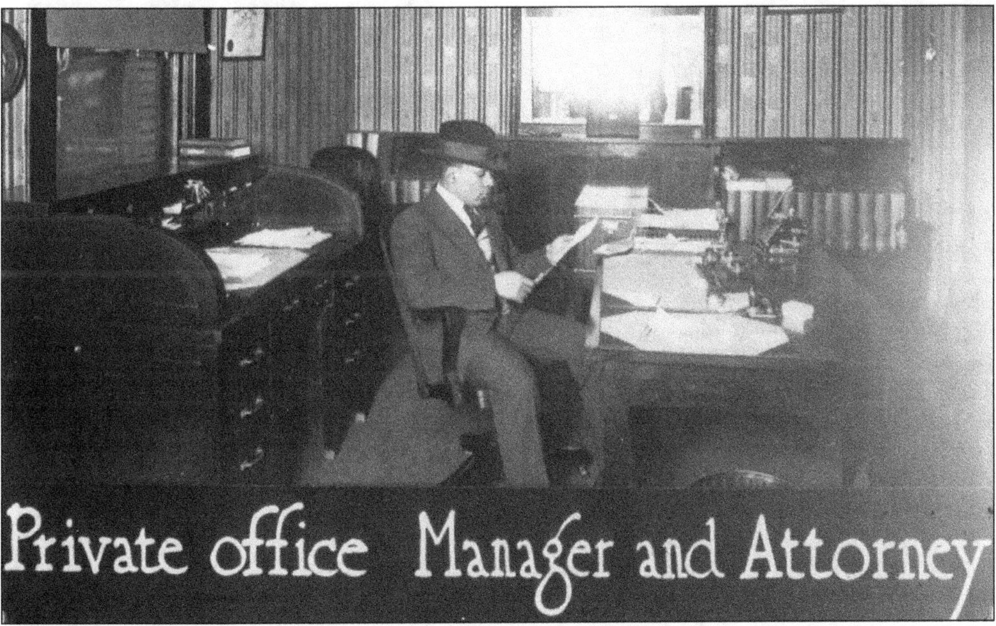

Trusted Counsel. Madam Walker hired Freeman Briley Ransom as her attorney and general manager, a position that today would be considered an executive vice president or chief operating officer. Born in Grenada, Mississippi, in 1882, he was valedictorian of his class at Nashville's Walden College. In the custom of the time, he "read law" at Columbia University before moving to Indianapolis. (Courtesy of Madam Walker Family Archives.)

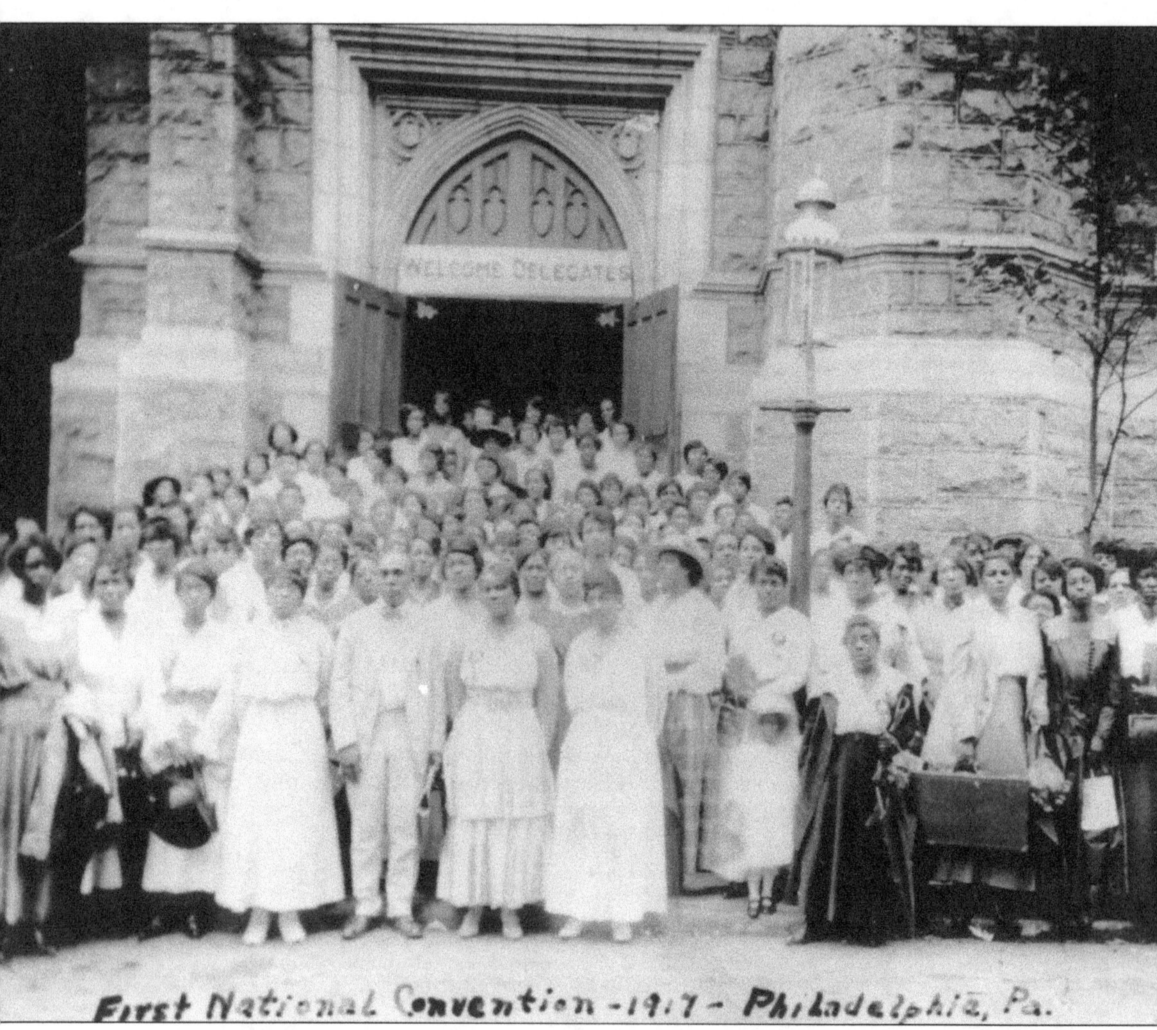

TAKING A STAND. In 1917, the year before cosmetics mogul Mary Kay was born, Madam Walker hosted her first sales convention of Walker agents in Philadelphia. Prizes went not only to women who sold the most products but also to those whose local Walker clubs had contributed the most to charity. Motivated by Walker's urgent appeal in the aftermath of racial violence in which nearly 40 black people were killed by a white mob in southern Illinois, the 200 politically conscious delegates sent a telegram to Pres. Woodrow Wilson urging him to support federal antilynching legislation. "This is the greatest country under the sun," she said. "But we must not let our love of country, our patriotic loyalty cause us to abate one whit in our protest against wrong and injustice. We should protest until the American sense of justice is so aroused that such affairs as the East St. Louis riot be forever impossible." (Courtesy of Madam Walker Family Archives.)

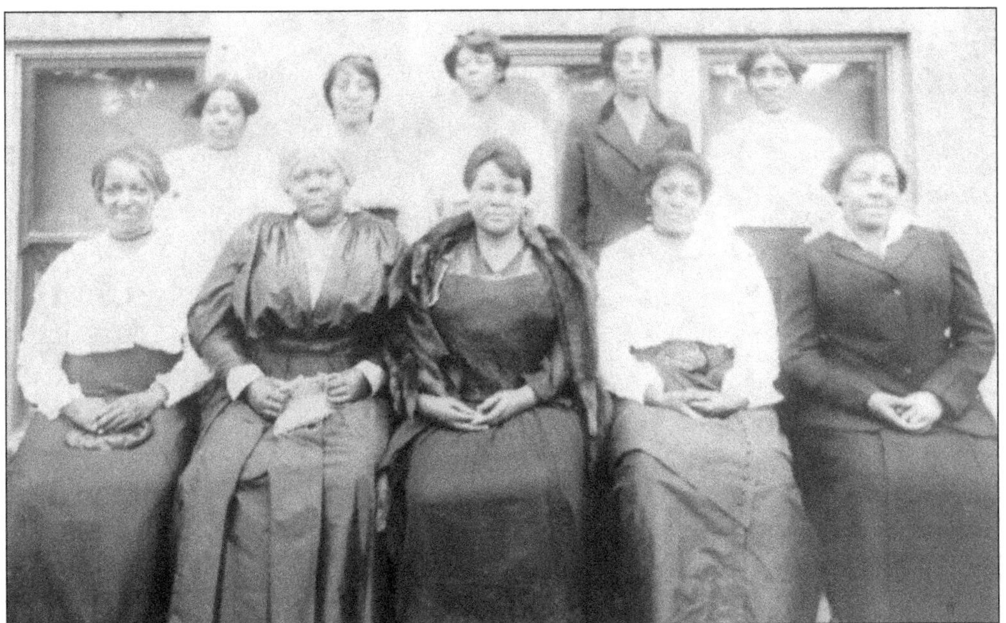

Organizing for Good. Even as a poor washerwoman in St. Louis, Madam Walker had witnessed the power of collective action by fellow church members who belonged to the National Association of Colored Women, a political and social service organization. Inspired by the NACW's structure and national network, she traveled throughout the United States in 1916 and 1917 organizing her agents into local and state chapters. (Courtesy of Madam Walker Family Archives.)

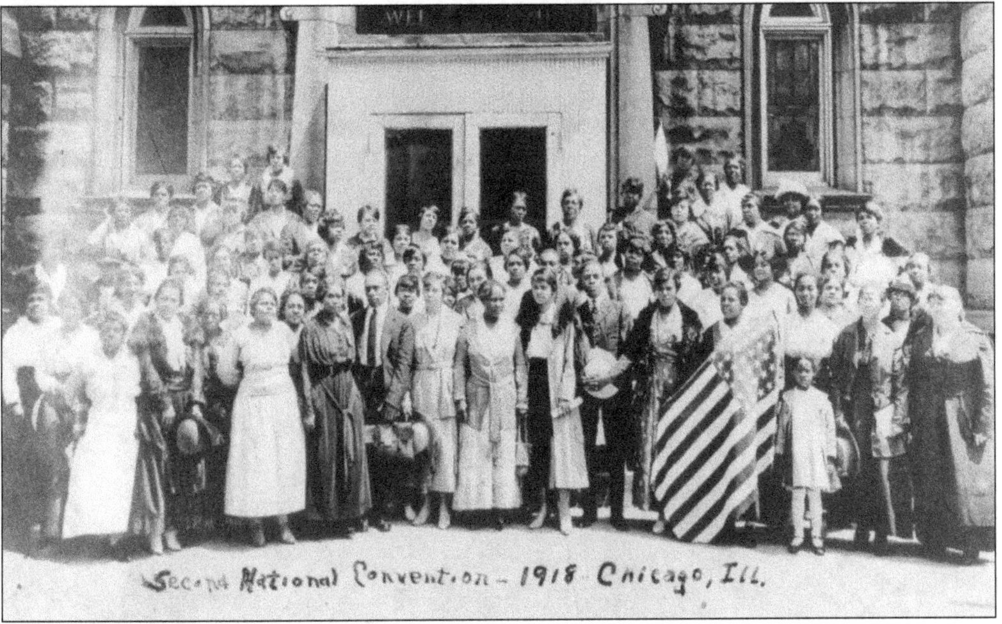

Meeting the War's Challenge. When the second-annual convention of Walker agents met at Chicago's Olivet Baptist Church, American soldiers were in Europe fighting in World War I. Concerned about the treatment of black troops serving in France in the segregated US Army, Madam Walker pledged "loyalty and patriotism" while also demanding equal rights and an end to discrimination. (Courtesy of Madam Walker Family Archives.)

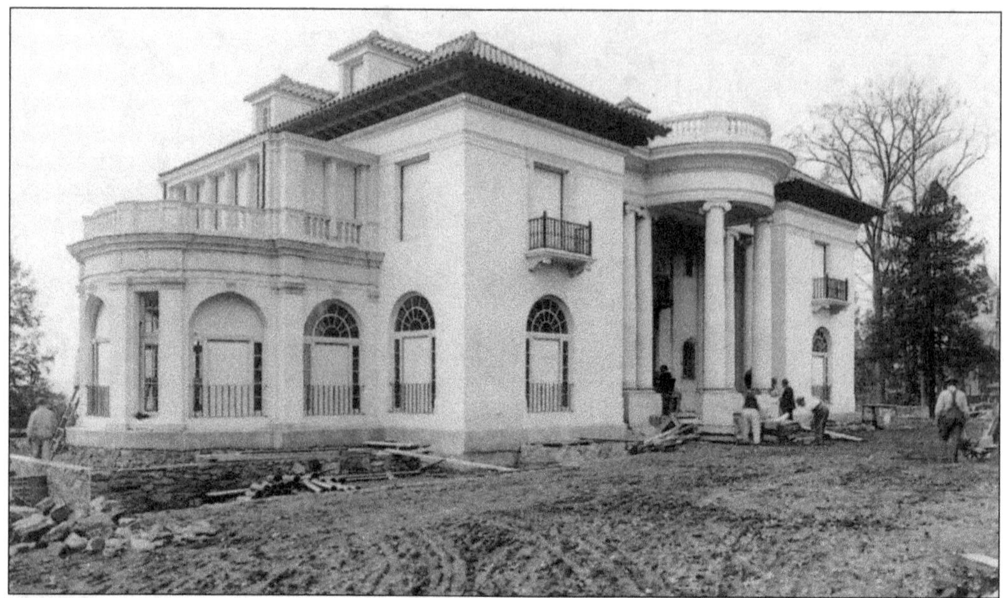

Her Dream of Dreams. In 1913, after A'Lelia Walker opened a Walker branch in Harlem, she urged her mother to join her. As Madam Walker's involvement in politics and the arts increased, she needed little convincing that Harlem—now a mecca of black activism and culture—should be her home. Construction began on her personal residence north of Manhattan in Westchester County in early 1917. (Courtesy of Madam Walker Family Archives.)

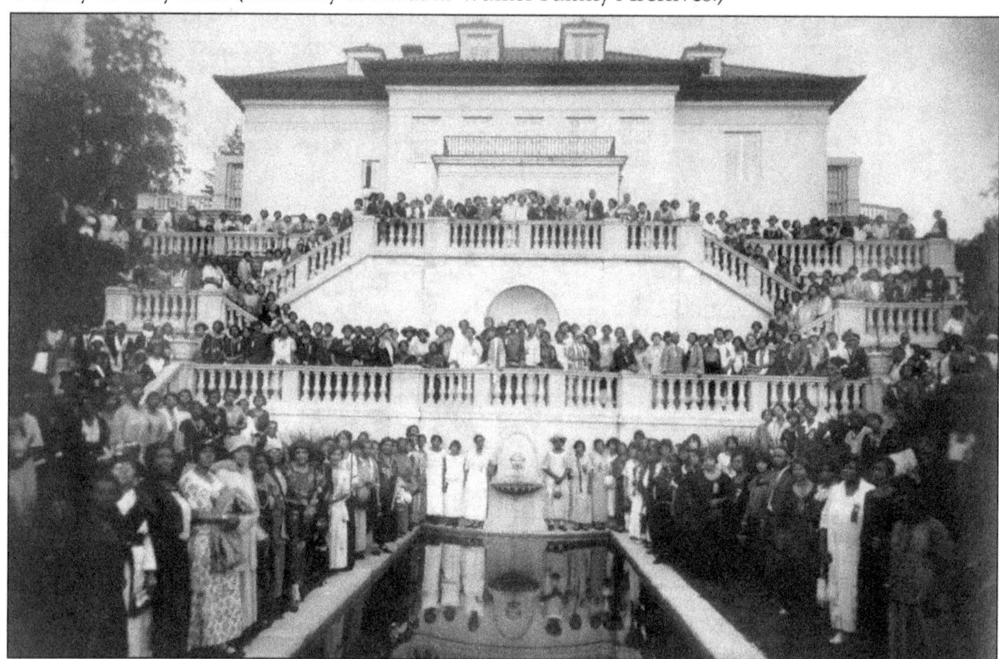

Villa Lewaro. At A'Lelia Walker's invitation, famed Italian opera tenor Enrico Caruso visited the property during construction. It so reminded him of homes in his native Naples that he suggested the name "Villa Lewaro," creating the acronym with the letters "Le" for A'Lelia, "Wa" for Walker, and "Ro" for Robinson, the surname of A'Lelia's first husband. (Courtesy of Madam Walker Family Archives.)

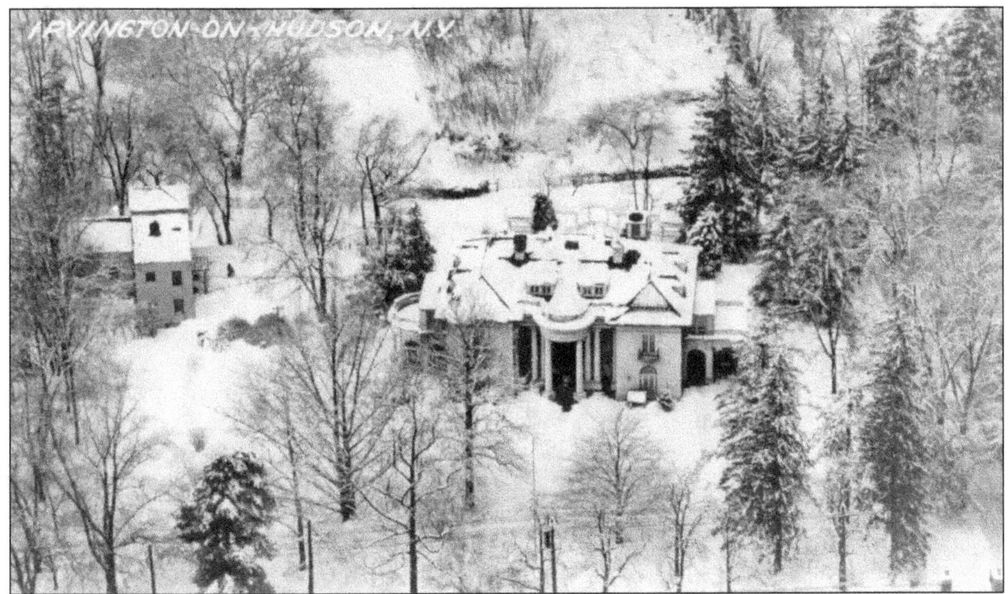

Christmas on the Hudson. Madam Walker moved into her mansion in June 1918, hosting a grand party that August honoring Emmett Scott, then-serving as special assistant to the US secretary of war in charge of Negro affairs. She celebrated Christmas and her 51st birthday that December. Sadly, she died in May 1919 after having lived at Villa Lewaro for less than a year. (Courtesy of Madam Walker Family Archives.)

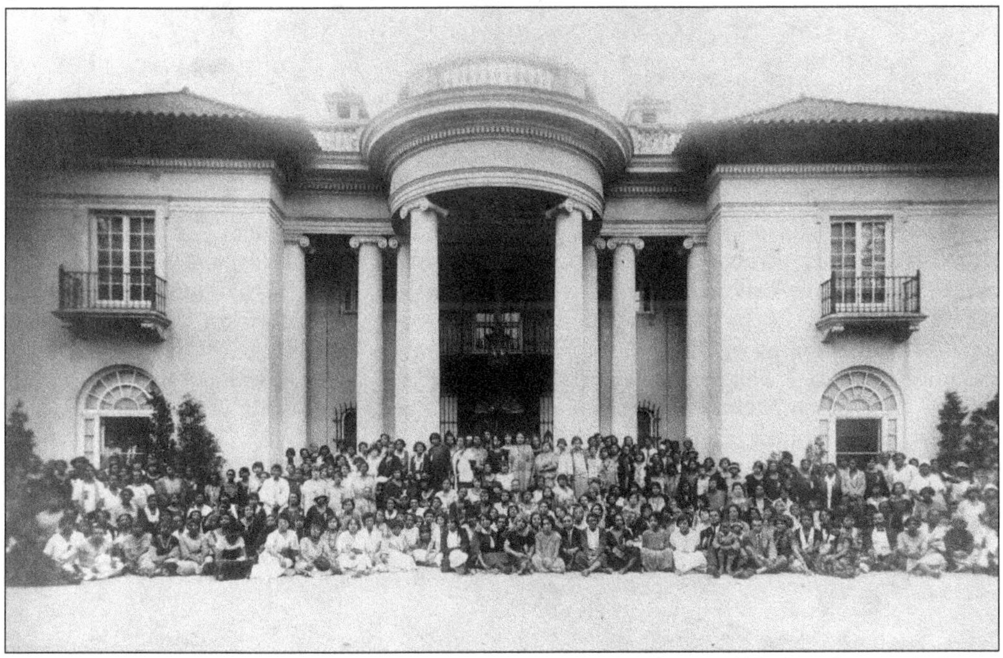

A Wonder House. Designed by Vertner Tandy, New York's first licensed black architect, the home was built with a view of the Hudson River in Irvington-on-Hudson, one of America's wealthiest towns; Villa Lewaro was not far from the estates of the Rockefellers, Goulds, Vanderbilts, and Tiffanys. The *New York Times Sunday Magazine* called it "a wonder house" and "one of the show places of the Hudson." (Courtesy of Madam Walker Family Archives.)

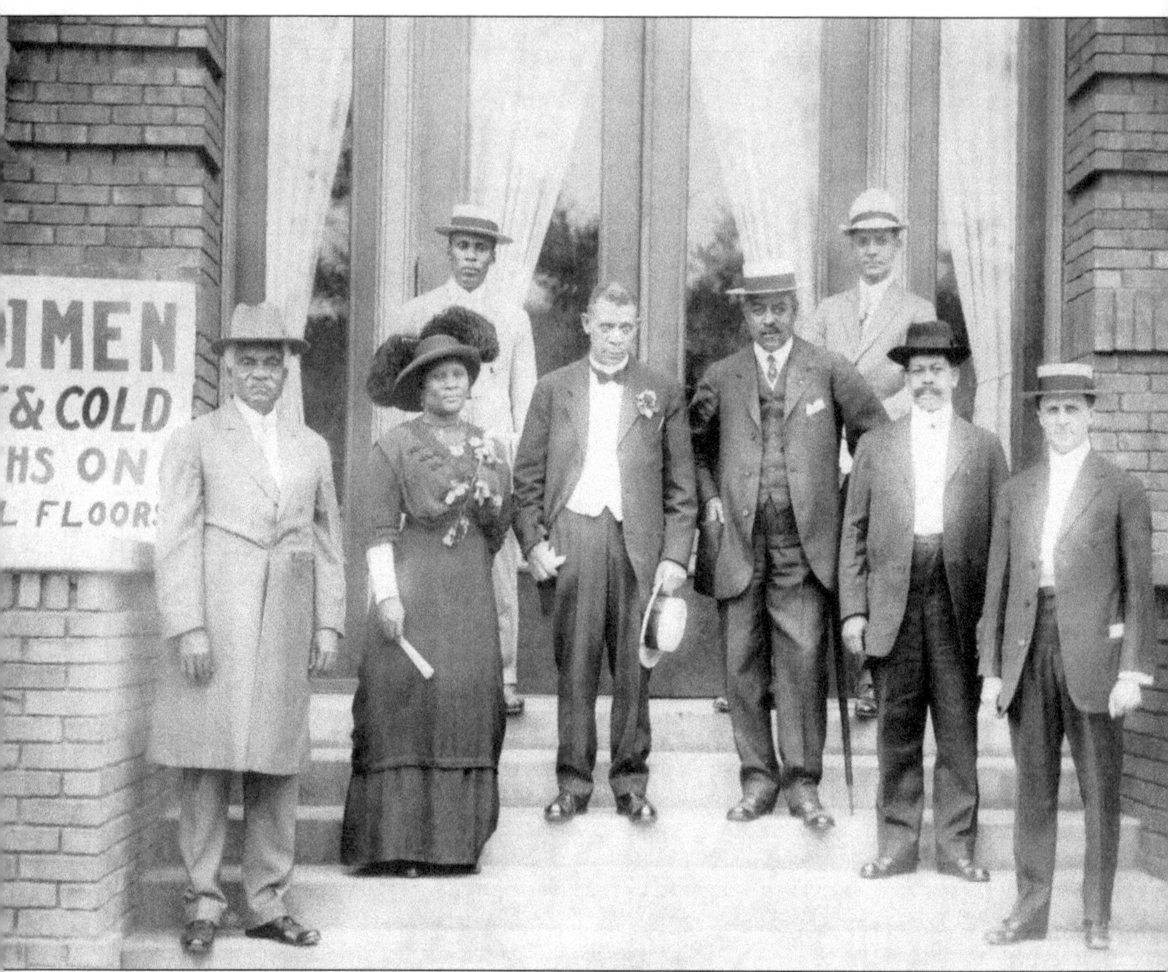

Sharing the Wealth. Shortly after she arrived in Indianapolis, Madam Walker contributed $1,000 to the Senate Avenue YMCA's building fund for a much-needed facility for black men and boys. At this 1913 dedication ceremony, Tuskegee Institute's Booker T. Washington (center) praised her for her gift, one of the many large donations she would make to black institutions. Walker combined philanthropy with political activism as a member of the NAACP's New York chapter executive committee. She counted among her friends Ida B. Wells, A. Philip Randolph, W.E.B. Du Bois, and William Monroe Trotter. She also was a life member of Washington's National Negro Business League. Shortly before her death, she pledged $5,000 to the NAACP's antilynching fund and bequeathed thousands of dollars to black schools and colleges. With Walker and Washington are, from left to right, *Indianapolis Freeman* publisher George Knox, F.B. Ransom, *Indianapolis World* publisher A.E. Manning, Dr. Joseph Ward, Louisville YMCA secretary R.W. Bullock, and Senate Avenue Y secretary Thomas Taylor. (Courtesy of Madam Walker Family Archives.)

Two

Anchoring the Avenue
Walker Headquarters

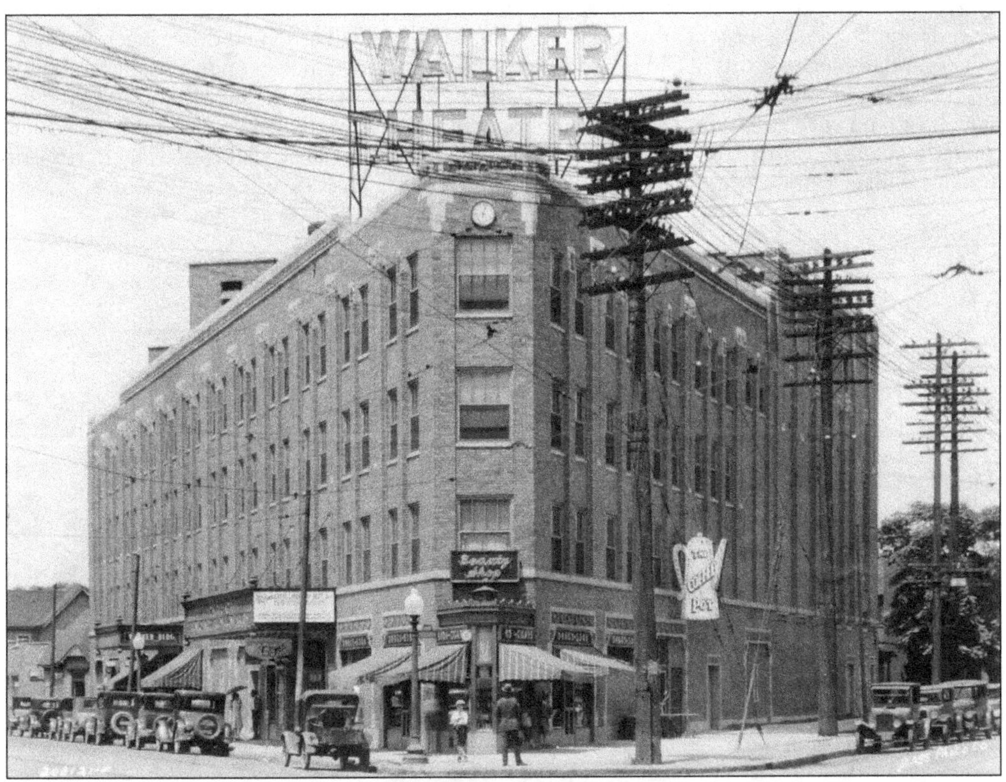

Anchoring the Avenue. In December 1927, the Madam Walker Company began moving into its new headquarters, a four-story, block-long, 48,000-square-foot flatiron structure. To a black community struggling against the forces of a Ku Klux Klan–controlled Indianapolis City Council, the building's movie theater, drugstore, restaurant, beauty salon, ballroom, and medical offices offered a welcomed haven. (Courtesy of Madam C.J. Walker Collection, Indiana Historical Society.)

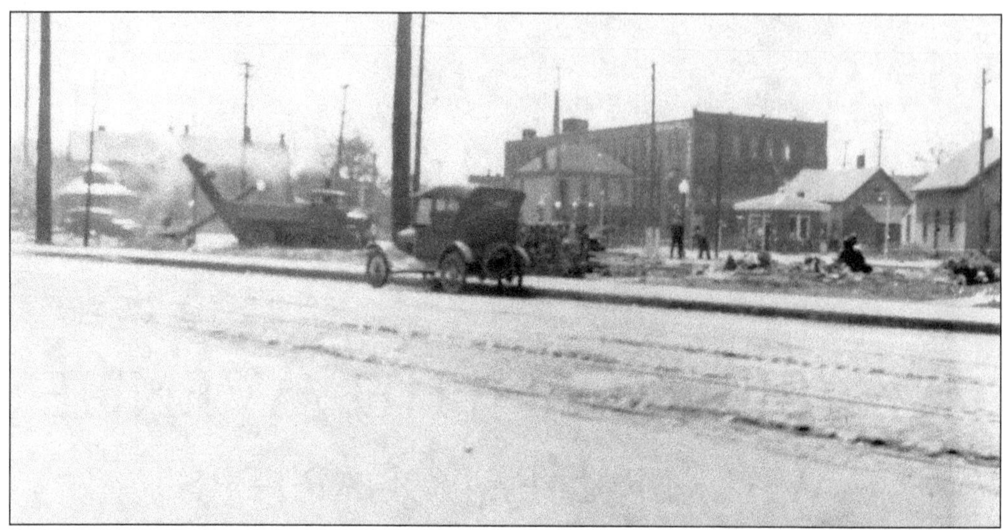

Transforming a Neighborhood. Surveyor Alexander Ralston created Downtown Indianapolis's original mile square plat in 1821. Modeled on the circles of Washington, DC, and Versailles, diagonal avenues radiated from a distinctive center. During the mid-19th century, African Americans began to cluster along the northwestern edge of the square in an area that was considered less than desirable because of a nearby canal. In 1910, Madam Walker joined other black business owners and residents in this neighborhood and vowed to improve living conditions. Planning for her new factory and office building began as early as 1914. By 1916, she had begun to purchase parcels of land with the intention of assembling a block-long triangular-shaped lot just outside the mile square. Construction for the Walker Building began in early 1927. (Above, courtesy of Madam Walker Family Archives; below, courtesy of Indiana Historical Society.)

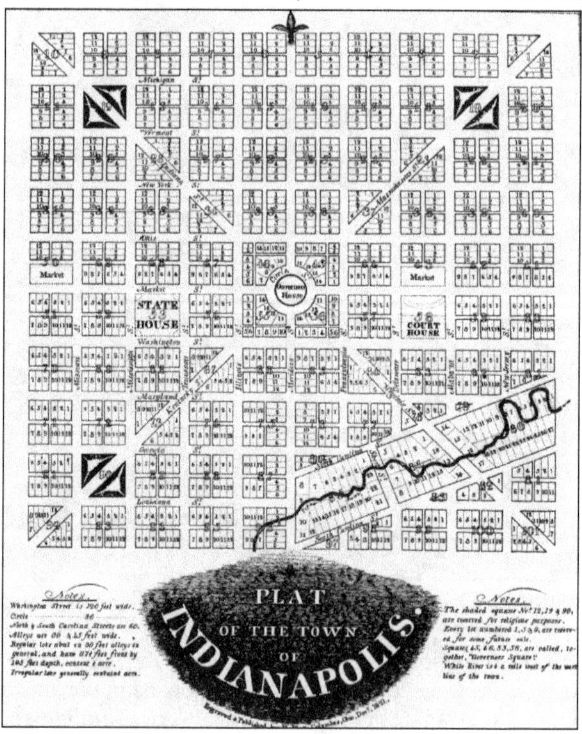

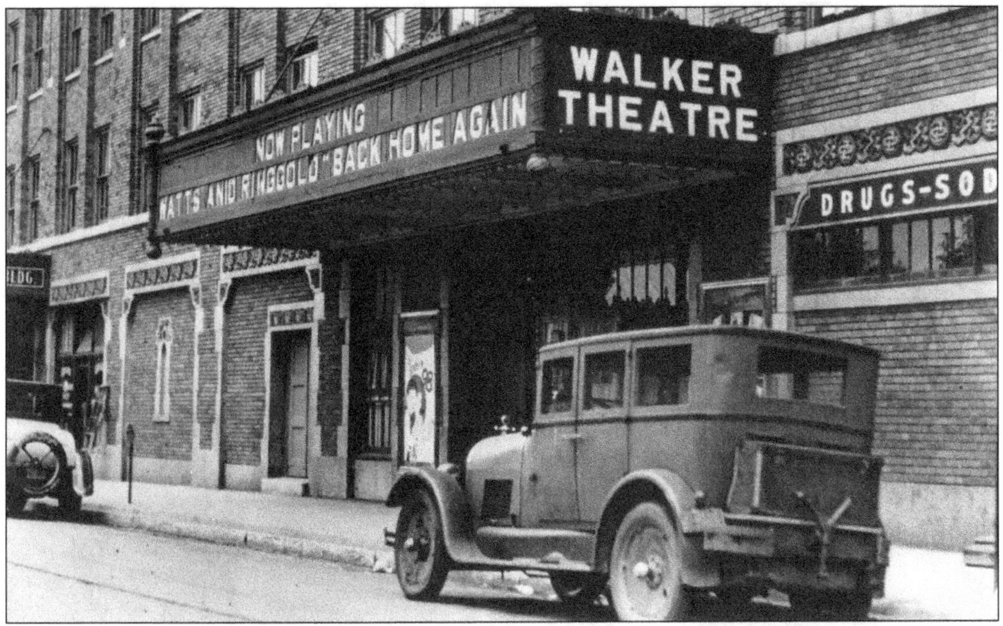

Standing Room Only. After a grand opening in December 1927, the Walker Theatre remained a popular venue for movies and vaudeville, with acts like Butterbeans and Susie, Mamie Smith and her Original Jazz Hounds, and the famed Whitman Sisters. Reginald DuValle, the Indianapolis pianist who taught composer Hoagy Carmichael to play ragtime and Jazz, led the Blackbirds, a favorite local orchestra. (Courtesy of W.H. Bass Collection, Indiana Historical Society.)

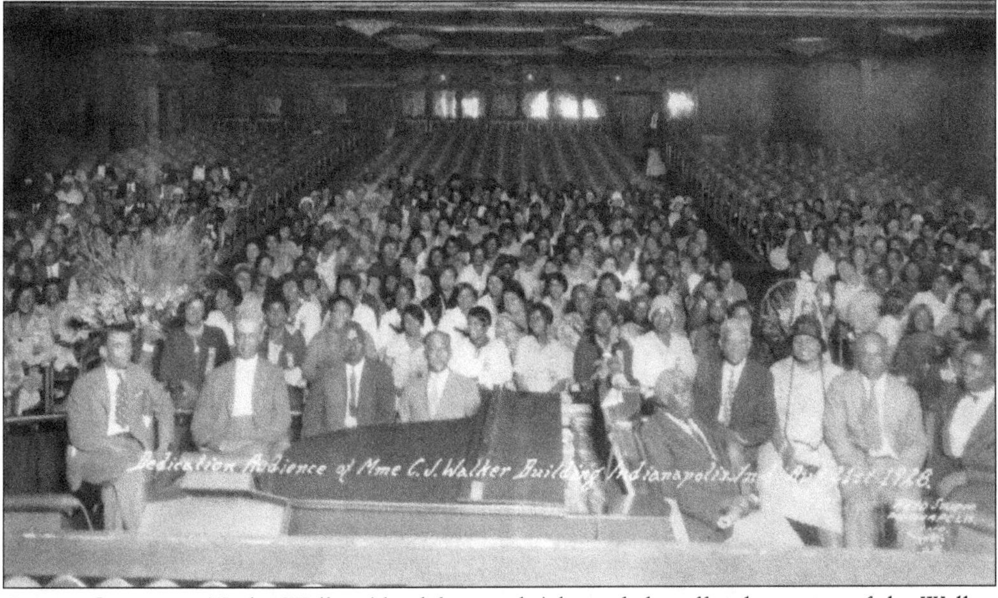

Grand Opening. A'Lelia Walker (third from right) hosted the official opening of the Walker Building in August 1928 during the 11th-annual National Convention of Walker Agents. Among the honored guests were composer J. Rosamond Johnson, Morgan State College dean William Pickens, North Carolina Mutual Insurance Company president C.C. Spaulding, Tuskegee president Robert R. Moton, and *Pittsburgh Courier* publisher Robert L. Vann. (Courtesy of Madam Walker Family Archives.)

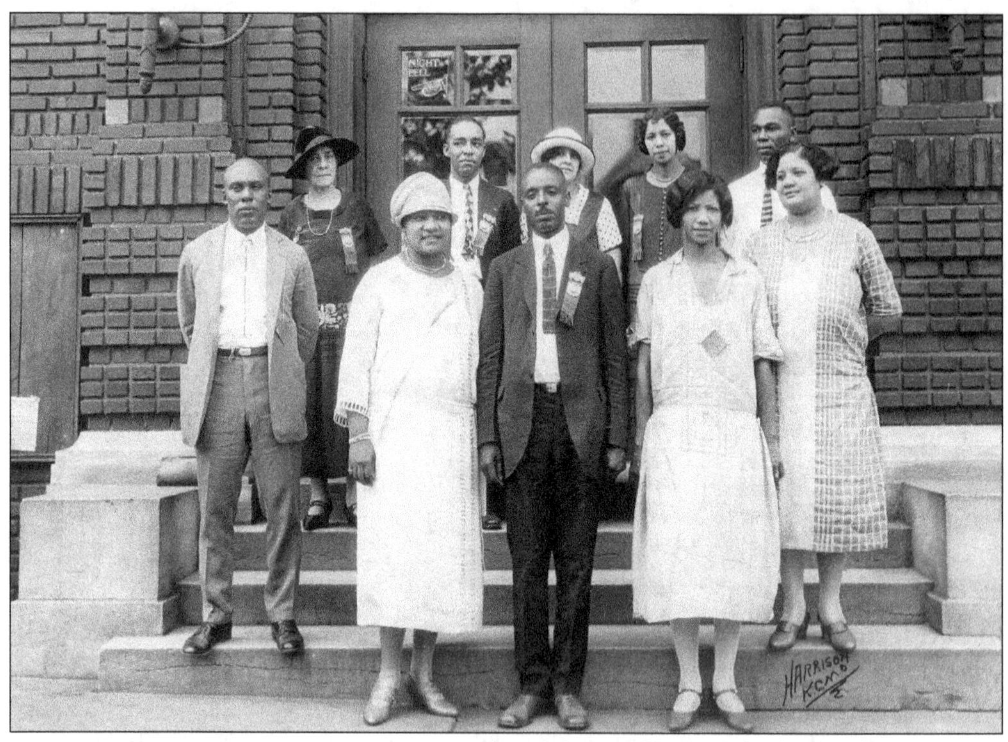

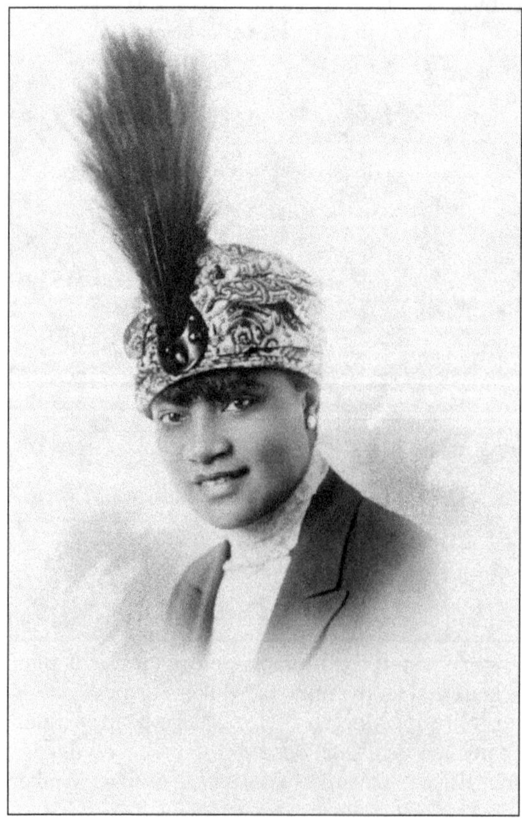

At the Helm. After her mother's death in May 1919, A'Lelia Walker was named Walker Company president. As she managed the Harlem office, F.B. Ransom and Alice Kelly directed Indianapolis operations. Wearing a white chapeau, she appears on the front row with Robert Brokenburr and Violet Reynolds. Immediately behind her are, from left to right, Ransom, Kelly, and advertising manager Harry Evans. Others are unidentified. (Courtesy of Madam Walker Family Archives.)

Harlem Hostess. A'Lelia Walker continued representing Walker Company interests at annual conventions and overseeing her New York school and salon, but as the Harlem Renaissance of the 1920s blossomed, she became immersed in the era's cultural activities. She converted a floor of her town house into a literary and music salon, hosting guests like Langston Hughes, Alberta Hunter, and Florence Mills, and Carl Van Vechten. (Courtesy of Madam Walker Family Archives.)

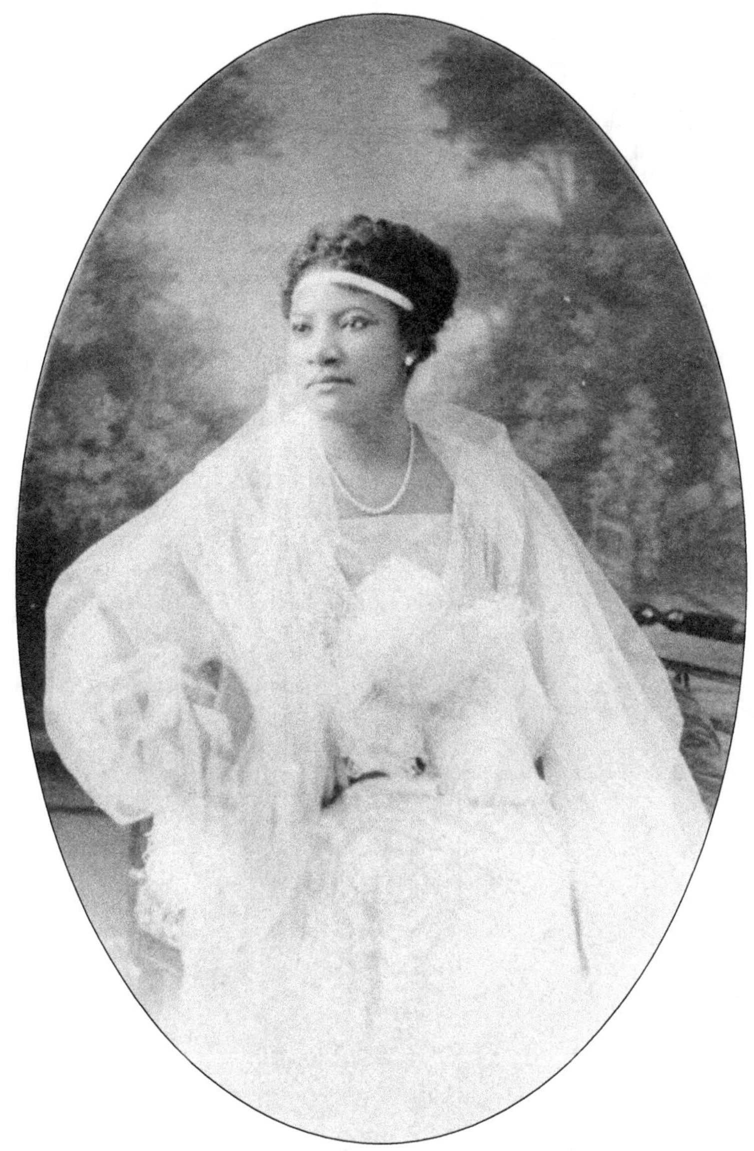

Joy Goddess of Harlem. Just three days after burying her mother in a private ceremony at Woodlawn Cemetery in the Bronx, A'Lelia Walker married her second husband, Dr. Wiley Wilson, but they soon separated. In November 1921, she sailed in a first-class cabin on the SS *Paris* for an eight-month excursion to Europe, Africa, and the Middle East. In Paris, she booked a suite at the Hotel Carleton on the Avenue des Champs-Élysées and was invited to a private jewelry showing at Cartier. She attended the opera at London's Covent Garden and witnessed the coronation of Pope Pius XI in Rome. In Cairo, she toured the pyramids on camelback and stayed at Shepherd's Hotel, a favorite haunt of wealthy Americans. In Ethiopia, she was granted an audience with Empress Zauditu. Her parties so defined the Harlem Renaissance that poet Langston Hughes crowned her "the joy goddess of Harlem's 1920s." (Courtesy of Madam Walker Family Archives.)

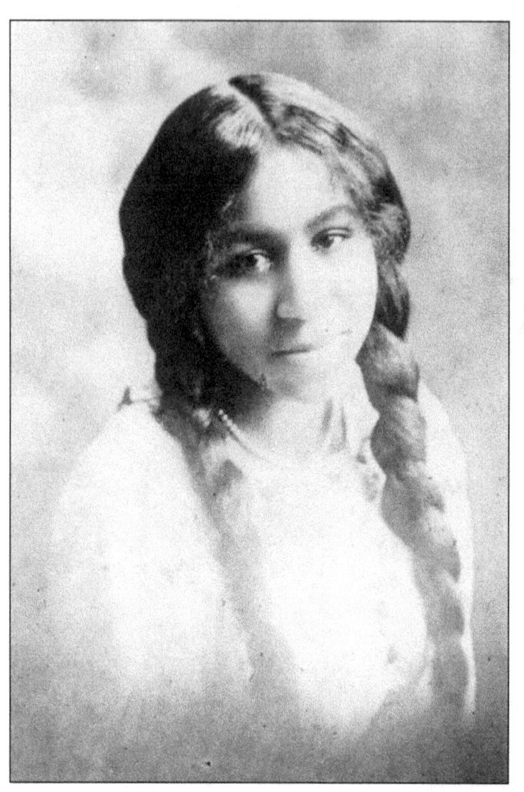

A Fairy Tale. Shortly after Madam Walker moved to Indianapolis, she met Semira Thomas Hammond, a neighbor whose granddaughter Fairy Mae Bryant began serving as a model for Walker's hair demonstrations. Her hip-length braids provided a perfect advertisement for Walker's Wonderful Hair Grower. Although two of Mae's ancestors had been free men of color, who served in the Continental Army from North Carolina during the Revolutionary War, her widowed mother, Sarah Hammond Bryant, struggled to rear her and her seven siblings. When A'Lelia Walker suggested adoption, Sarah Bryant reluctantly agreed when the Walkers promised to educate Mae and allow her to maintain contact with her family. Fairy Mae, who became known as Mae Walker, graduated with honors from Spelman Seminary in 1920. She was Walker Company president from 1931 until her death in 1945. (Both, courtesy of Madam Walker Family Archives.)

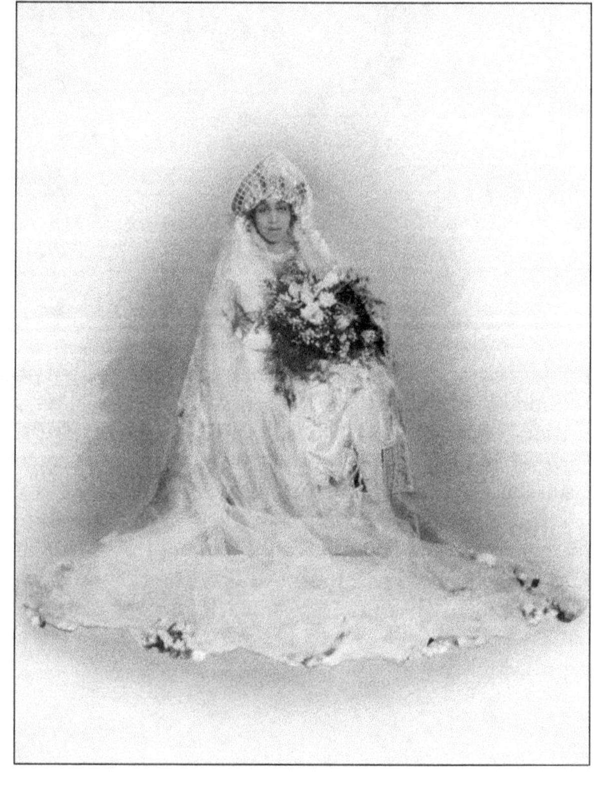

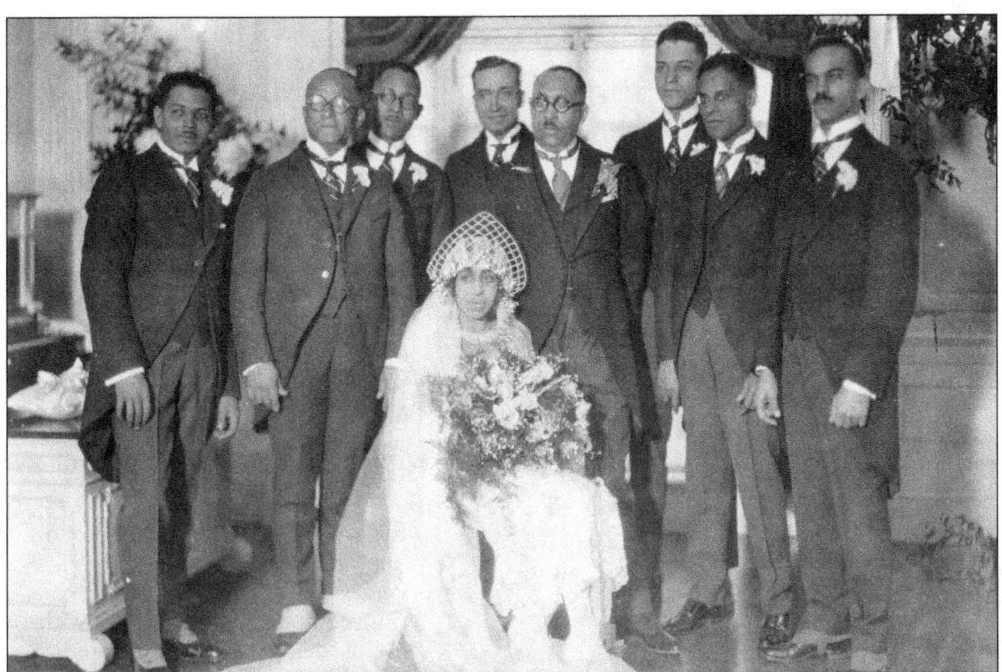

Social Event of the Season, 1923. Mae Walker married Dr. Gordon H. Jackson, fifth from left, the grandson of a wealthy entrepreneur, in a November 1923 wedding arranged by A'Lelia Walker. Mae's sad face tells the story as she sits surrounded by Gordon's groomsmen, all of whom were physicians, dentists, and lawyers. Her bridesmaids—dressed in custom-gowns and handmade shoes—also were from prominent families. The ceremony at Harlem's St. Philip's Episcopal Church was featured in all major black newspapers and several white dailies. A'Lelia Walker, who had sent souvenir invitations to Walker agents, considered the $40,000 tab valuable publicity for the Walker Company. (Both courtesy Madam Walker Family Archives.)

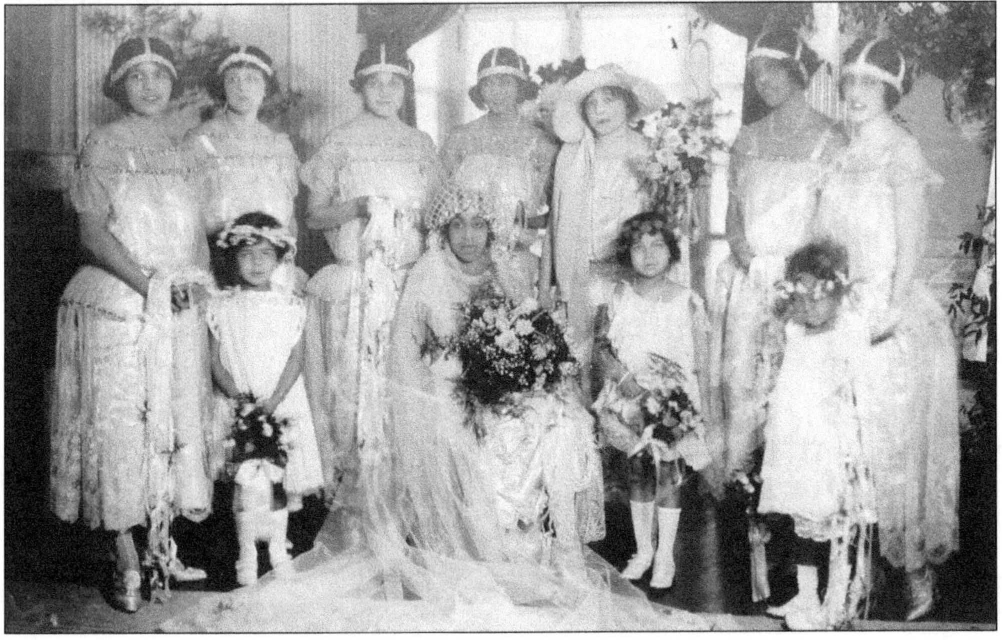

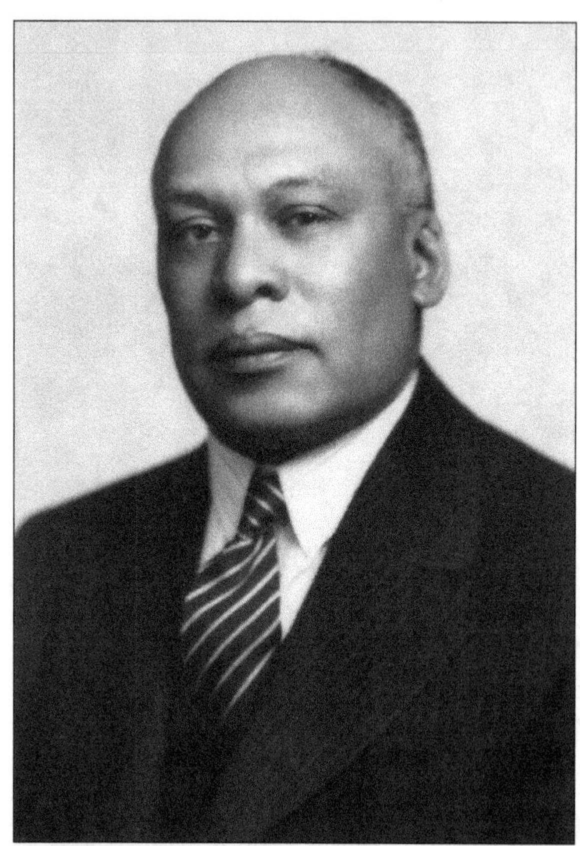

A Tight Ship. Freeman Briley Ransom served as Walker Company attorney and general manager from 1911 until his death in 1947. His political sophistication and legal and financial skills were critical to the ongoing operation of the enterprise after Madam Walker's death and the construction of the Walker Building. Ransom was elected to the Indianapolis City Council in 1938 and served on several civic boards. (Courtesy of Madam Walker Family Archives.)

Family Man. F.B. Ransom, second from right, and his wife, Nettie Cox Ransom, seated, celebrate their 25th anniversary in 1937 with five of their six children. Clifford is seated. Standing are, from left to right, Willard, Robert, Frederic, and A'Lelia Emma, who was named for her godmother, A'Lelia Walker. Son Frank is not pictured. (Courtesy of the Ransom family.)

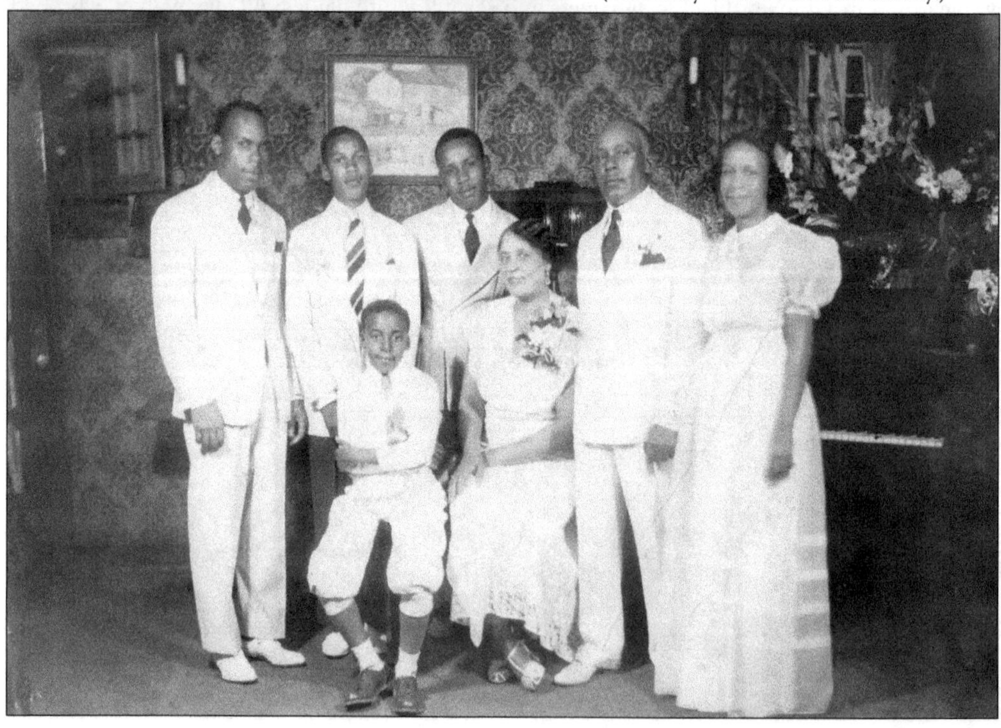

Close Confidante. When Madam Walker met Alice Kelly around 1909, she persuaded Kelly to leave her position as a Latin teacher at Eckstein-Norton Institute in Cane Springs, Kentucky, and become her factory "forelady." Kelly also served as traveling companion and tutor to Walker, who was determined to improve her communications skills. Walker left Kelly $10,000 in her will and entrusted her with her secret formula. (Courtesy of Madam Walker Family Archives.)

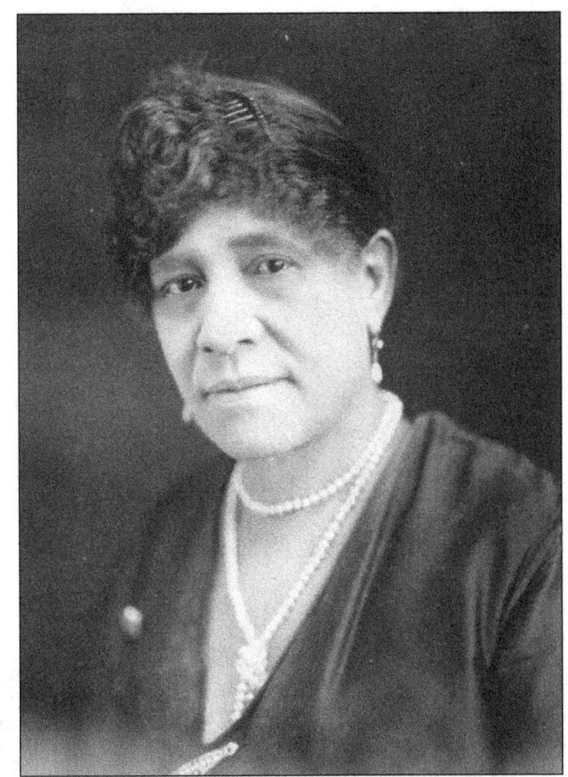

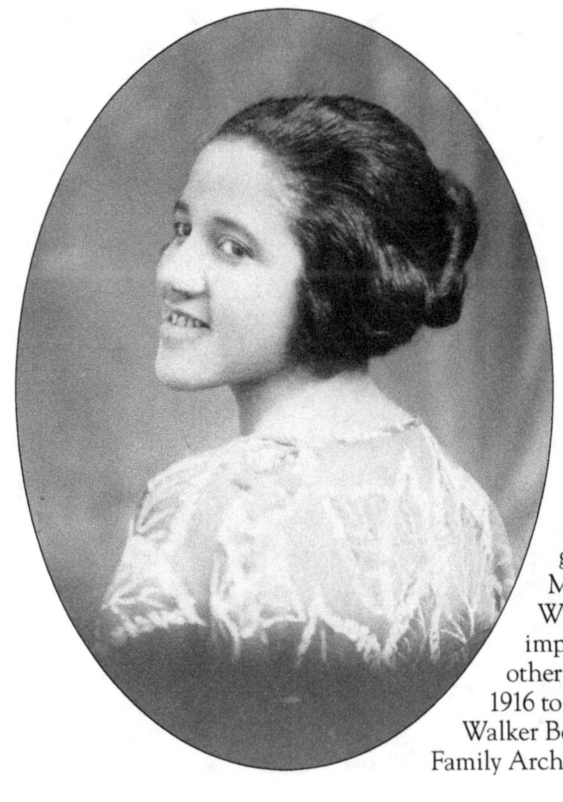

Dynamo. A talented orator and natural leader, Marjorie Stewart Joyner already had graduated from Chicago Musical College and Moler Beauty School when she met Madam Walker in 1916. Joyner's hairstyling skills so impressed Walker that she hired her to train other women. A Walker Company employee from 1916 to 1963, she served as national supervisor of 12 Walker Beauty Schools. (Courtesy of Madam Walker Family Archives.)

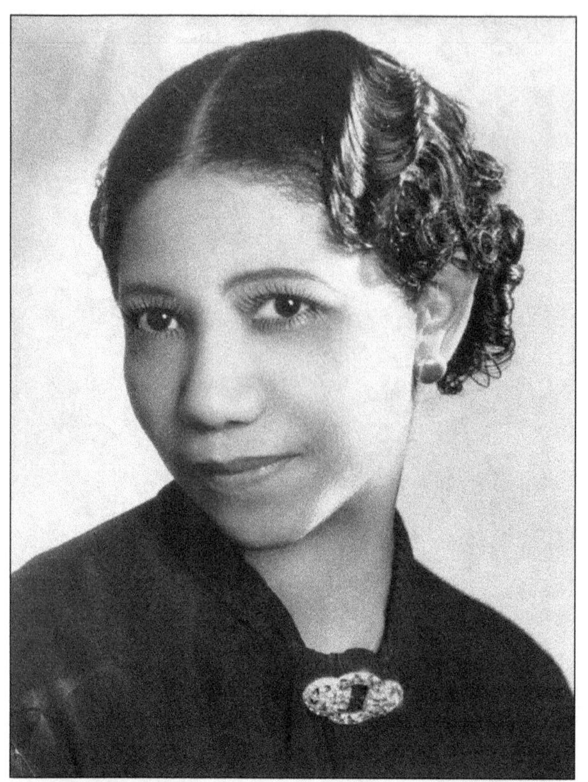

Keeper of the Flame. Violet Davis Reynolds was only 16 years old in 1914 when Madam Walker recruited her to work as a secretary. A Birmingham, Alabama, native and former Eckstein-Norton student of Alice Kelly's, Reynolds retired in 1982 as secretary of the Walker board of trustees. A *Remarkable Woman,* her brief Walker biography, was invaluable. (Courtesy of Madam Walker Family Archives.)

Barrier Breaker. Madam Walker enlisted attorney Robert Lee Brokenburr, a graduate of Hampton Institute and Howard University Law School, to file her official articles of incorporation in 1911. Elected the first black Indiana State senator in 1940, Brokenburr appears with Tony Reynolds, son of Walker secretary Violet Reynolds, in the Indiana Statehouse in 1946. (Courtesy of the Reynolds family.)

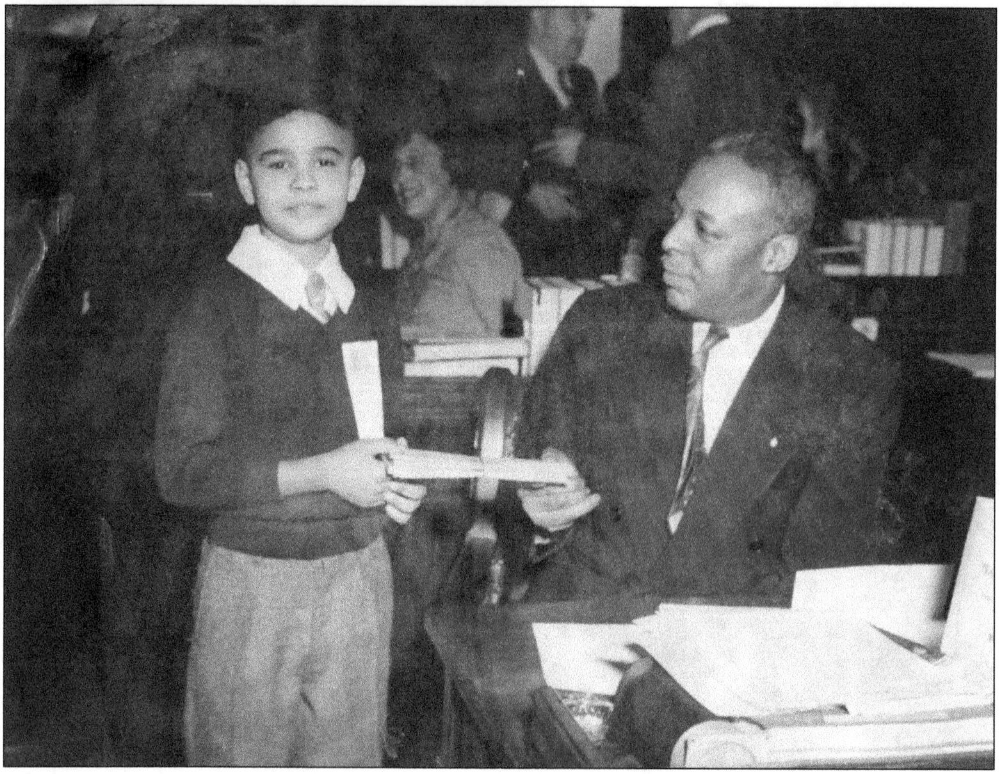

Three

Beauty to Ballroom
A City within a City

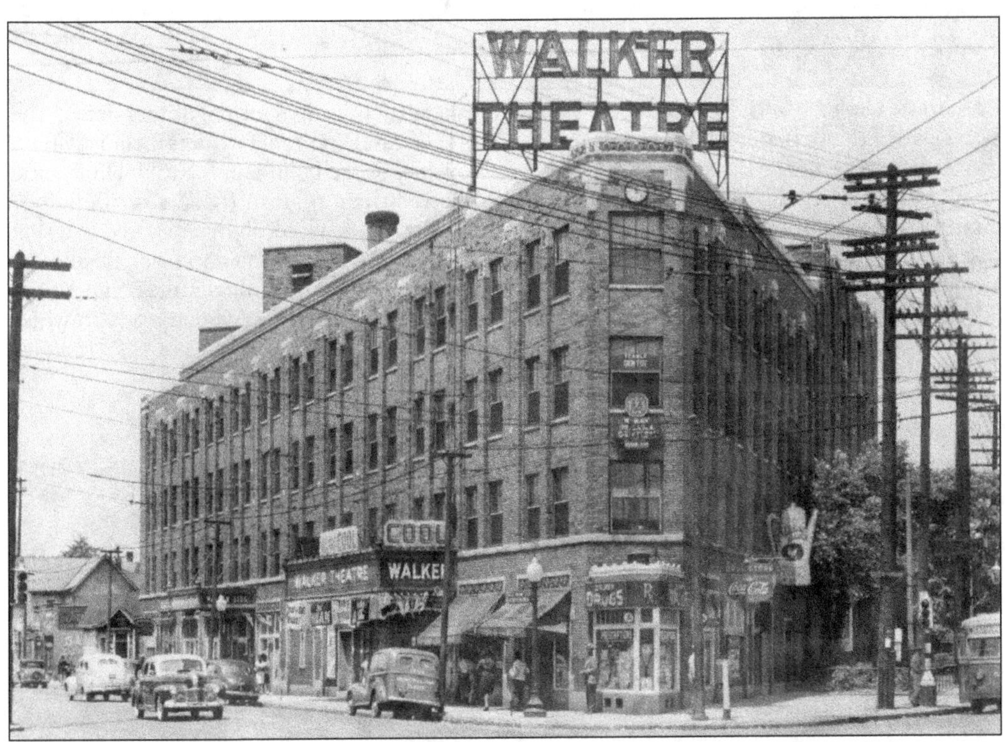

City within a City. The Walker Building had something for everyone. As the corporate headquarters, it provided jobs and pride for the city's black residents. Its hairstylists were among the best in the country. The doctors and dentists were graduates of the nation's top schools. The theater showed only first-run movies, and the popcorn was always fresh. (Courtesy of Madam C.J. Walker Collection, Indiana Historical Society.)

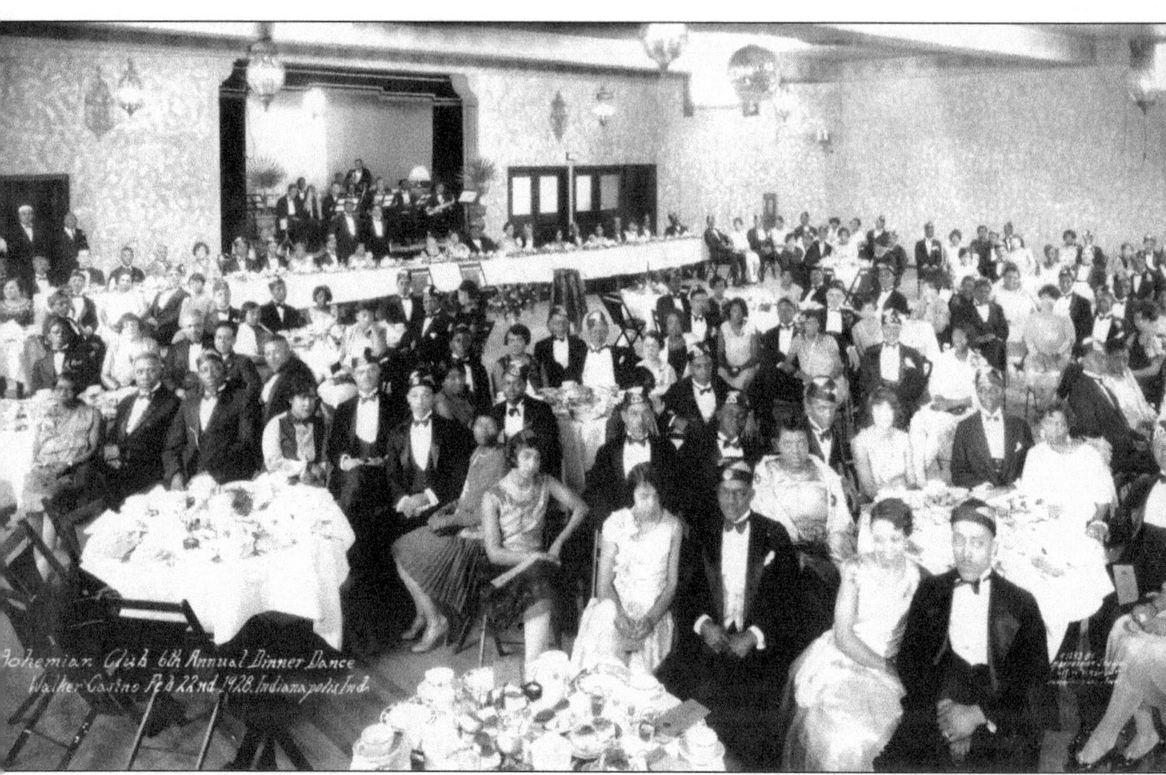

Bohemian Club, 1928. To ensure nonstop live music at their annual formal dinner dance, the 50 couples of the Bohemian Club usually hired two orchestras. Perennial favorites included Frank Fowler Brown's Bammy Boys, Kioda Barber's Jazz Hoppers, Russell Williams's Rinky Dinks, and Frank Hines's Margulators. In February 1928, they hosted their affair in the Walker Building's Grand Casino Ballroom, one of the first halls in Indianapolis with a revolving mirrored ball that cast swirling rainbow lights and prisms across the dance floor. With the men in black tie and the women in silk and chiffon, the couples had prepared for weeks for the annual waltz competition. As the evening ended, 50 bright yellow taxis assembled along Indiana Avenue ready to whisk the revelers home. (Courtesy of Madam Walker Theatre Center.)

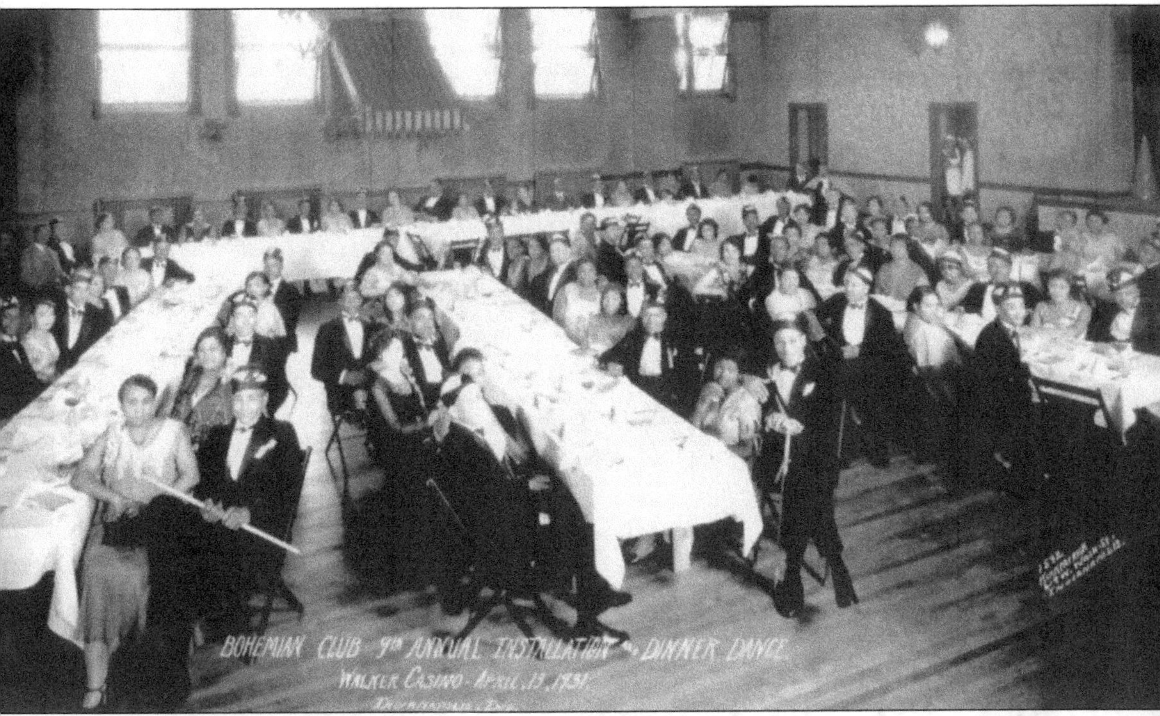

Bohemian Club, 1931. Perhaps a reflection of hard times brought on by the Stock Market Crash of 1929, the Bohemian Club attendance had dropped for its ninth annual dinner dance. Nevertheless, the members maintained their elegance. Their all-day gathering—often noteworthy enough to be covered by the *Chicago Defender* and *Pittsburgh Courier*—usually began with orations and the installation of officers. One year's menu included cream of tomato soup with whipped cream, boiled pork tenderloin, cream peas in patties, hot rolls, and ice cream. Through the years, other black social clubs, fraternities, sororities, churches, and schools hosted luncheons, cotillions, graduation ceremonies, and proms in the Casino. (Courtesy of Madam Walker Theatre Center.)

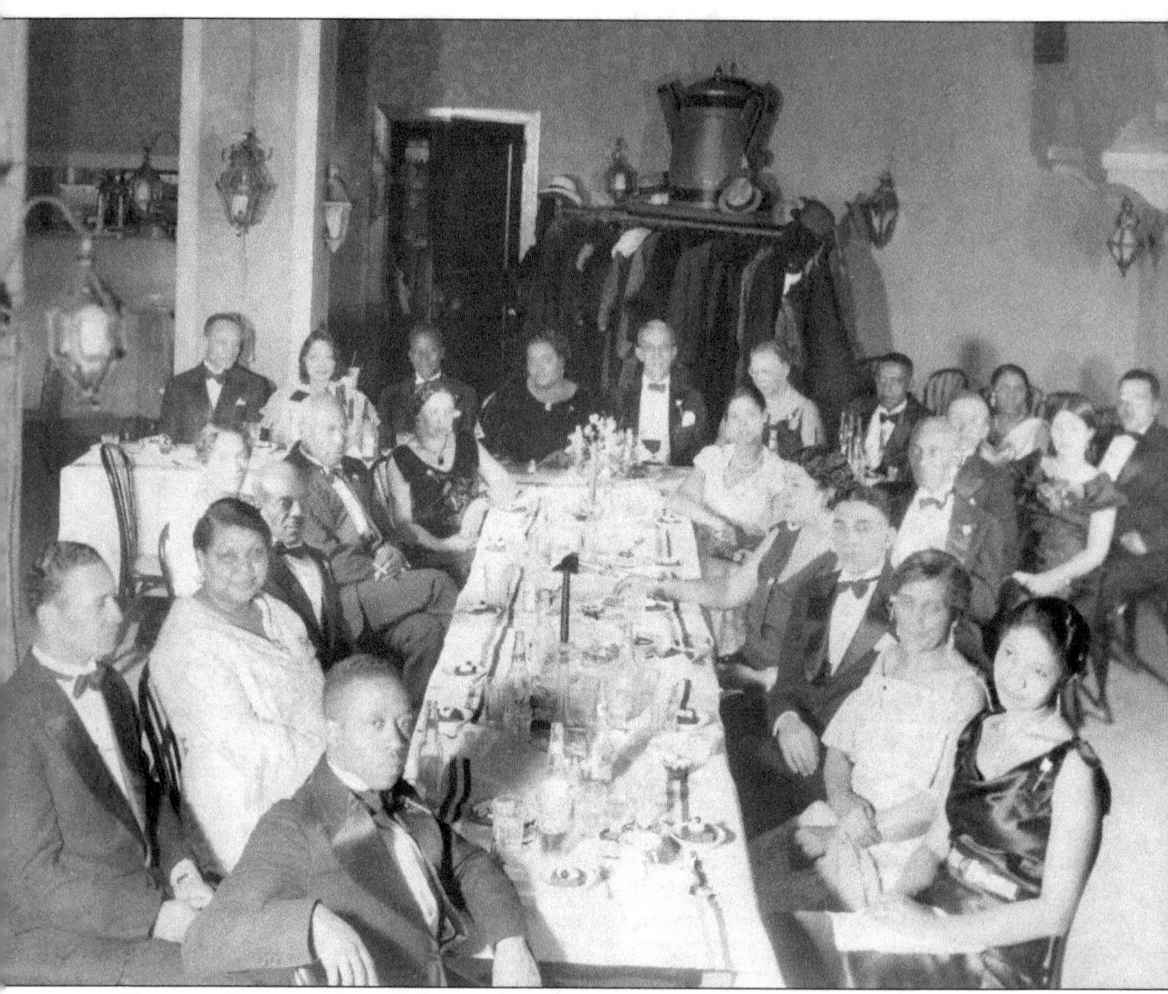

Elegant Evening. For smaller, more intimate gatherings, the Walker Coffee Pot provided the perfect setting. Its signature over-sized coffee pot sits atop the coat rack in the back of the room. This group of elegantly attired diners includes longtime Walker Company secretary, Violet Reynolds, front right in black dress. For Sunday afternoon dinners, "meet me at the Coffee Pot" was a popular refrain. Decorated in Spanish tile, the restaurant's motif evoked an outdoor garden. Breakfast was served from 7:30 a.m. until 11:30 a.m. Dinner entrees included T-bone steak for $1.50, shrimp for 95¢, pork chops for 90¢, and fried chicken for 85¢. (Courtesy of the Reynolds family.)

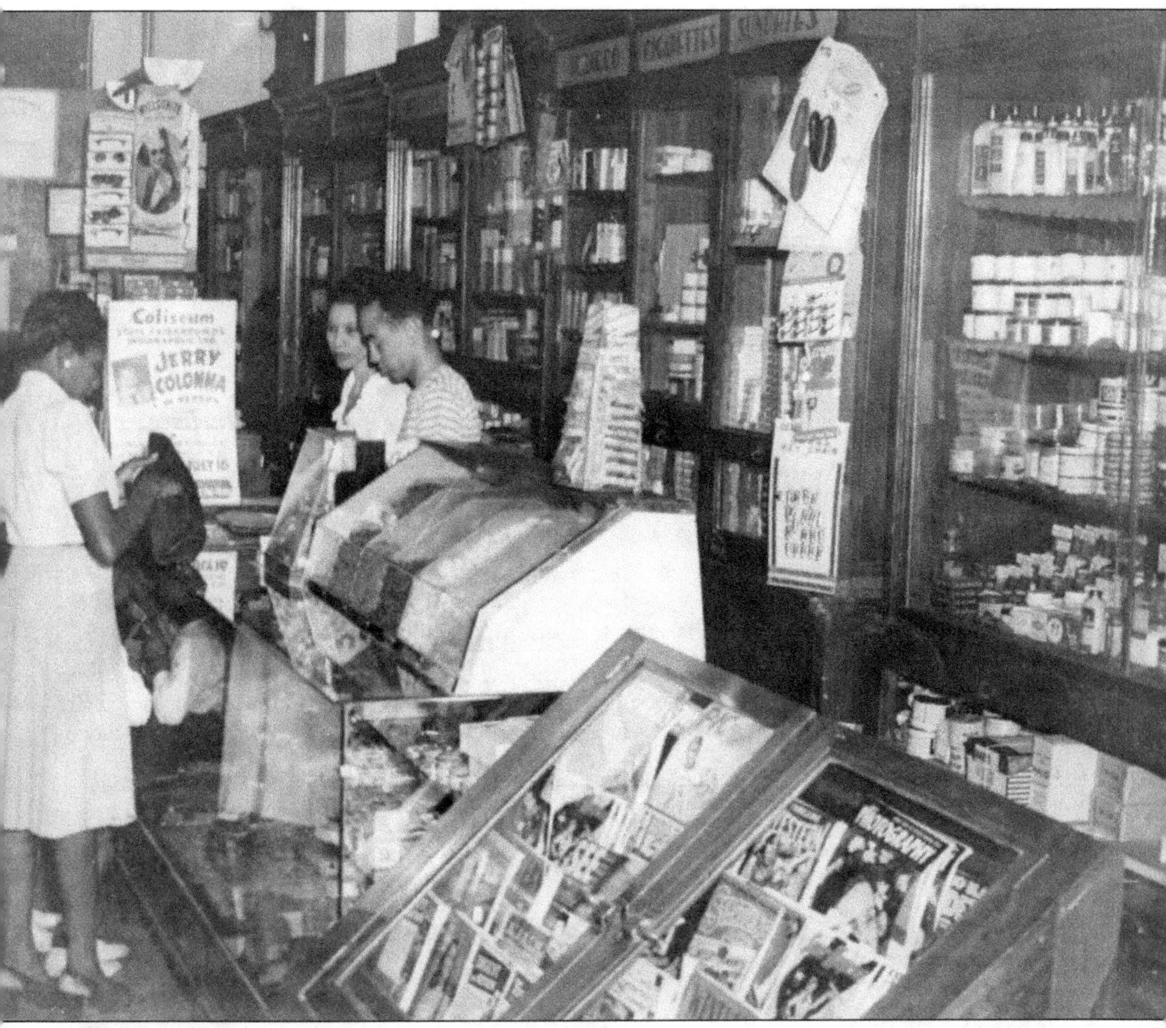

WALKER DRUGSTORE, 1946. The Walker Drugstore occupied the triangular point of the building where Indiana Avenue met West Street (now Dr. Martin Luther King Jr. Street). Striped awnings above its display windows welcomed customers who could purchase everything from magazines and sunglasses to aspirin and, of course, Walker products. Students walking home from nearby Crispus Attucks High School and Public Schools Nos. 1 and 24 flocked to the ice cream freezer for Dreamsicles, Drumsticks, and Popsicles. The management promised "positively no stale seconds, inferior or refuse merchandise will be used, stocked, or sold." Behind the counter is Walker Gordon Perry, son of Mae Walker and Dr. Gordon Jackson. Adopted as a toddler by Mae's second husband, Marion Perry, he was a graduate of Pennsylvania's Lincoln University. (Courtesy of Madam Walker Family Archives.)

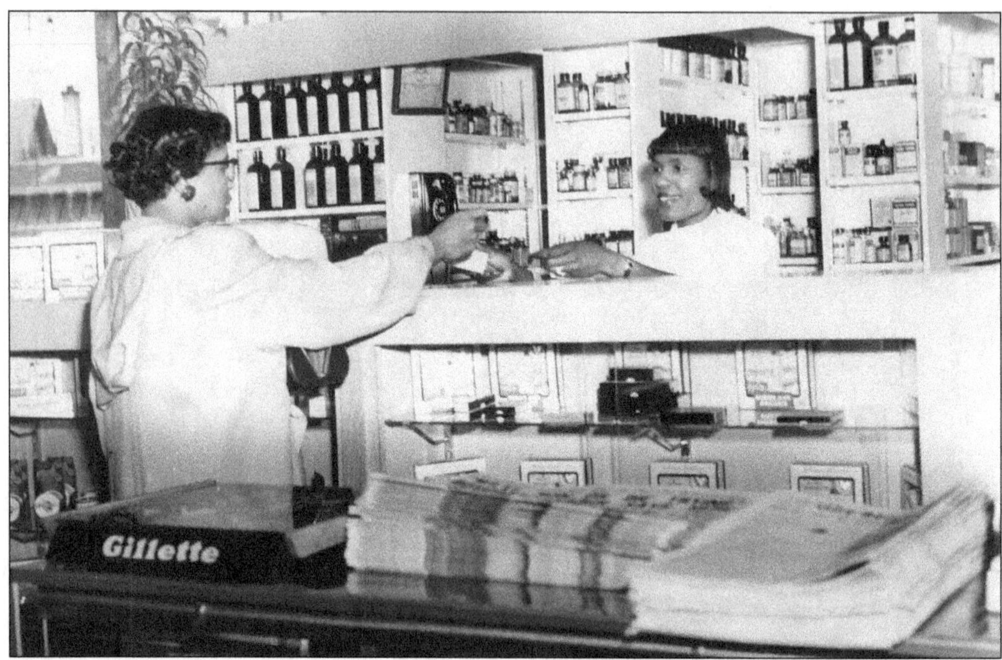

First-class Pharmacy. Elsie Jefferson, one of the few licensed women pharmacists in Indiana during the 1950s, was on the Walker Drugstore staff. With doctors' and dentists' offices upstairs and two hospitals nearby, there was a ready-made clientele for prescriptions. (Courtesy of Madam Walker Family Archives.)

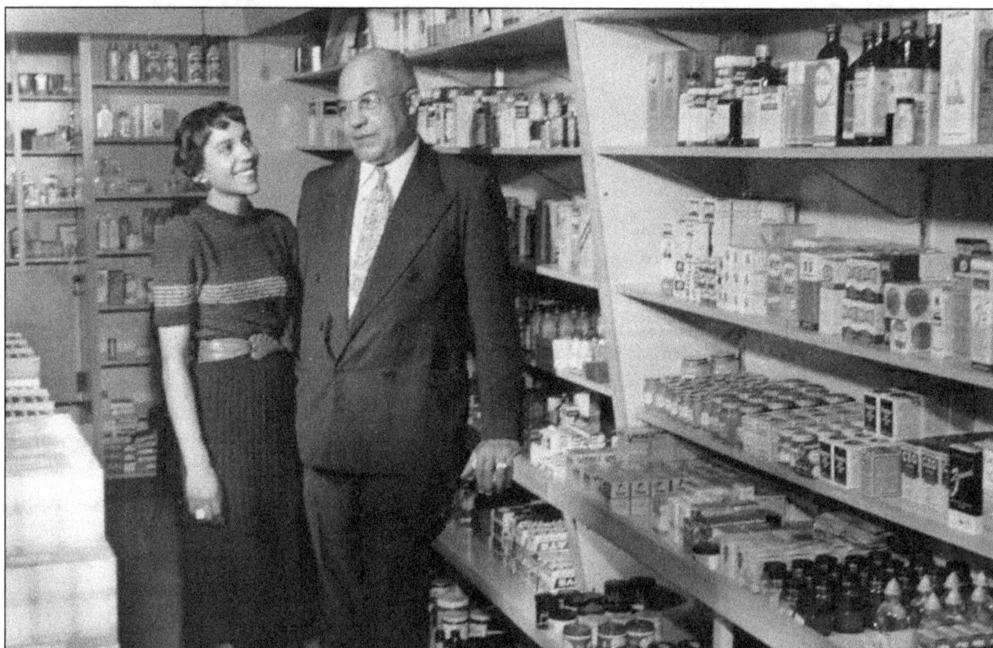

In the Family. Marion R. Perry, Mae Walker's second husband whom she married in 1927, was an attorney and a trustee of the Sarah Walker Estate. Shown here with his daughter A'Lelia Mae Perry Bundles, he managed the Walker Drugstore during the mid-1950s. (Courtesy of Madam Walker Family Archives.)

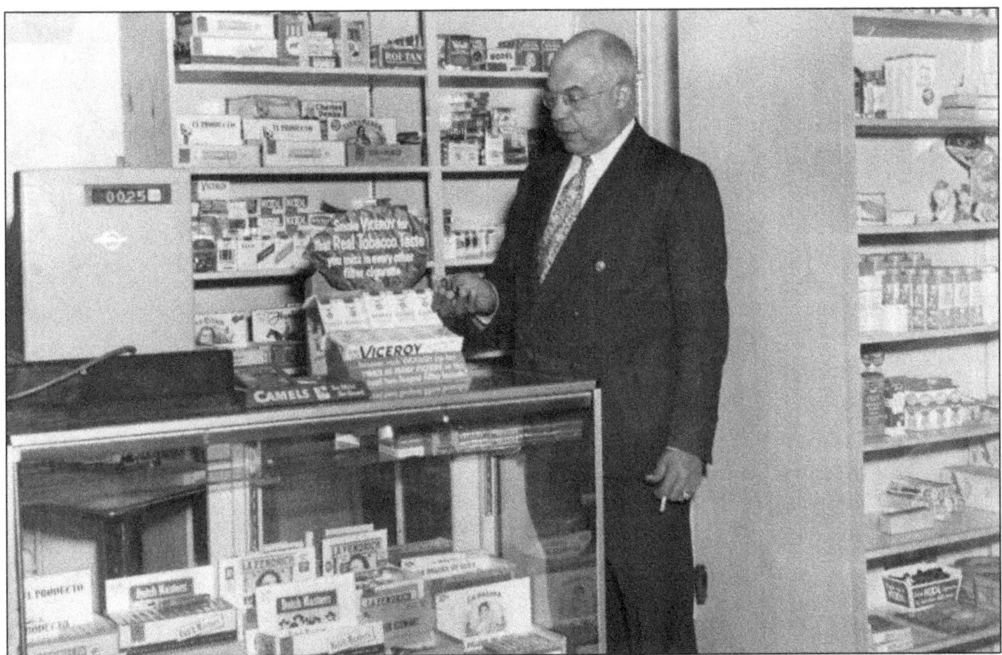

A Fine Selection. Born in 1892, Marion Perry, was a graduate of Lincoln University and University of Pittsburgh's Law School. A few years before the surgeon general's 1964 report warned of the link between smoking and cancer, Perry proudly displays his selection of cigars and cigarettes. In his left hand is a half-smoked Lucky Strike. (Courtesy of Madam Walker Family Archives.)

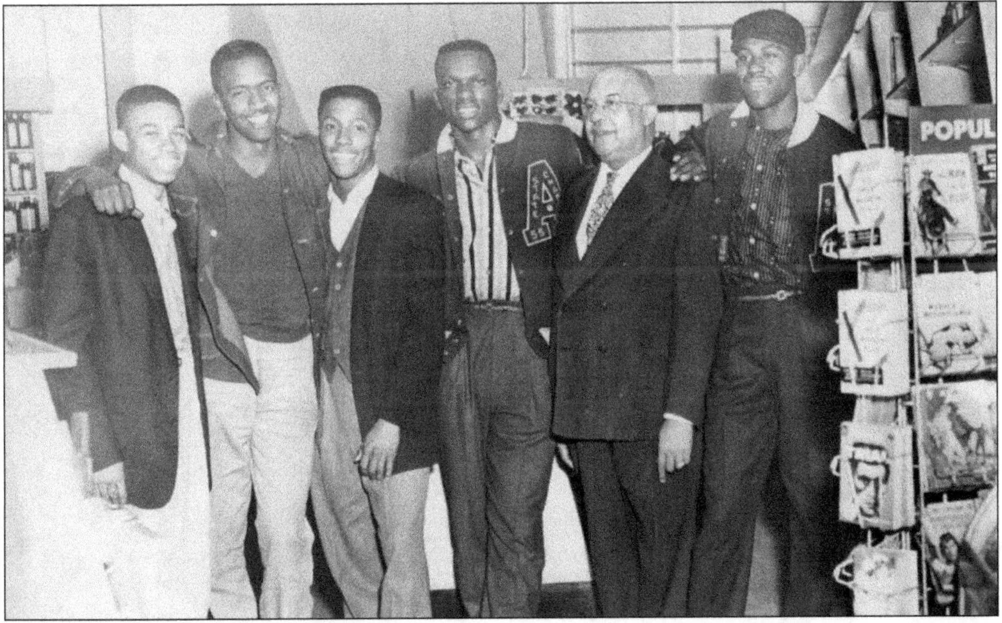

Basketball Champions, 1956. Located just a few blocks from the Walker Building, Crispus Attucks High School became the first school in Indiana history to win the state basketball championship in an undefeated season. In the starting five was the legendary Oscar Robertson. Marion Perry poses with other members of the team who were regular customers. (Courtesy of Madam Walker Family Archives.)

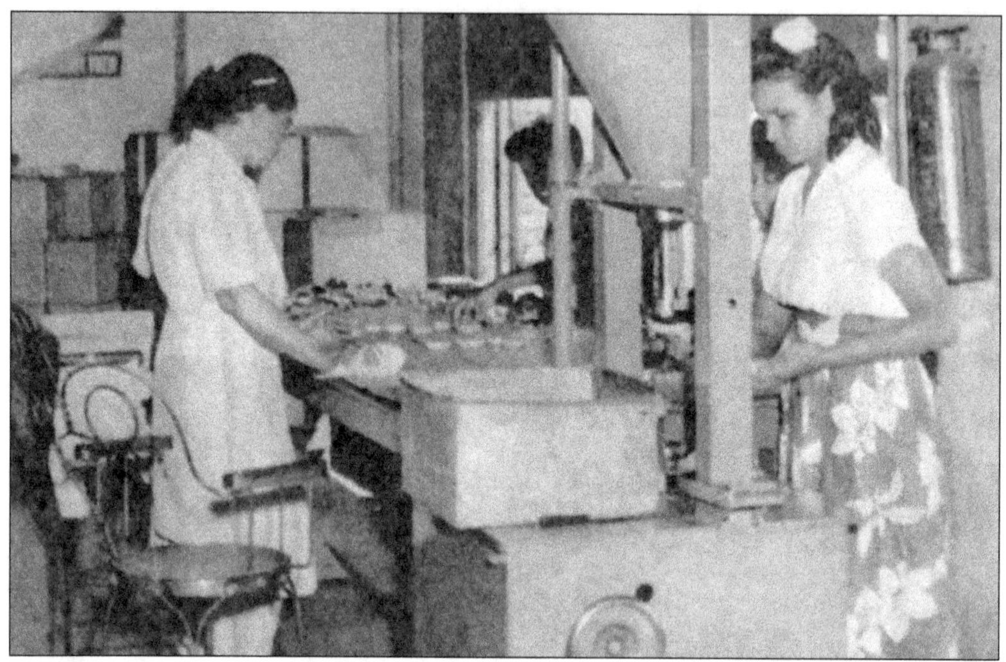

Handled with Care. From the clerical staff to the shipping room, most of the Walker Company employees were women, a legacy of Madam Walker's interest in helping other women to become economically independent. Each jar or tin of ointment was filled by hand, sealed, and boxed, then sent to the shipping room. (Courtesy of Madam Walker Family Archives.)

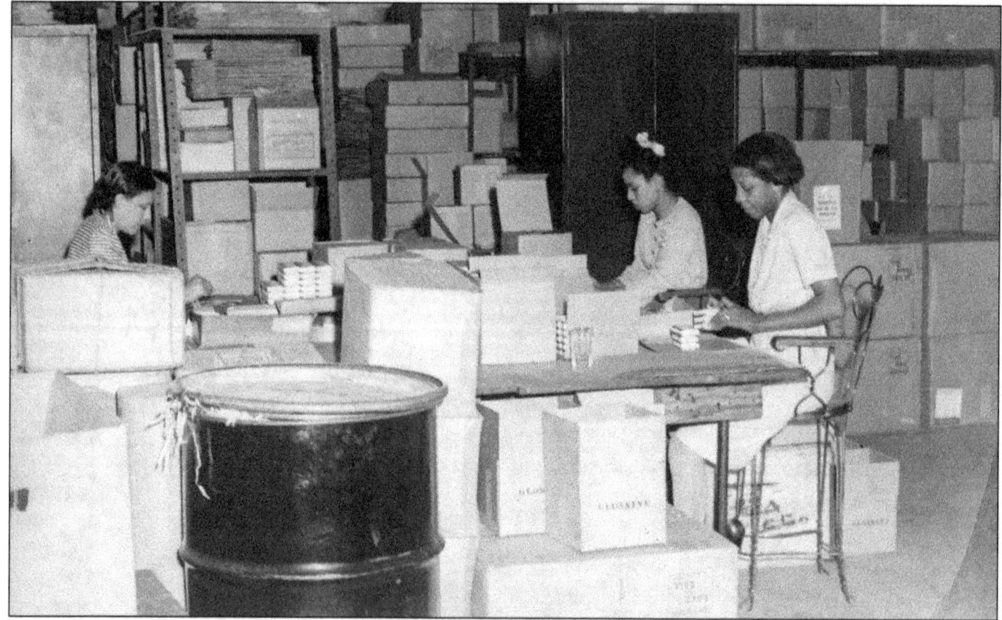

Getting It Right. The morning mail brought hundreds of orders. On a clunky machine called an Address-o-graph, secretaries typed each new address onto small metal rectangles, similar to dog tags, to create a permanent plate for future orders. In the shipping room, paper labels printed from the Address-o-graph were pasted onto boxes and then double-checked for accuracy. (Courtesy of Madam Walker Family Archives.)

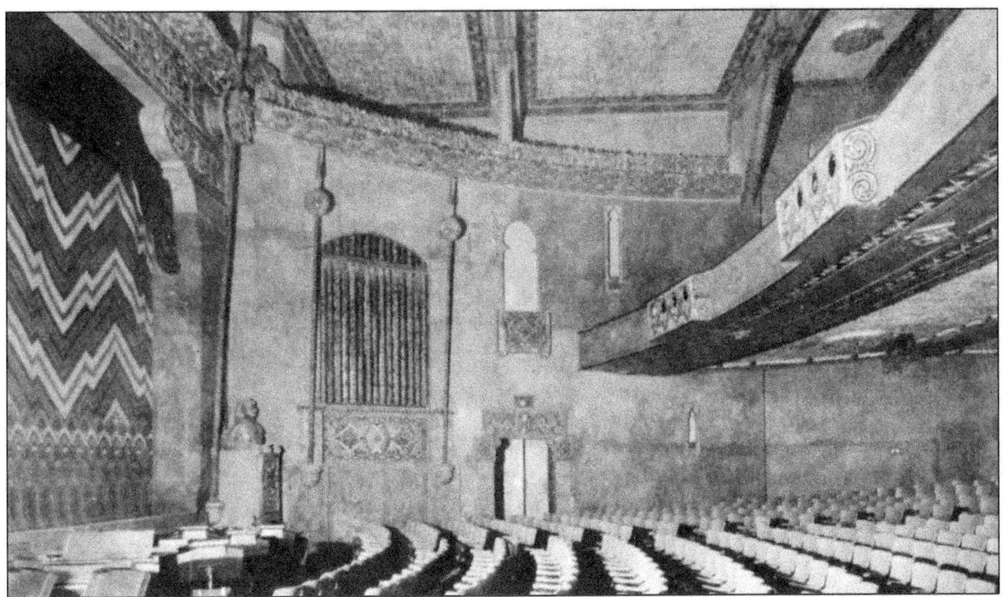

African Heritage. With the Indiana Roof Ballroom designed the same year as the Walker Building, architects Preston Rubush and Edgar Hunter applied Spanish Baroque details to both. For the Walker's audience, they added Egyptian and African touches throughout the building. (Courtesy of Madam Walker Family Archives.)

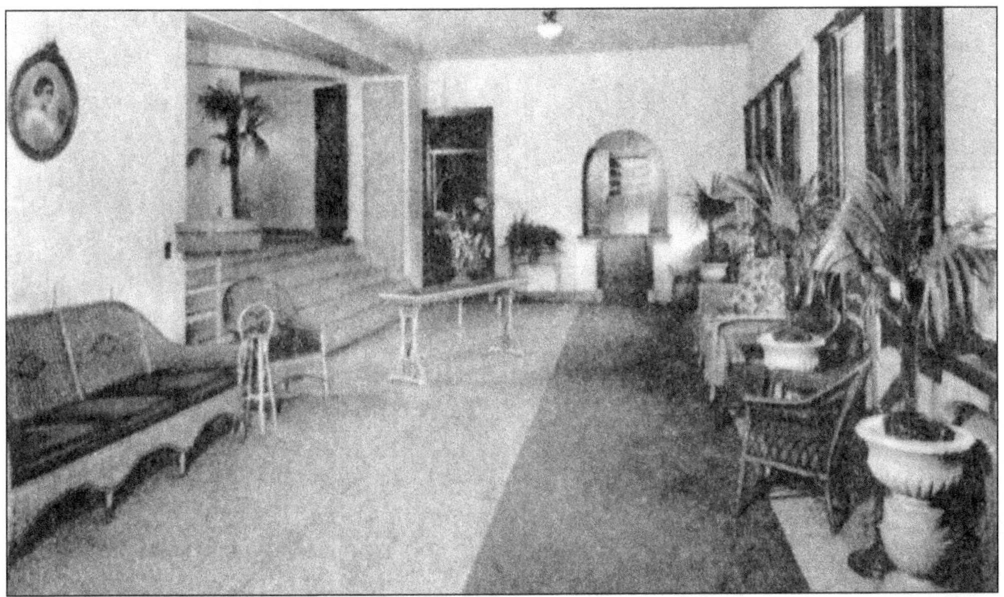

Before the Ball. Visitors to the Casino Ballroom took a short ride up the elevator to the fourth level and stepped out onto a crimson-flecked terrazzo floor. Those with Walker Company business entered the corporate office in the doorway in the center. (Courtesy of Madam Walker Family Archives.)

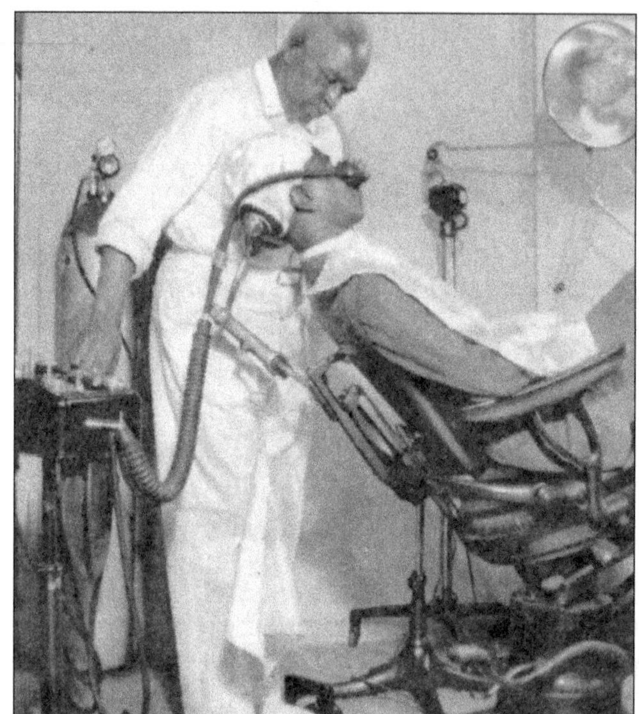

RENAISSANCE MAN. Dr. Theodore Cable conducted his dental practice in the Walker Building until he moved to New York in the late 1940s. A graduate of Indiana University School of Dentistry, he broke Harvard's hammer throw record while an undergraduate student there in 1912. He also was elected to city council and the state legislature. His mother, Mary Cable, founded Indianapolis's NAACP chapter. (Courtesy of Madam Walker Family Archives.)

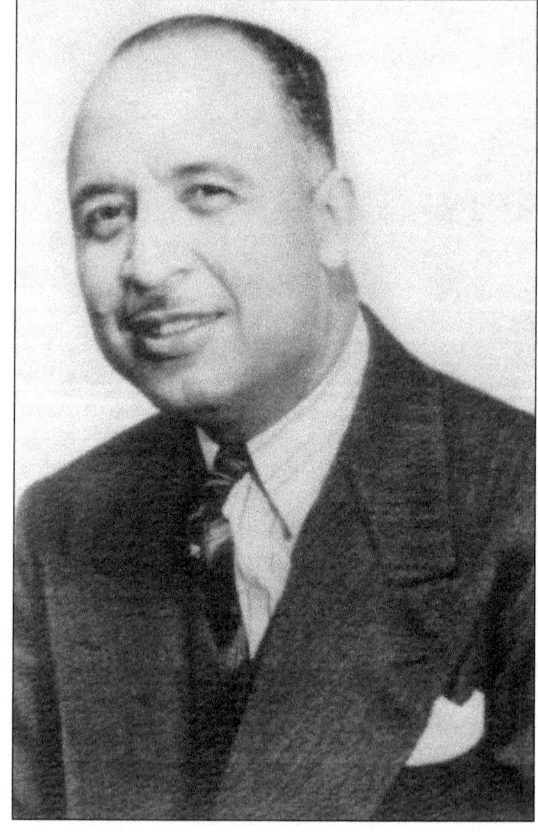

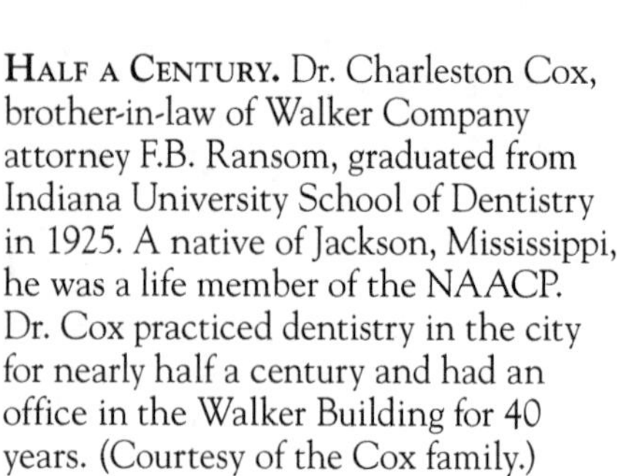

HALF A CENTURY. Dr. Charleston Cox, brother-in-law of Walker Company attorney F.B. Ransom, graduated from Indiana University School of Dentistry in 1925. A native of Jackson, Mississippi, he was a life member of the NAACP. Dr. Cox practiced dentistry in the city for nearly half a century and had an office in the Walker Building for 40 years. (Courtesy of the Cox family.)

Four

Road to Success
A Career in Beauty Culture

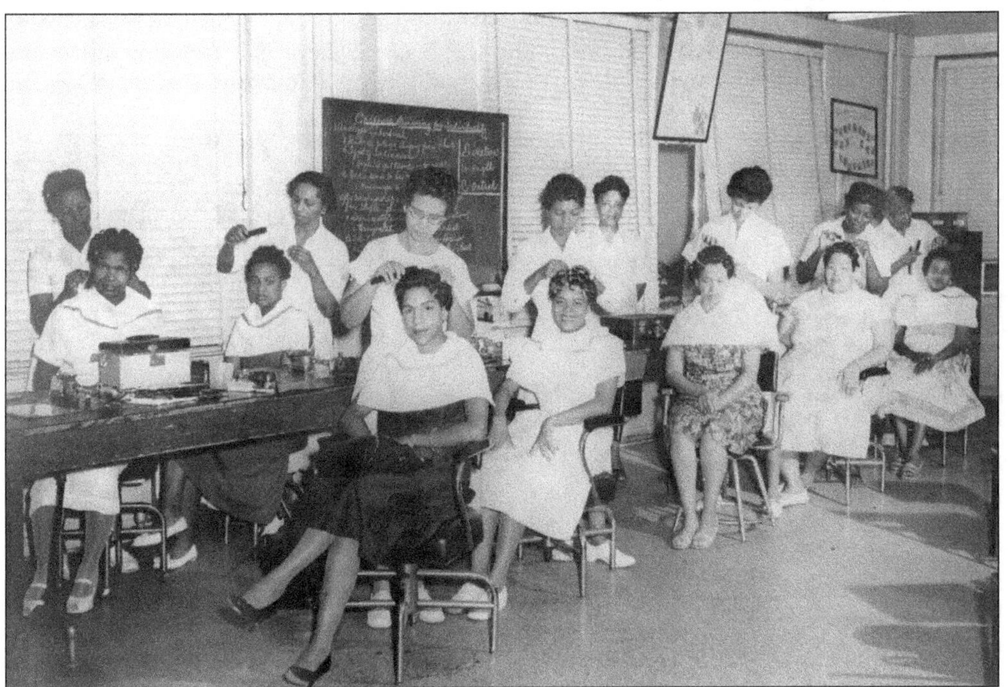

Road to Success. From the start, Madam Walker saw beauty culture as a path to financial independence. A Walker Beauty School diploma, her advertisements promised, was "insurance against hard times." A star pupil in this Indianapolis class creates a coif for A'Lelia Mae Perry Bundles, Walker's great-granddaughter (in black dress), who served as vice president of the Walker Company from 1955 to 1975. (Courtesy of Madam Walker Family Archives.)

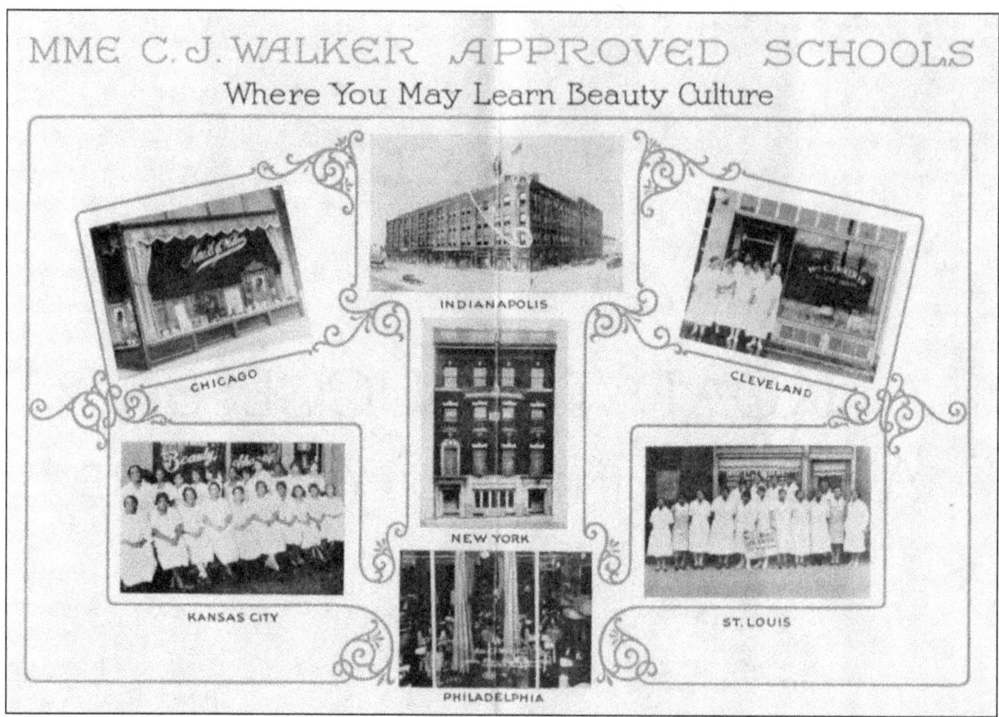

NATIONAL NETWORK. By the late 1920s, there were seven Walker Beauty Schools in Indianapolis, New York, Chicago, Kansas City, St. Louis, Philadelphia, and Cleveland. Traveling instructors provided classes in towns and cities with no formal facility. (Courtesy of Madam Walker Family Archives.)

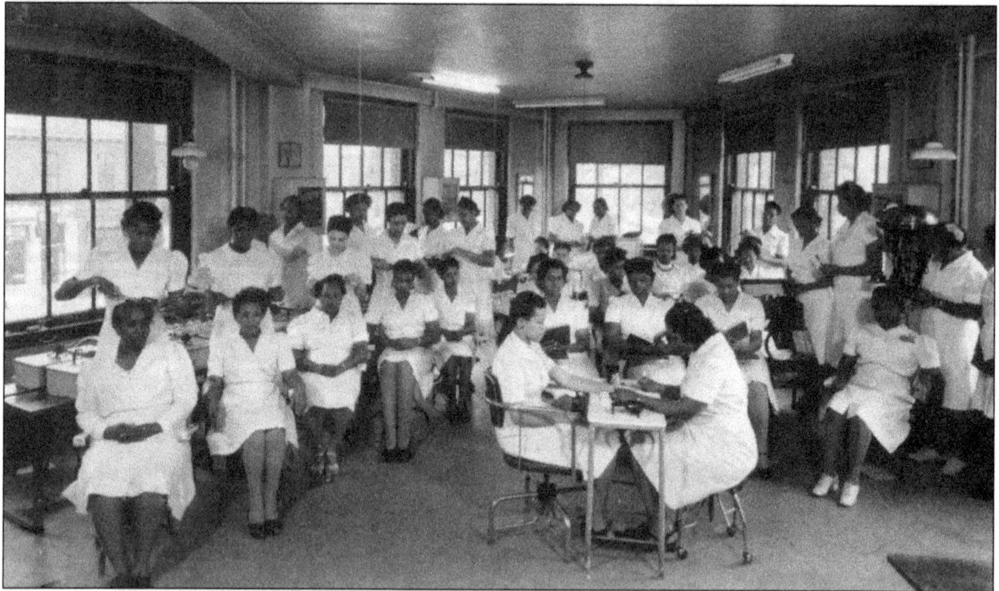

FLAGSHIP. The Indianapolis school was the largest and most popular. In the late 1930s, tuition was $100 with a small down payment due at enrollment. Students had to be 17½ years old with an eighth-grade education. To graduate, students were required to complete 1,000 hours of instruction. (Courtesy of Madam Walker Family Archives.)

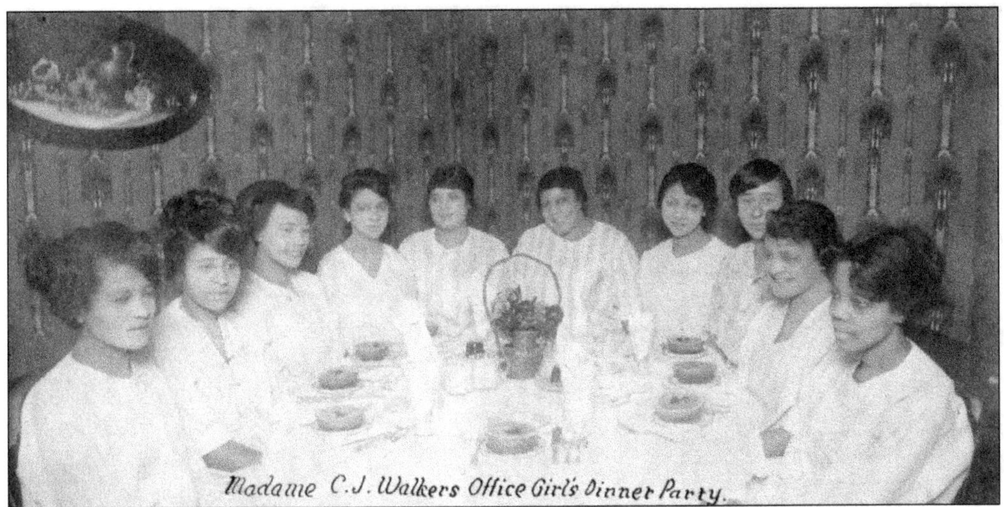

Dinner Party. Walker Company staff members, who were in charge of enrolling students and keeping track of their hours, enjoy a special dinner party. Violet Reynolds, an assistant to F.B. Ransom after Madam Walker's death, is fourth from right. Some beauty school graduates later became company employees. (Courtesy of the Reynolds family.)

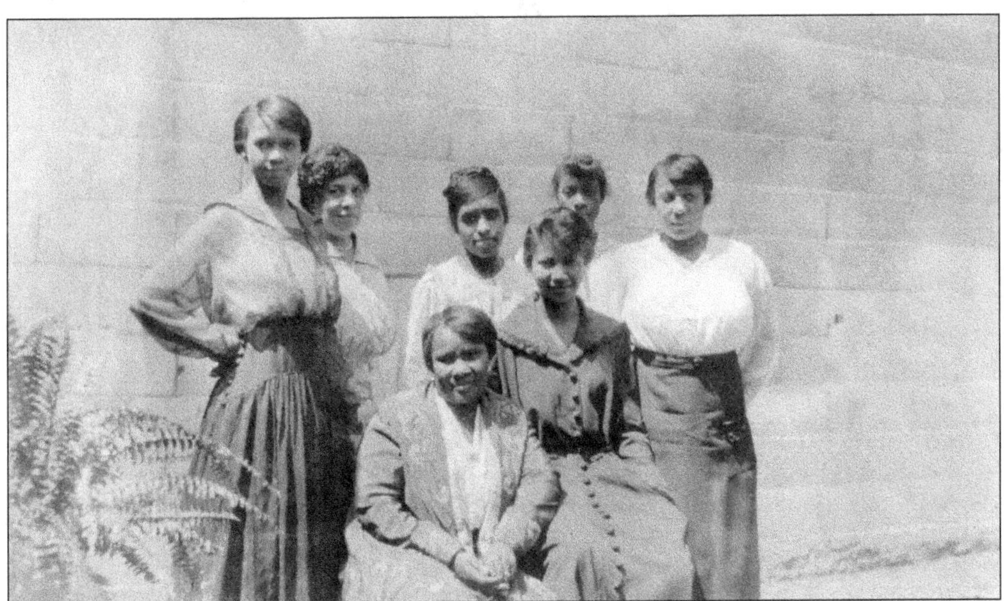

Inspiration. Every graduate of the Walker Beauty School was required to learn the history of founder Madam Walker. Those who knew the early hardships she faced, often were inspired to overcome their own obstacles. Surrounded by her office and factory staff, Walker is seated. To her right is Violet Davis Reynolds. (Courtesy of the Reynolds family.)

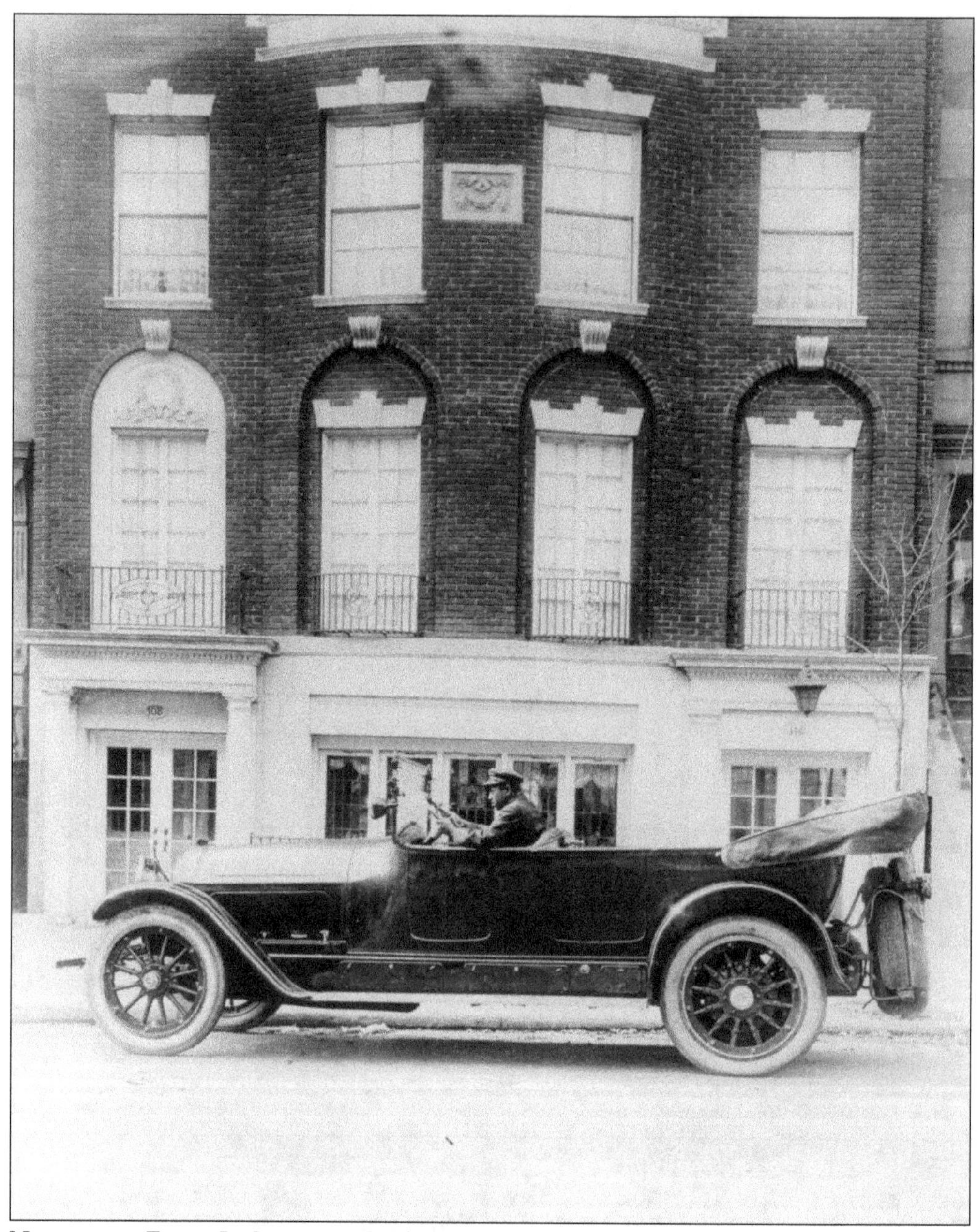

Nothing to Equal It. In 1913, as Harlem was emerging as the nation's center of black culture and politics, A'Lelia Walker persuaded her mother to establish a Walker presence there. Architect Vertner Tandy remodeled this townhouse at 108–110 West 136th Street into a combination residence, beauty salon, and school. "It's just impossible for me to describe it to you," Madam Walker wrote after seeing the renovation. "The decorators said that of all the work they had done here in that line there is nothing to equal it, not even on Fifth Avenue." The *Indianapolis World* pronounced the salon "an exquisite beauty palace." In October 1927, A'Lelia Walker converted the top floor of the home into the Dark Tower, a gathering place for artists, musicians, and writers of the Harlem Renaissance, like Countee Cullen and Zora Neale Hurston. (Courtesy of the Byron Collection, Museum of the City of New York.)

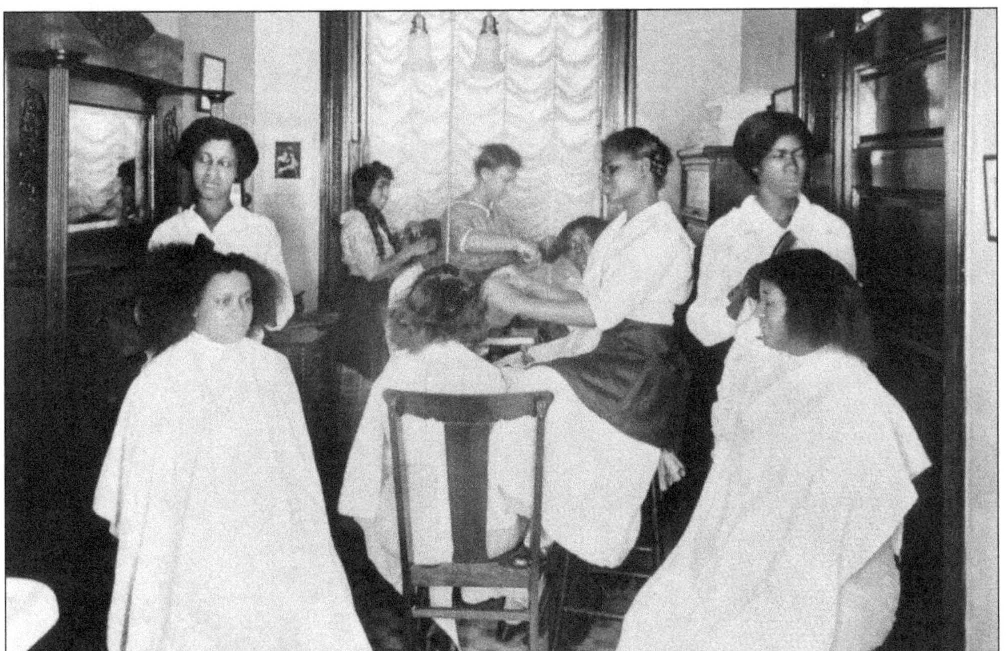

Take the A Train. The Harlem branch of Lelia College of Beauty Culture occupied the Walker townhouse's first floor. Located in the heart of Harlem, the school attracted women from all along the East Coast. A'Lelia Walker, seated front left, and Mae Walker, third from left in back, often led the classes. (Courtesy of the Byron Collection, Museum of the City of New York.)

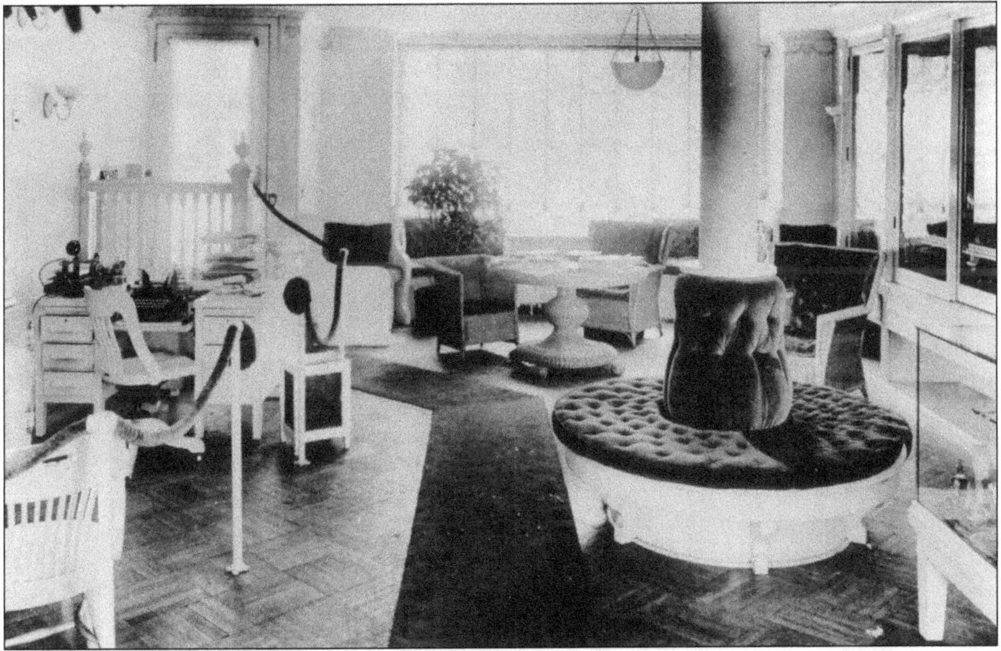

Beauty Palace. A'Lelia Walker spared no expense in furnishing her Harlem salon. Clients stepped onto a deep-pile blue carpet and walked past a navy velvet banquette to her Japanese-themed relaxation room or courtyard garden where they enjoyed tea as they awaited their appointments. (Courtesy of the Byron Collection, Museum of the City of New York.)

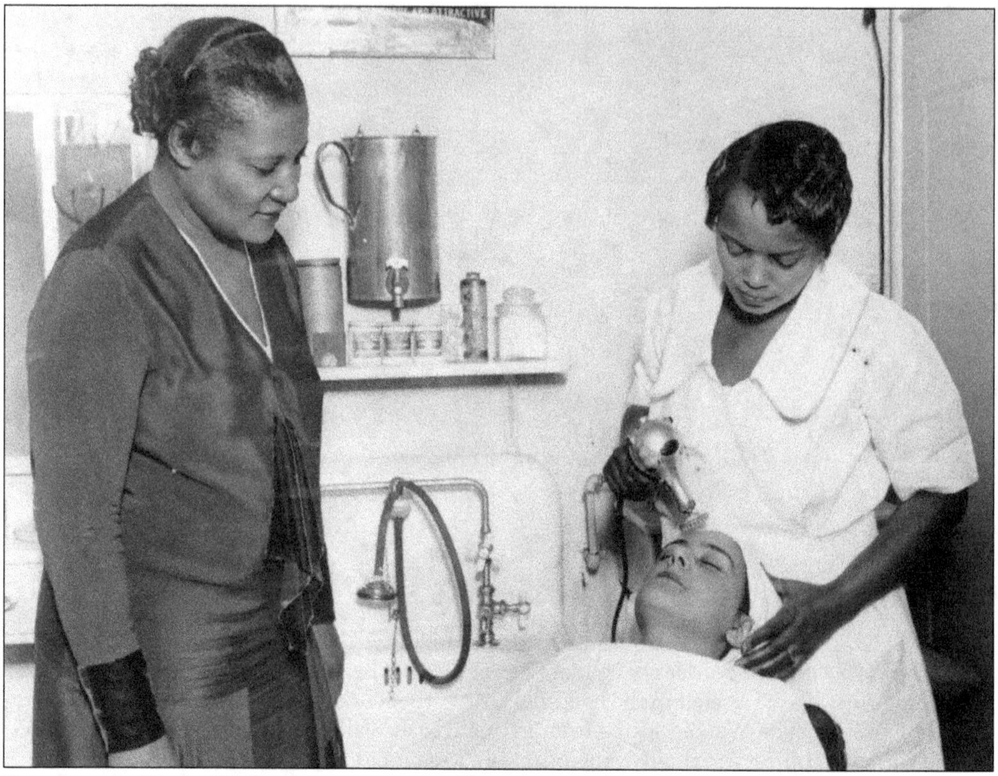

PAMPERING. A'Lelia Walker observes one of her New York aestheticians administering a facial massage. In addition to its original hair care line, the Walker Company marketed cold cream, witch hazel, and other skin care products. (Courtesy of Madam Walker Family Archives.)

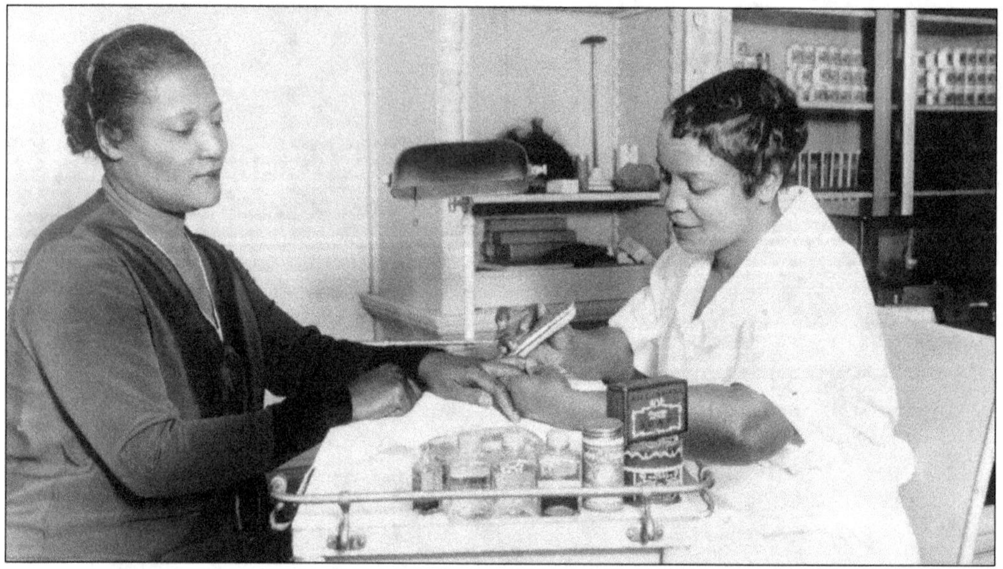

GROOMING REGIMEN. As president of the Walker Company after her mother's death in 1919, A'Lelia Walker knew it was essential that she always be well groomed. Cosmetics on the table and in the display cases reflect a new packaging design introduced during the early 1920s. (Courtesy of Madam Walker Family Archives.)

Harlem Renaissance. During the 1920s, A'Lelia Walker continued managing the New York office and opened a Walker salon on Seventh Avenue in the ritzy Dunbar Apartments. Lucille Green Randolph, wife of civil rights activist A. Philip Randolph, was a Walker trained beautician who helped run the Harlem operation. (Courtesy of Madam Walker Family Archives.)

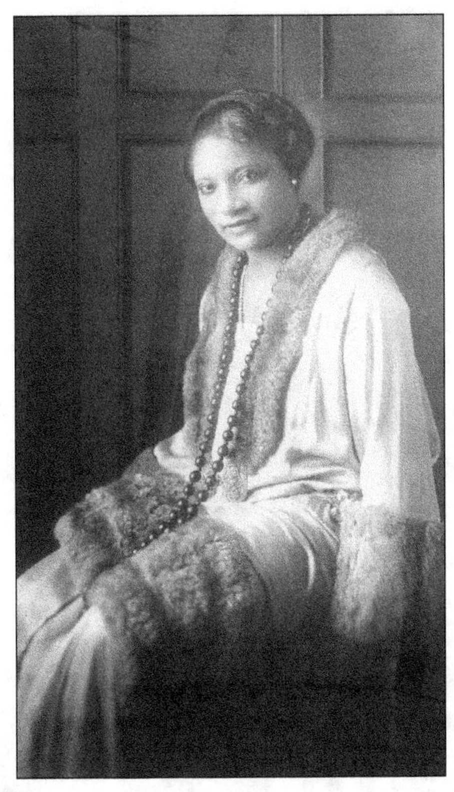

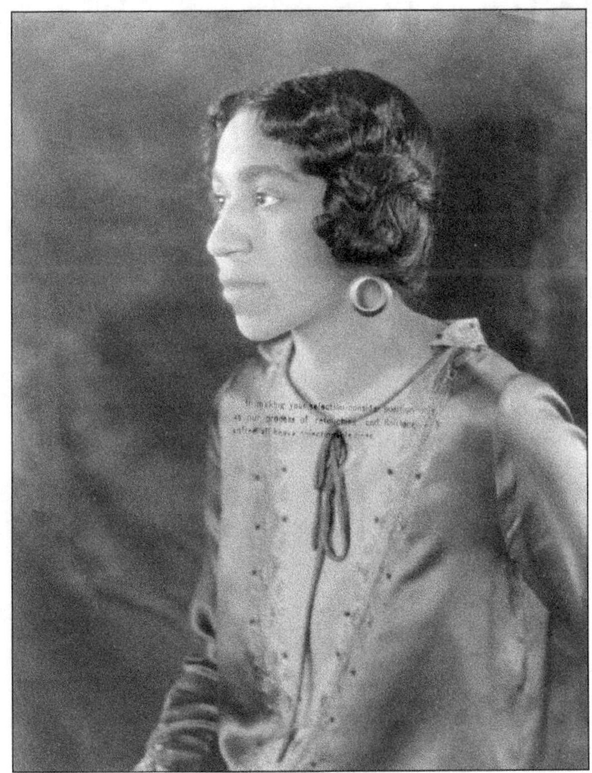

Heiress. After divorcing Dr. Gordon Jackson, Mae Walker moved from Chicago to New York with her young son, Walker Gordon Jackson. Trained personally by Madam Walker as well as at Chicago's Burnham Beauty School, she supervised some classes and occasionally modeled for hair demonstrations. She was Walker Company president from 1931 to 1945. (Courtesy of Madam Walker Family Archives.)

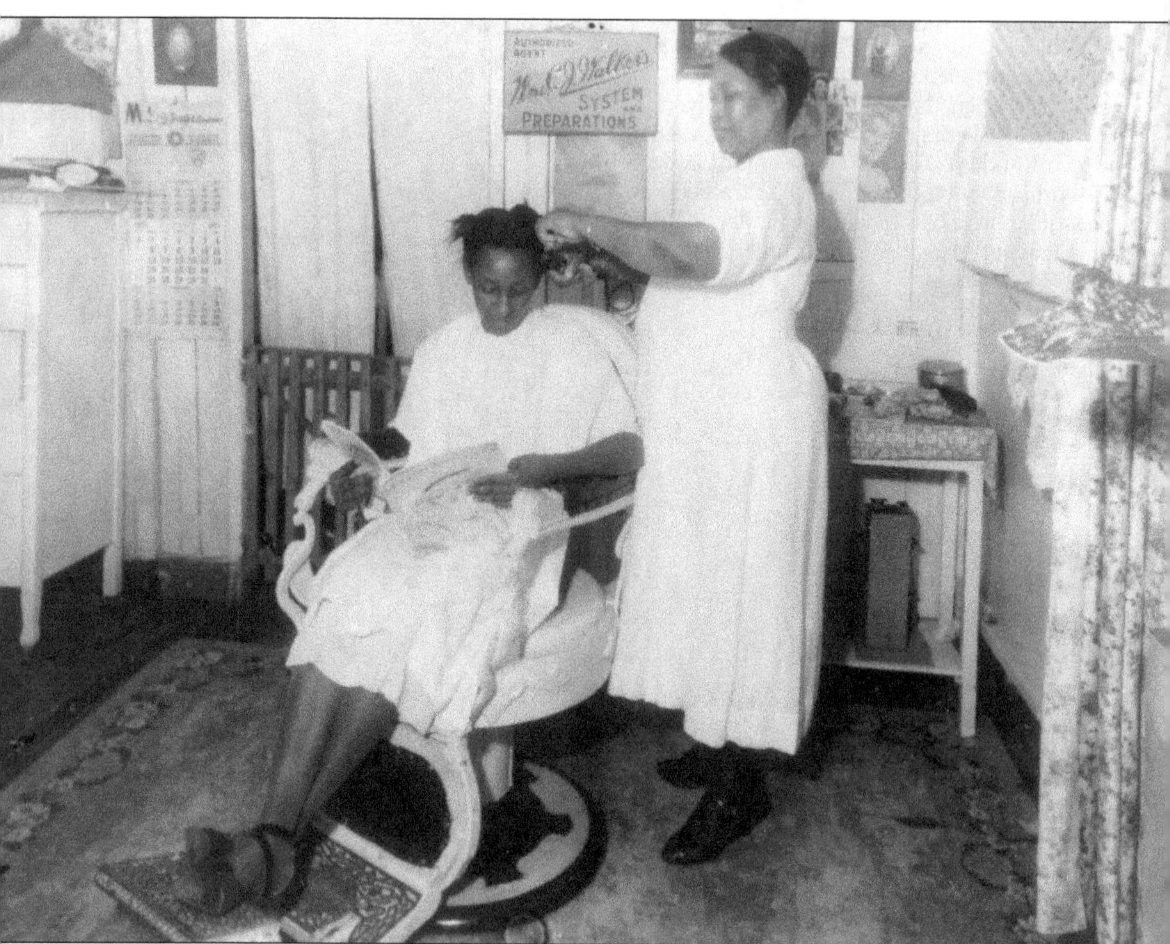

A WORLD OF POSSIBILITY. In the early 1900s, when Madam Walker founded her business, most African Americans lived in towns and on farms of the Southern United States. Educational and career opportunities were extremely limited in a world of Jim Crow segregation and political disenfranchisement. To supplement their family incomes, many black women worked outside the home. While a few were teachers, nurses, and secretaries, most worked in rural areas picking cotton and other crops or in cities as cooks, maids, and laundresses for pay as low as $1 a week. Becoming a Walker beautician offered prosperity beyond anything they ever had imagined. One satisfied agent wrote to Madam Walker, "You have made it possible for a colored woman to make more money in a day selling your products than she could in a month working in somebody else's kitchen." This graduate proudly displays her "authorized agent" sign. (Courtesy of Madam Walker Family Archives.)

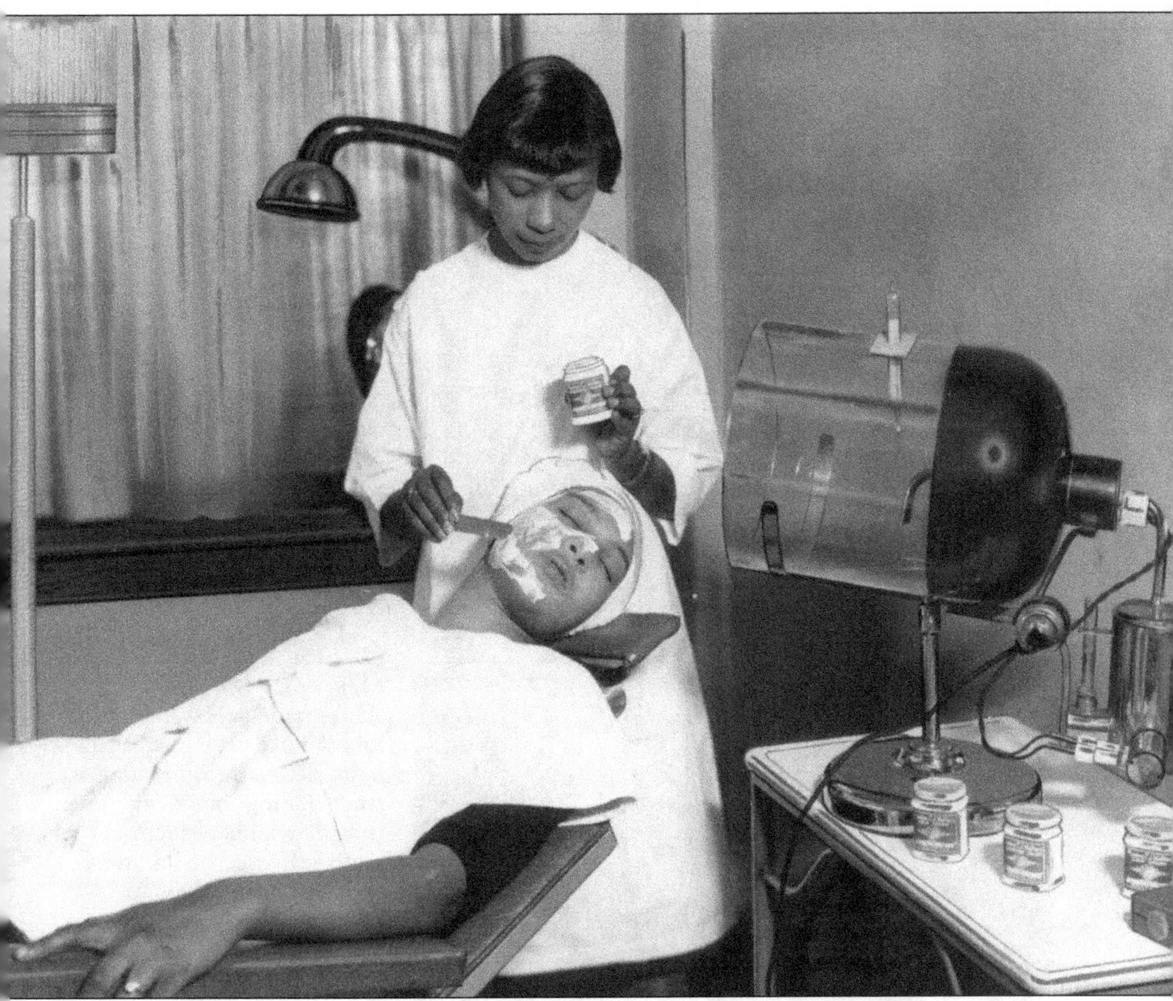

Best Face Forward. Skin care was just as important as hair care at the Walker Beauty Schools. Students learned to administer facials as well as anatomy, histology, chemistry, bacteriology, physiology, sanitation, and sterilization. Instructors insisted on proficiency in eyebrow arching as well as the proper application of artificial eyelashes, mascara, eye shadow, rouge, lipstick, and powder. As with hair care, the emphasis was on clean, healthy skin. All graduates took manicuring classes and learned to perform hand and arm massages. The Walker Company sold a range of cosmetics, including five shades of Superfine Face Powder and three shades of rouge and lipstick: orange, poppy, and medium. A 1930s Walker brochure made the following assurance: "Nothing is overlooked in a Madam C.J. Walker Course. It covers all one needs to know to become an operator, manager, or shop owner." (Courtesy of Madam Walker Family Archives.)

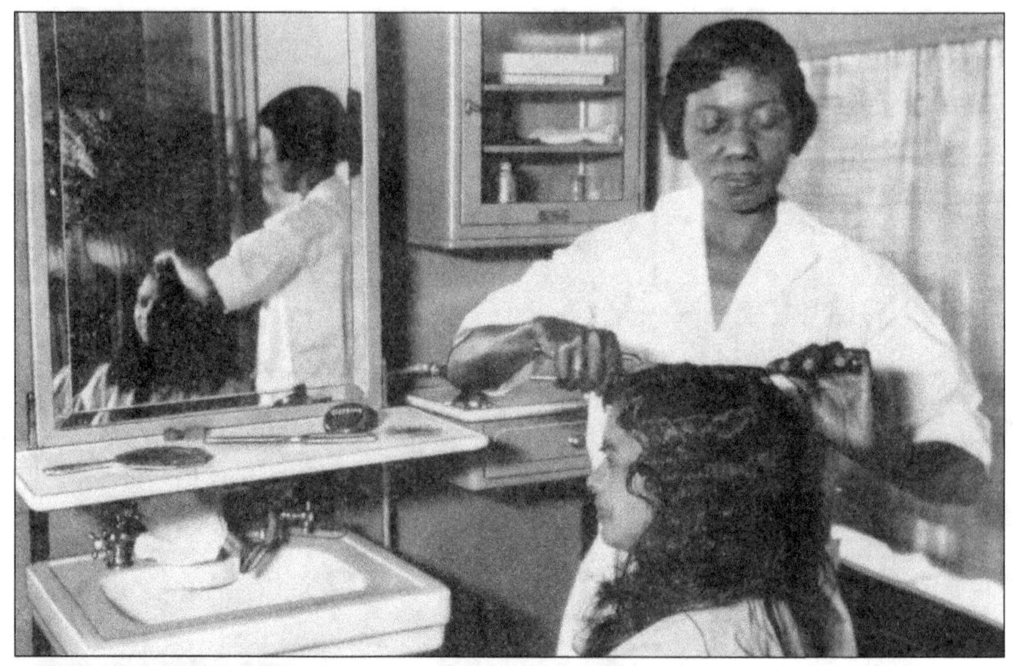

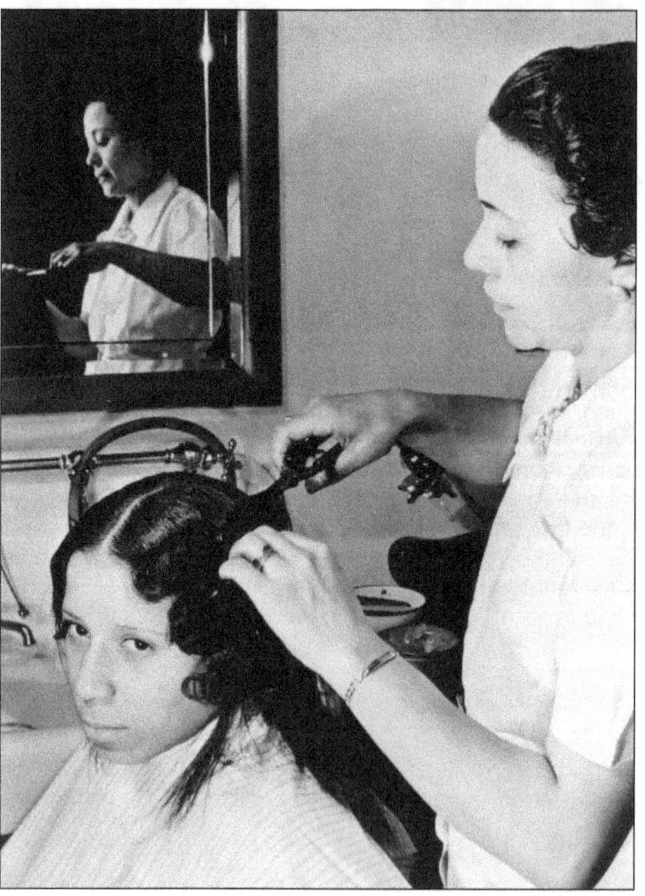

Mastering the Marcel. Walker graduates were known for their expertise in creating hairstyles with curling irons, straightening combs, and other heated metal implements. Unlike the electric flat irons and blow dryers of today, the implements these two Walker beauty culturists used were heated on miniature stoves with open flames. Each student was required to demonstrate her skill at creating what were called Marcel, croquignole, finger, and water waves. Despite a widespread myth that many believe, Madam Walker did not invent the hot comb, a steel device that was used to straighten hair. In fact, hot combs were sold in Sears, Roebuck & Company's and Bloomingdale's catalogs as early as the 1890s, which was more than a decade before she started her business. (Both, courtesy of Madam Walker Family Archives.)

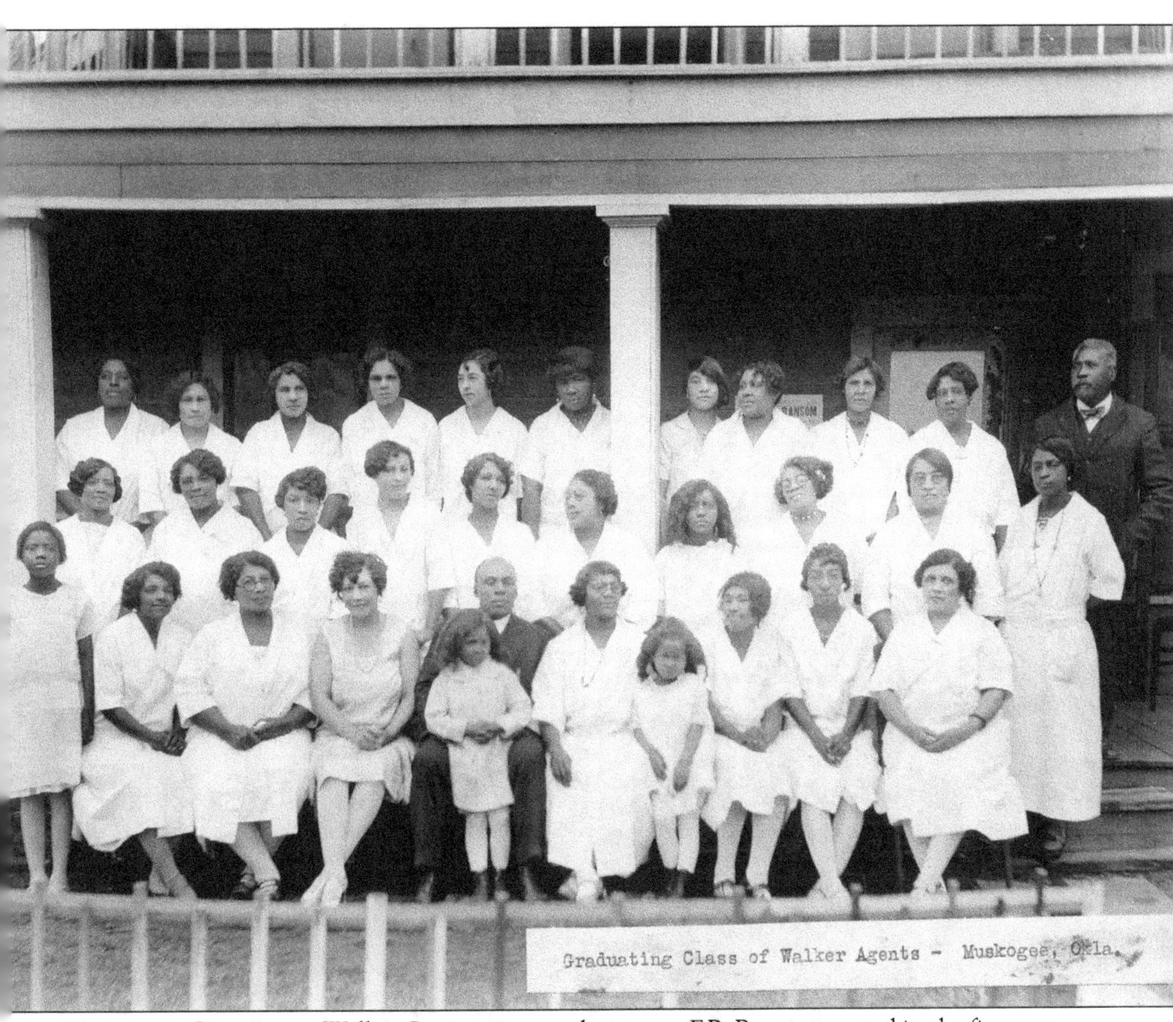

Muskogee, Oklahoma. Walker Company general manager F.B. Ransom, seated in the first row, is joined by national sales representative Alice Burnett, seated to his left. In August 1919, a few years before this photograph was taken, the third annual Walker convention, which was the first one after Madam Walker's death, was held in Muskogee. Mae Walker represented the family in the absence of A'Lelia Walker, who was in California on her honeymoon with her second husband, Dr. Wiley Wilson. Several Walker representatives traveling from Southern states engaged a private Pullman car to avoid traveling in Jim Crow accommodations. Muskogee was one of more than 50 all-black or predominantly black Oklahoma towns founded between 1865 and 1920. After the Civil War, freedmen affiliated with the Five Civilized Tribes created settlements in Indian Territory. The Oklahoma Land Rush of 1889 attracted even more African Americans who envisioned a "Promise Land" where they could govern themselves. By 1919, Muskogee's 10,000 residents supported 3 banks, 3 dentists, 18 doctors, 14 lawyers, and 50 merchants. (Courtesy of Madam C.J. Walker Collection, Indiana Historical Society.)

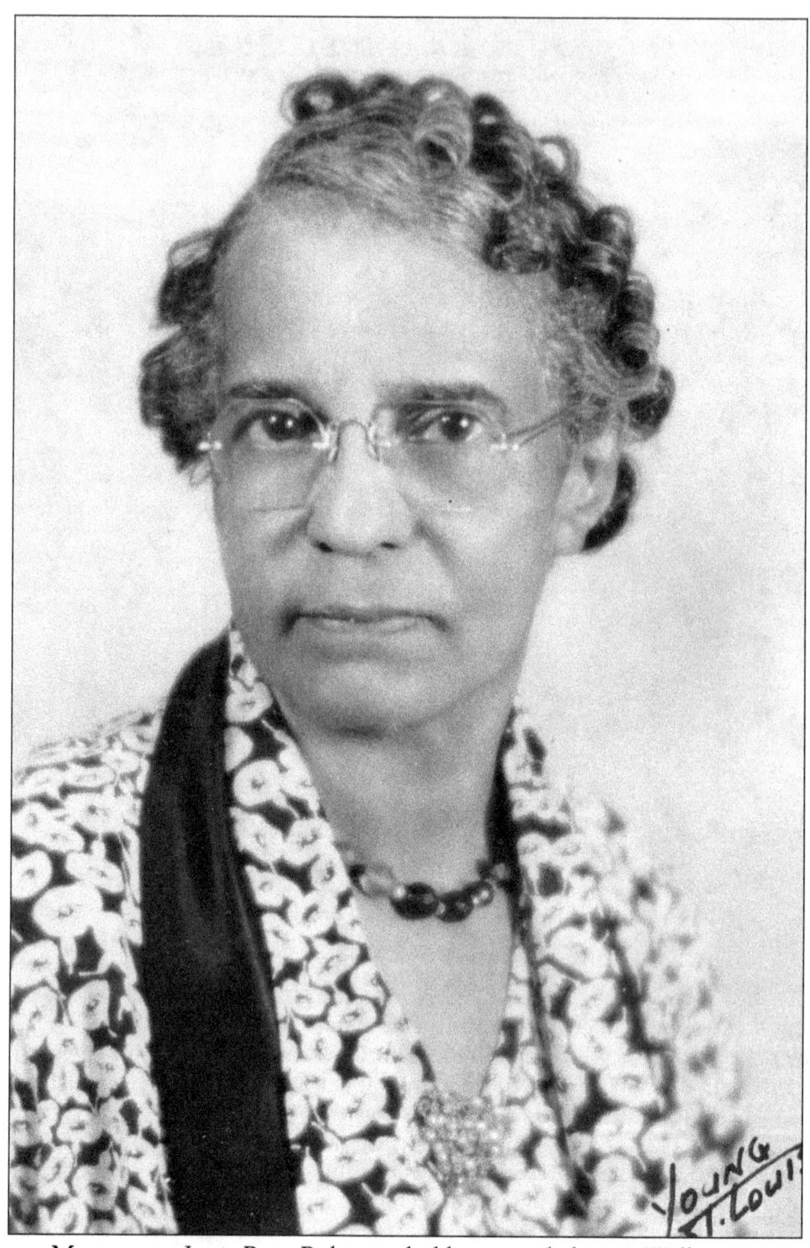

Mentor and Motivator. Jessie Batts Robinson holds a special place in Walker Company history and Madam Walker's life. An 1889 graduate of St. Louis's renowned Sumner High School, she taught at Banneker Elementary School. A member of St. Paul AME Church, she was among the middle-class women who assisted Sarah Breedlove when she first arrived in the city. After marrying Christopher Robinson, publisher of the *Clarion* and supreme grand secretary of the black Knights of Pythias, she was elected head of the national Court of Calanthe, the group's women's auxiliary. As a trusted friend and associate, Robinson was granted the St. Louis Walker school and salon franchise, which she operated for many years on bustling Market Street. It was in Robinson's home where Walker became so ill during the spring of 1919 that she was transported in a private train car back to Villa Lewaro, where she died several weeks later. (Courtesy of Madam Walker Family Archives.)

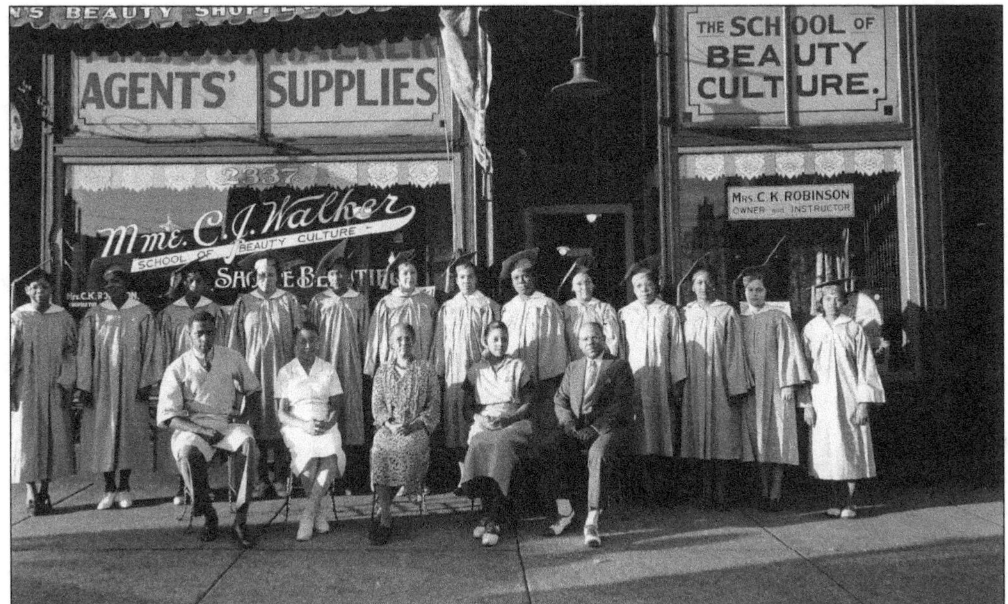

BUSINESSWOMAN. Here, Jessie Robinson, seated at center, presides over this 1938 St. Louis graduation. After Walker's death, Robinson oversaw the distribution of $11,000 in Walker bequests to St. Louis's YMCA, YWCA, Colored Orphan's Home, Colored Old Folks Home, and St. Paul's Mite Missionary Society. Jessie Robinson died in February 1946. Mae Walker's husband, Marion Perry, is seated at the far right. (Courtesy of Madam C.J. Walker Collection, Indiana Historical Society.)

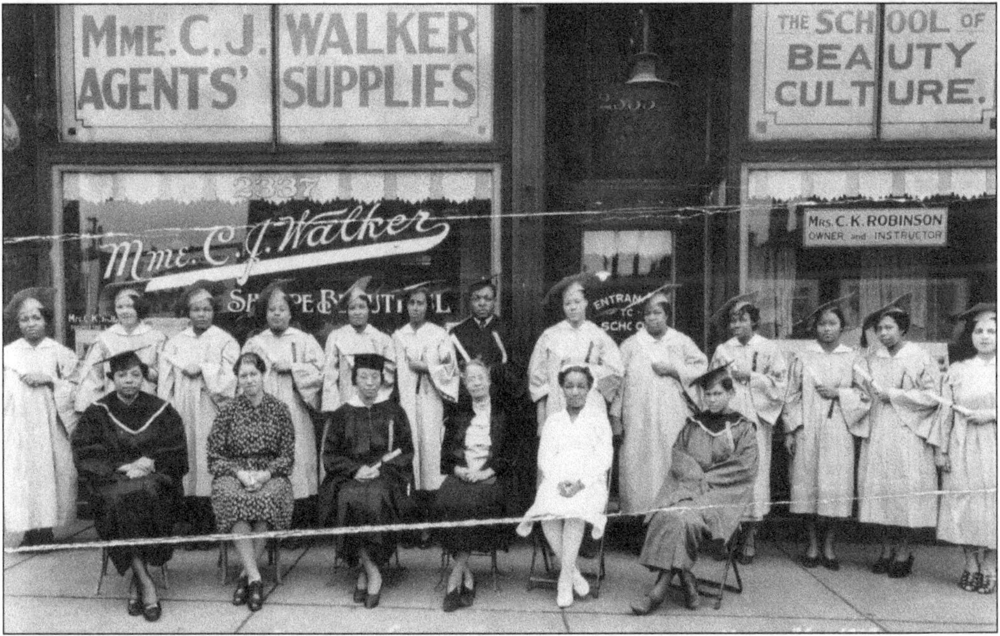

MORTARBOARD AND TASSLES. Diplomas in hand, these 1939 spring semester graduates join St. Louis principal Jessie Robinson, seated fourth from left. Before founding the school, she was one of the city's first black social workers. After the July 1917 East St. Louis riot, she worked alongside Red Cross relief workers assisting victims from the town across the Mississippi River. (Courtesy of Madam Walker Family Archives.)

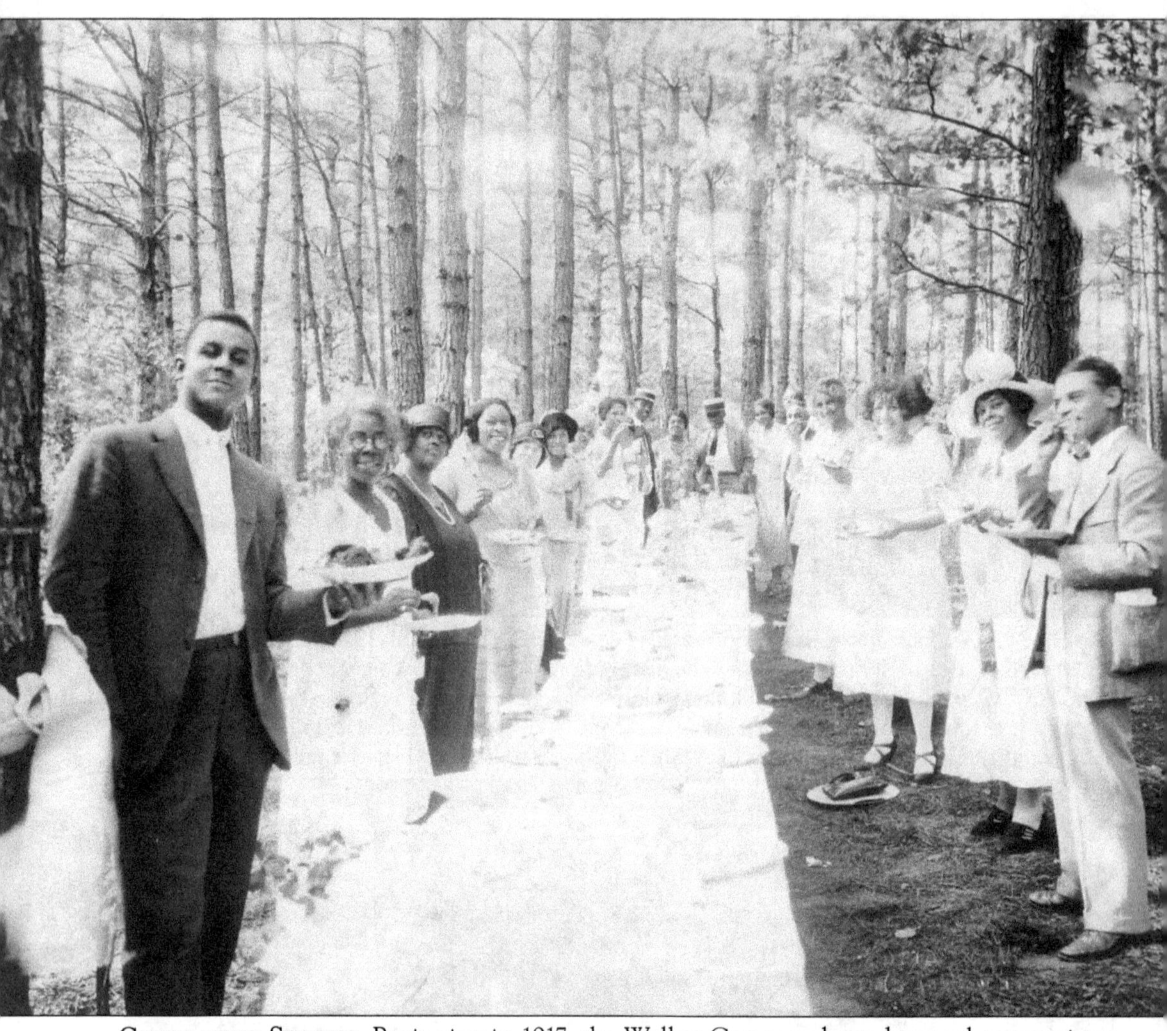

Celebrating Success. Beginning in 1917, the Walker Company hosted annual conventions where sales agents joined top executives for refresher courses in hair care techniques, an awards ceremony, and motivational speeches by distinguished educators, publishers, ministers, and civil rights leaders. The first convention at Philadelphia's Union Baptist Church was followed in 1918 with a gathering at Chicago's Olivet Baptist Church, where delegates were addressed by George W. Ellis, former US minister to Liberia, and by *Chicago Defender* publisher Robert Sengstacke Abbott. The sight of well-dressed Walker agents sporting bright-yellow convention badges made quite an impression at conventions in Indianapolis, Detroit, Kansas City, and New York. Longtime Walker Company employees who appear in this undated picnic photograph are general manager F.B. Ransom, standing at the far end of the table at center in a straw hat; vice president and national representative Alice Burnett, third from right; and advertising manager Harry Evans, first on right. (Courtesy of Stanley Nelson.)

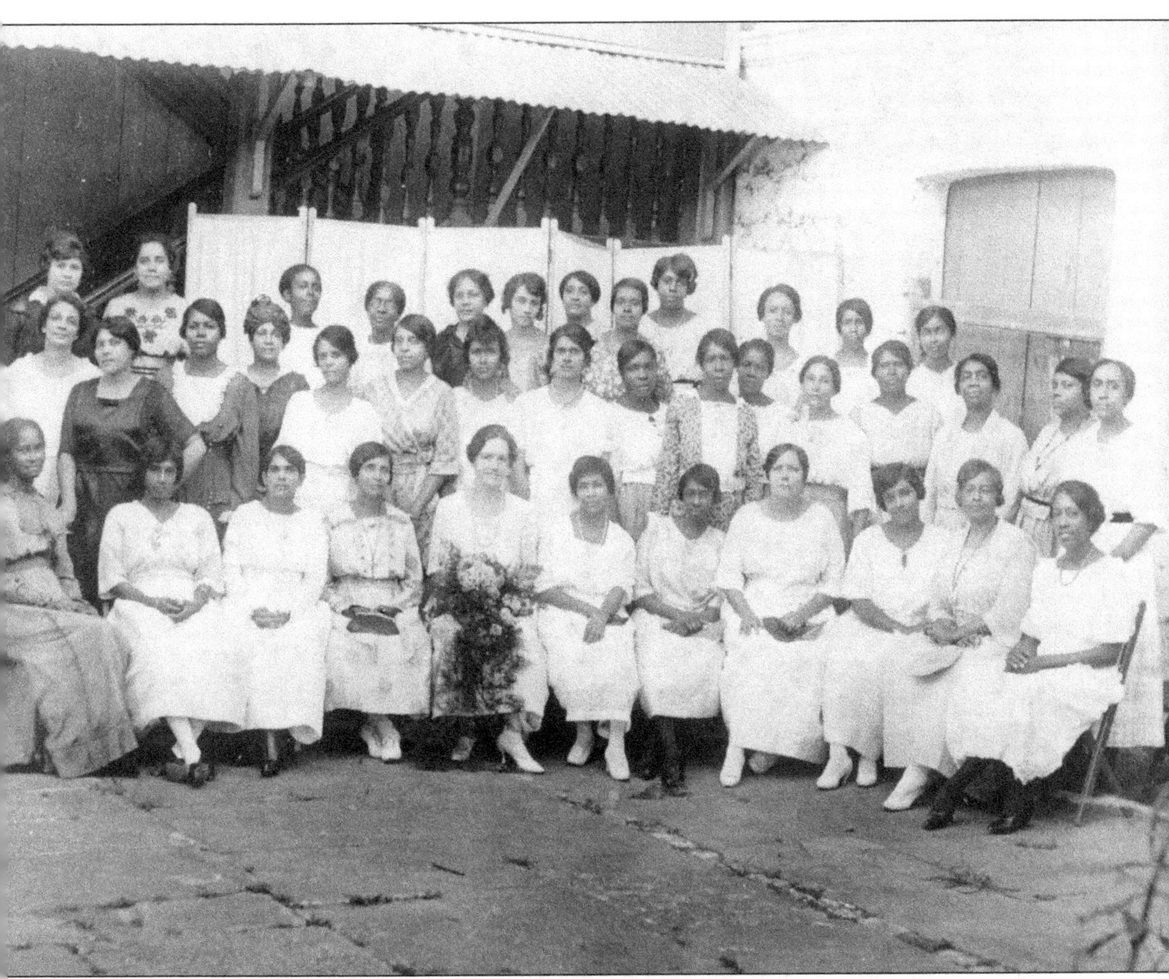

International Outreach. These Bridgetown, Barbados, agents were among many Central American and West Indian Walker graduates. Madam Walker also targeted Panama in her early business development strategy because of the sizeable black population attracted there during the construction of the Panama Canal. In November 1913, she traveled by steamer *Oruba* from New York to Jamaica. Also on board was her friend Madame Anita Patti Brown, a coloratura soprano, who had toured the Caribbean and Central America a year earlier. In Kingston, Brown introduced Walker to prominent officials. From there Walker visited Haiti, Costa Rica, Cuba, and Panama training new sales agents and enjoying the tropical weather during North America's winter months. Her daughter, A'Lelia Walker, and granddaughter, Mae, later visited Panama in 1919 to continue building their international customer base. For many years, the Walker Company engaged the services of a bilingual representative, who created Spanish language advertisements and translated correspondence. (Courtesy of Madam Walker Family Archives.)

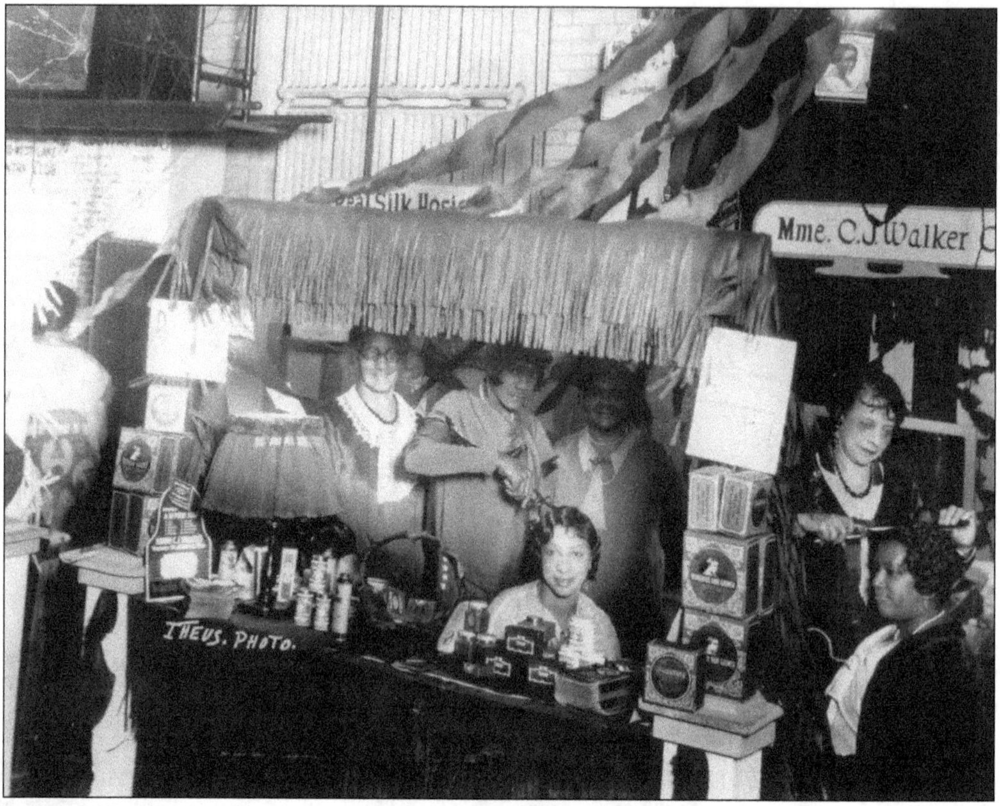

BUSINESS RULES. In addition to mastering hair care and styling, Walker students were required to take a course in business ethics and management to learn about operating a salon, customer service, bookkeeping, insurance, state laws, commercial licenses, and taxes. "Building a large, well paying business is the aim," a Walker handbook advised. (Courtesy of Madam Walker Family Archives.)

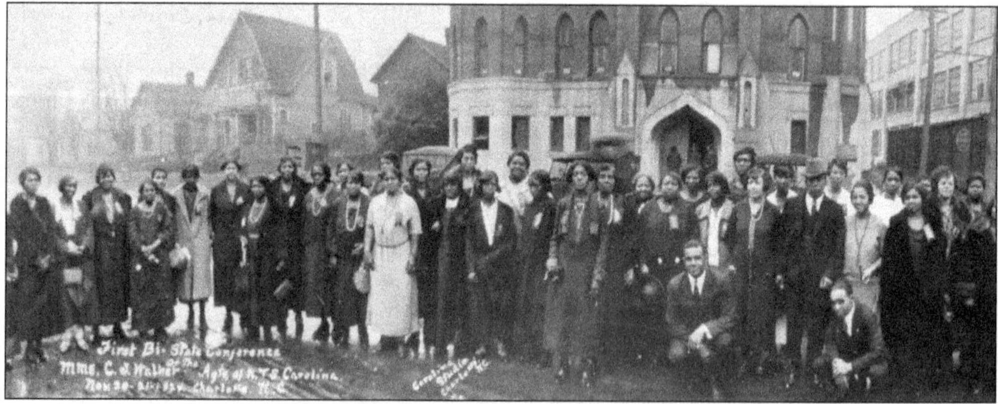

CAROLINA CONVENTION. To keep the momentum going between national conventions, Walker agents from North Carolina and South Carolina gather in Charlotte for their first bistate regional conference in November 1924. They are joined by F.B. Ransom, who is standing on the right between traveling instructor Alice Burnette and national beauty school supervisor Marjorie Joyner. (Courtesy of Madam Walker Family Archives.)

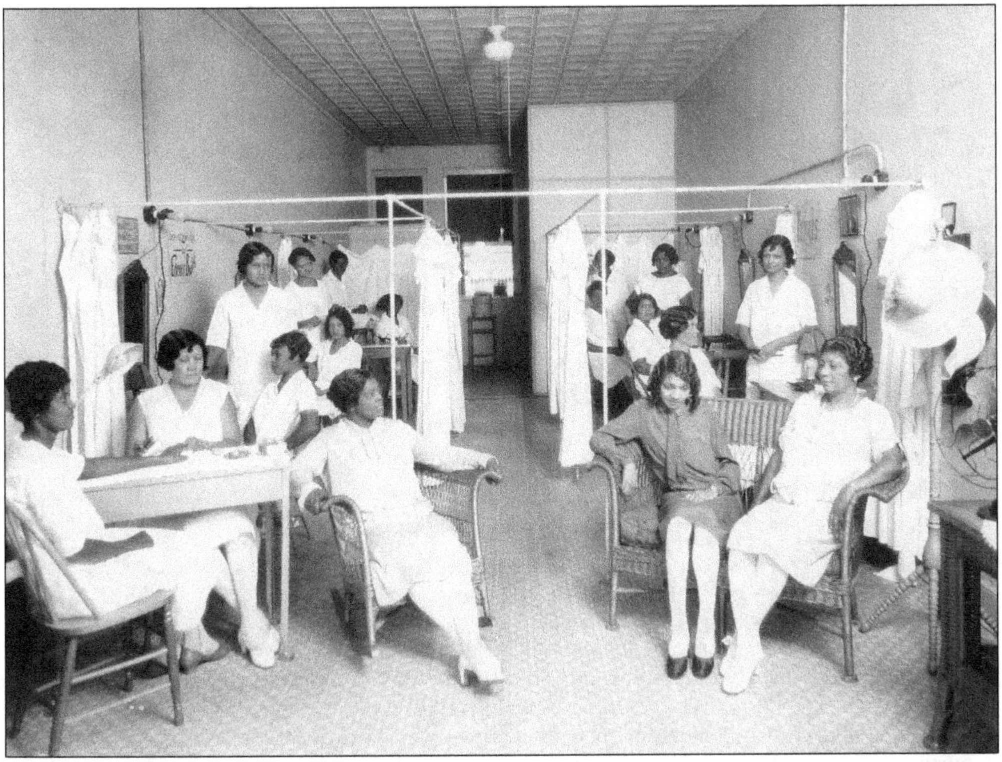

Southwest Sales. In 1907, when Madam Walker was establishing her company, she visited Texas, Oklahoma, Kansas, Arkansas, Louisiana, Mississippi, and Alabama. That early effort and those relationships continued to pay off with enough business in the Southwest to eventually established beauty schools in Dallas, Houston, Austin, and Tulsa. Dallas graduates opened this comfortable, pristine salon. (Courtesy of Madam Walker Family Archives.)

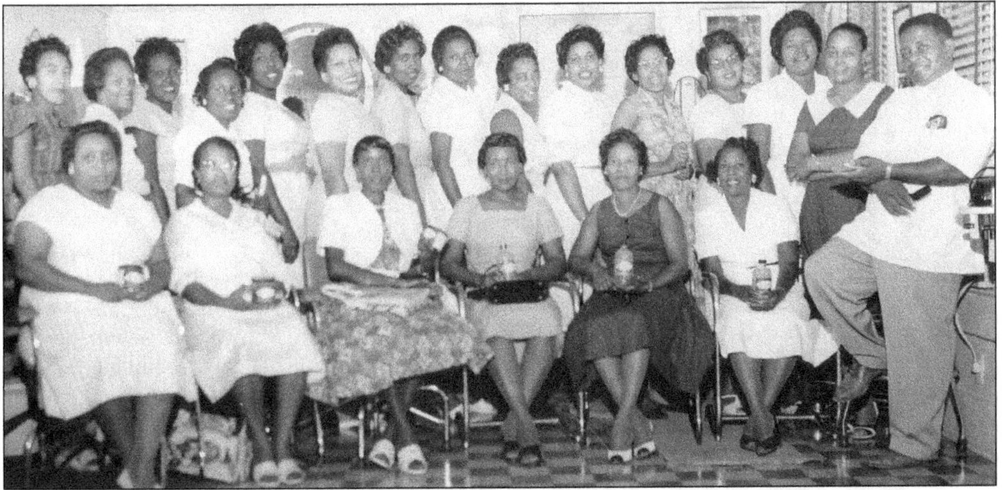

Lone Star State. During her 1907 Texas trip, Madam Walker visited Dallas, Tyler, Houston, and Galveston where she scheduled training classes at local churches and lodges. Nearly 50 years later in Beaumont, special Walker Company representative George Washington demonstrates two new products, Satin Tress Crème Press and Satin Tress Crème Rinse. (Courtesy of Madam Walker Family Archives.)

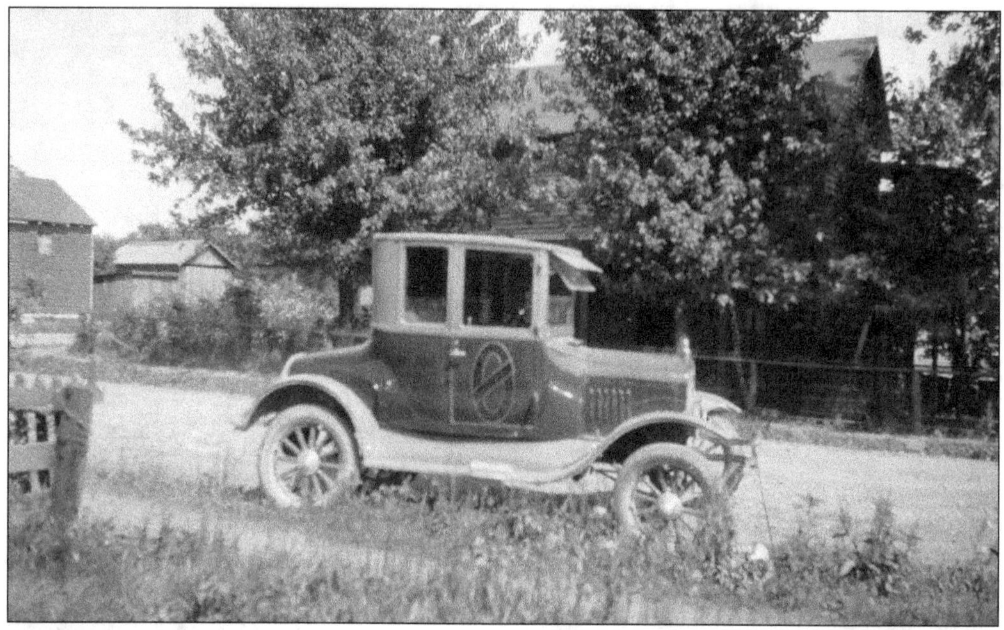

On the Road. With Walker agents located in large cities, small towns, and out-of-the-way hamlets, a range of distribution strategies were necessary. Most orders were shipped by train and delivered via the US Postal Service. In cities with Walker schools, agents picked up their weekly supplies. Cars like this—complete with Walker logo—were awarded as prizes to top sales agents. (Courtesy of Madam Walker Family Archives.)

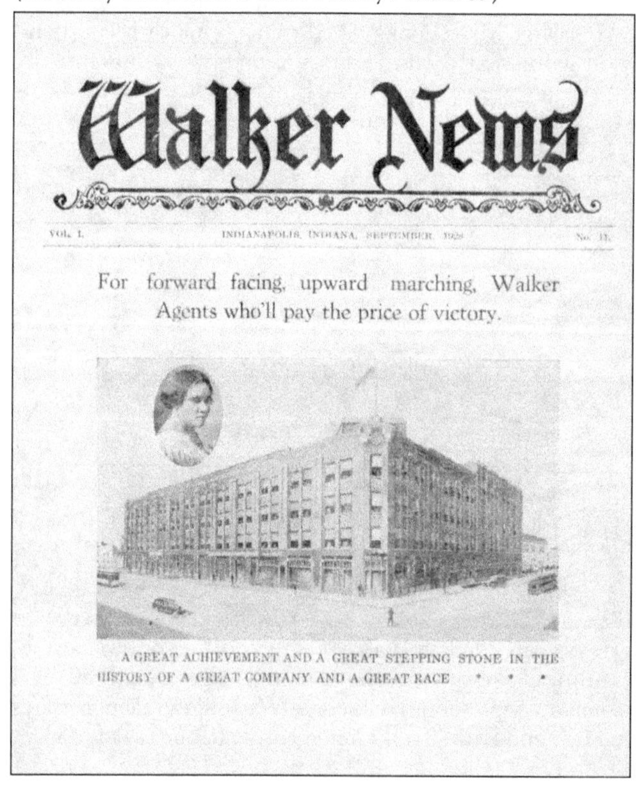

Walker News

VOL. I. INDIANAPOLIS, INDIANA, SEPTEMBER 1928

For forward facing, upward marching, Walker Agents who'll pay the price of victory.

A GREAT ACHIEVEMENT AND A GREAT STEPPING STONE IN THE HISTORY OF A GREAT COMPANY AND A GREAT RACE . . .

Spreading the News. Madam Walker always understood the power of the press, buying her first advertisement in the *Denver Statesman* in 1906. Many black newspaper publishers said she helped keep them in business. In 1928, the Walker Company began publishing the *Walker News*, a monthly newsletter for agents and employees with salesmanship tips and business and personal family news. (Courtesy of Madam Walker Family Archives.)

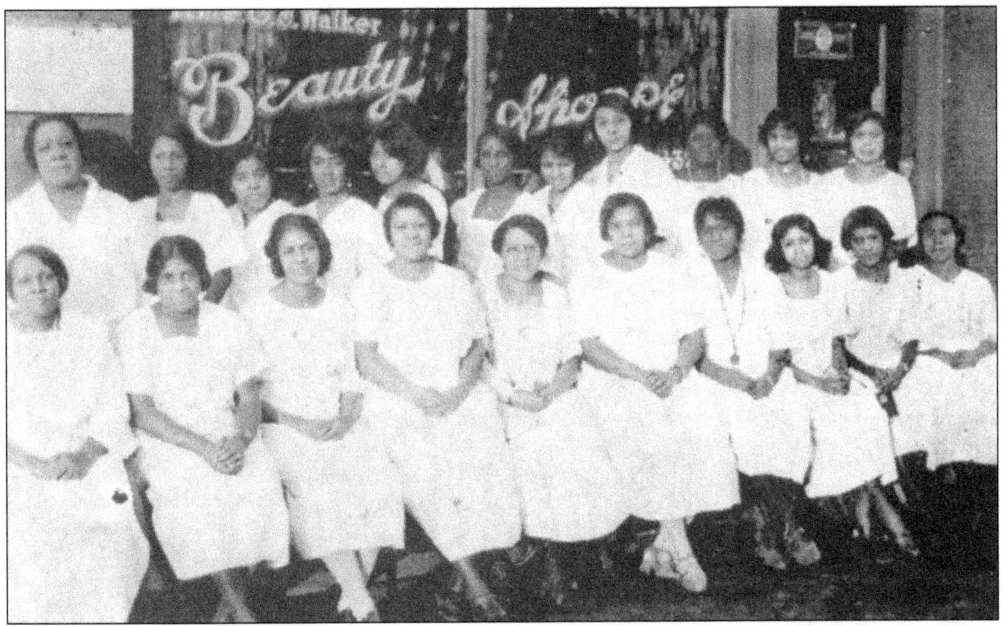

Kansas City, 1924. The Madam Walker salon and school Kansas City, Missouri, were located at 1834 Paseo Boulevard, just a few blocks away from the corner of Twelfth and Vine Streets in the area known for its jazz and blues clubs. The local black branch of the Young Men's Christian Association was a block away at Eighteenth and Vine Streets. (Courtesy of Madam Walker Family Archives.)

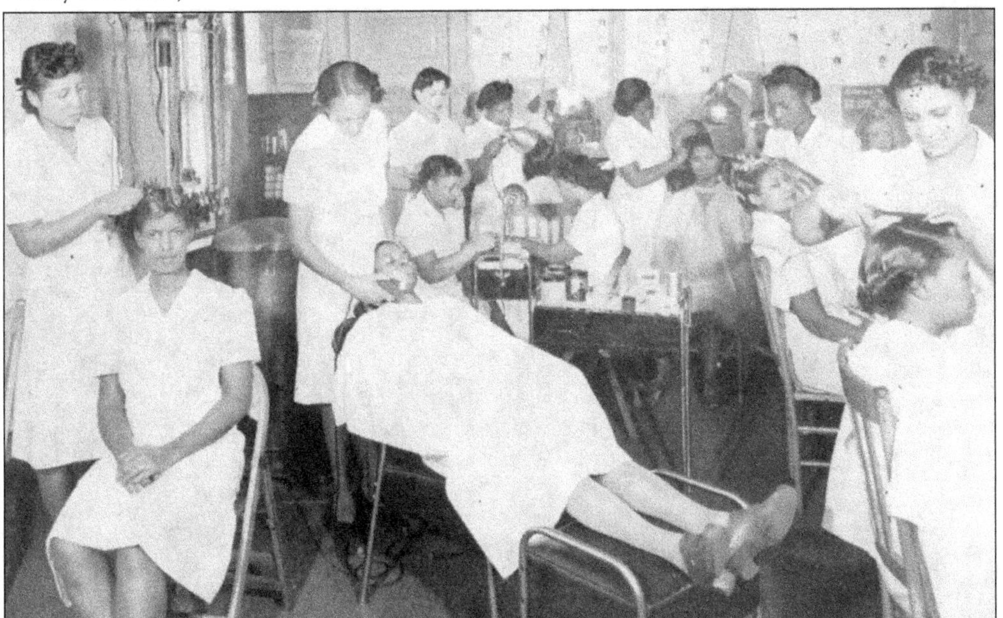

$100 a Week. A 1930s Walker catalogue comparing pay scales for several trades and professions helped sell these students on careers in beauty culture. Nurses, it said, earned $25 a week after three years of training. Stenographers might make $18 after six-month preparation. Walker graduates, it claimed, could earn from $10 to $100 after just a few weeks of instruction. (Courtesy of Madam Walker Family Archives.)

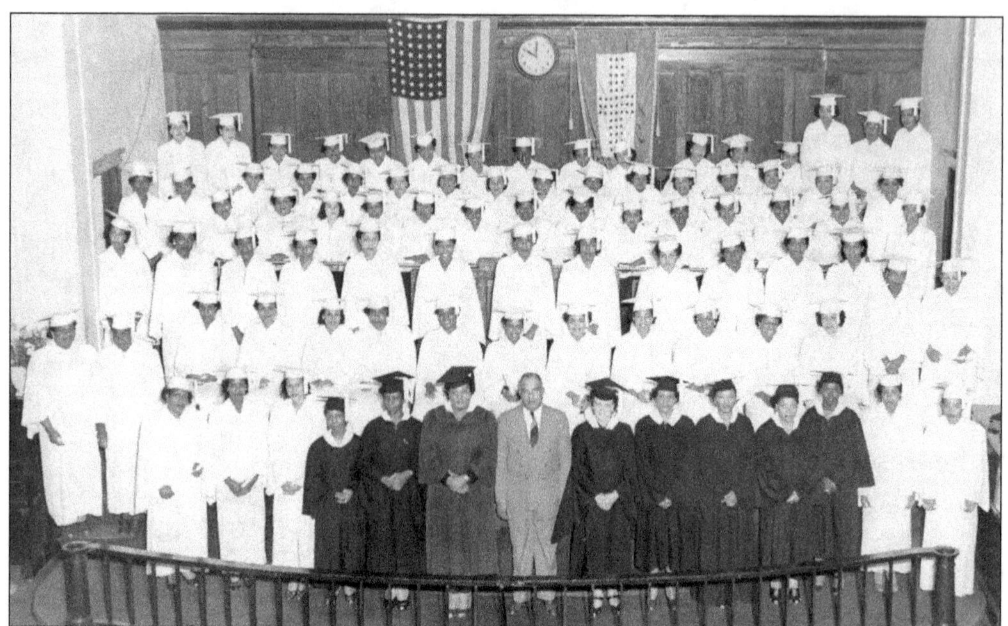

Kansas City Graduation, 1946. The Kansas City school maintained strong enrollment numbers for students who attended classes in what a promotional brochure described as a "commodious up-to-date building, spacious class rooms, lecture quarters, and practice booths." This graduation ceremony opened with "Life Every Voice," the Negro National Anthem. Talented students performed "Go Down Moses" and "Ave Maria." (Courtesy of Madam Walker Family Archives.)

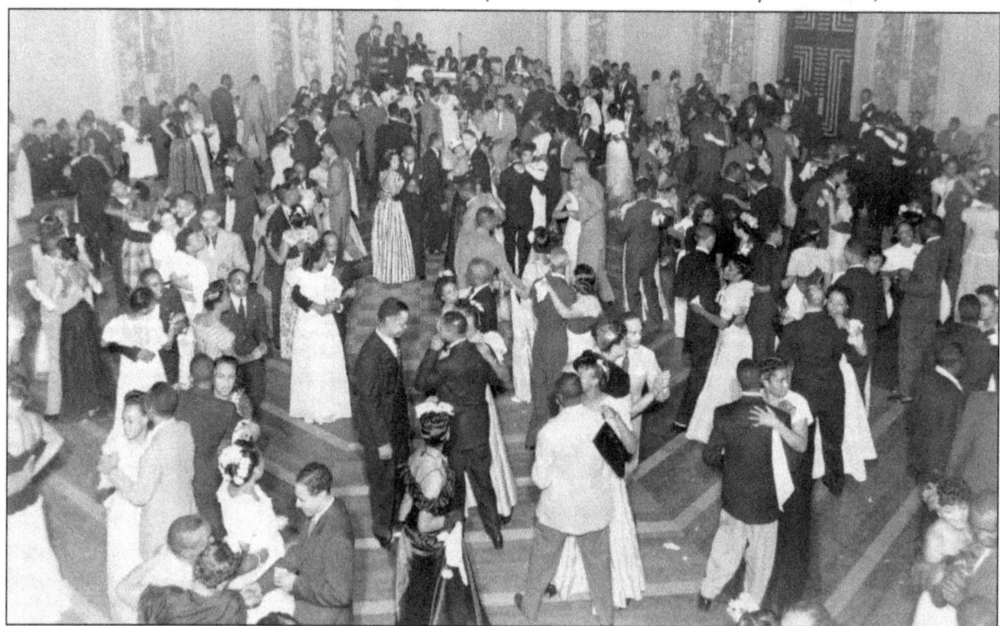

At the Prom, 1946. During the mid-1940s, fewer than half of all American teenagers graduated from high school. The rate for African Americans was even lower. But for these students at the annual Walker prom, the future was bright as they danced at Kansas City auditorium's octagonal Little Theater Ballroom. Many would go on to own their own salons. (Courtesy of Madam Walker Family Archives.)

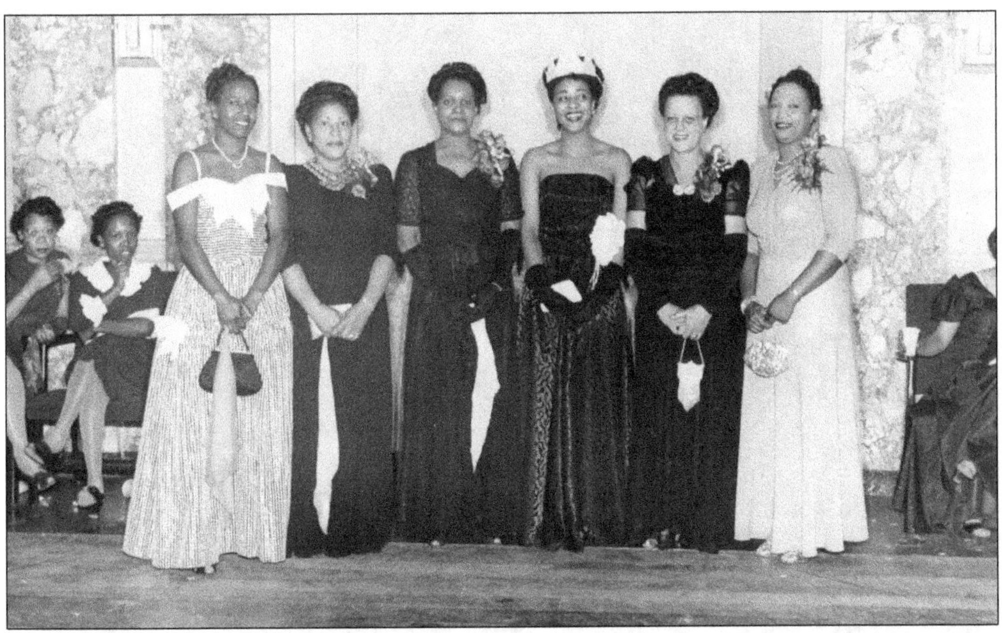

Kansas City Principal. Roberta Nelson Aiken, second from right next to the 1946 prom queen, was principal of the Tulsa Walker Beauty School from 1934 until 1940, when she was promoted to the larger school in Kansas City, Missouri. A native of Illinois and graduate of Texas's Prairie View College, she had been a teacher in Kansas City and Dallas. (Courtesy of Madam Walker Family Archives.)

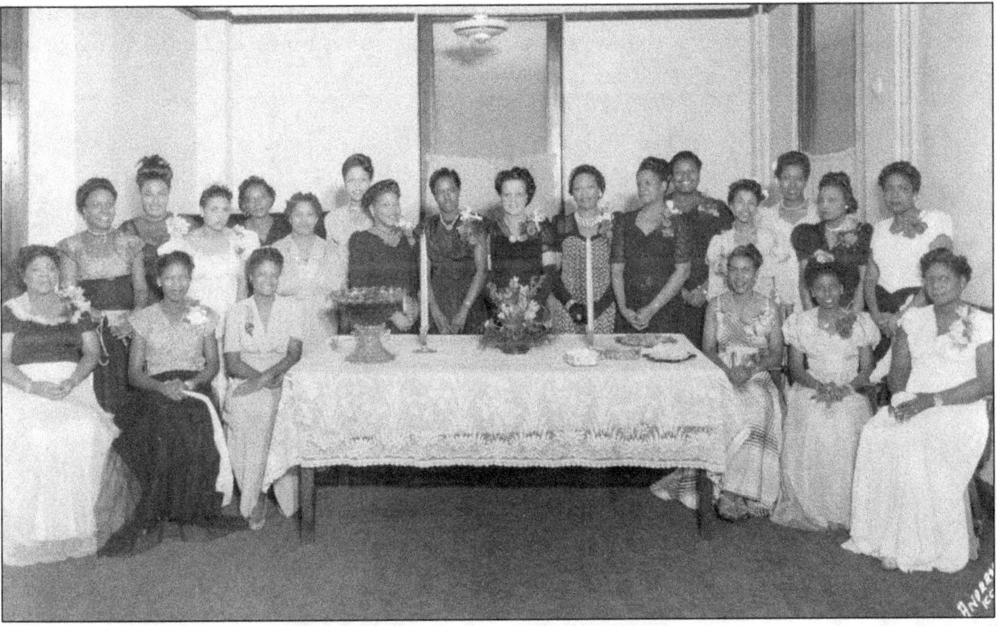

Setting an Example. Kansas City principal Roberta Nelson Aiken, center behind floral arrangement, was a leader of the National Beauty Culturists League (NBCL), a black beauticians organization founded in 1919. Her skill as a premier hairstylist led to her role as chairman of the NBCL's hairstyling competition committee; she was of great benefit to students, who join her in this photograph at the 1946 prom. (Courtesy of Madam Walker Family Archives.)

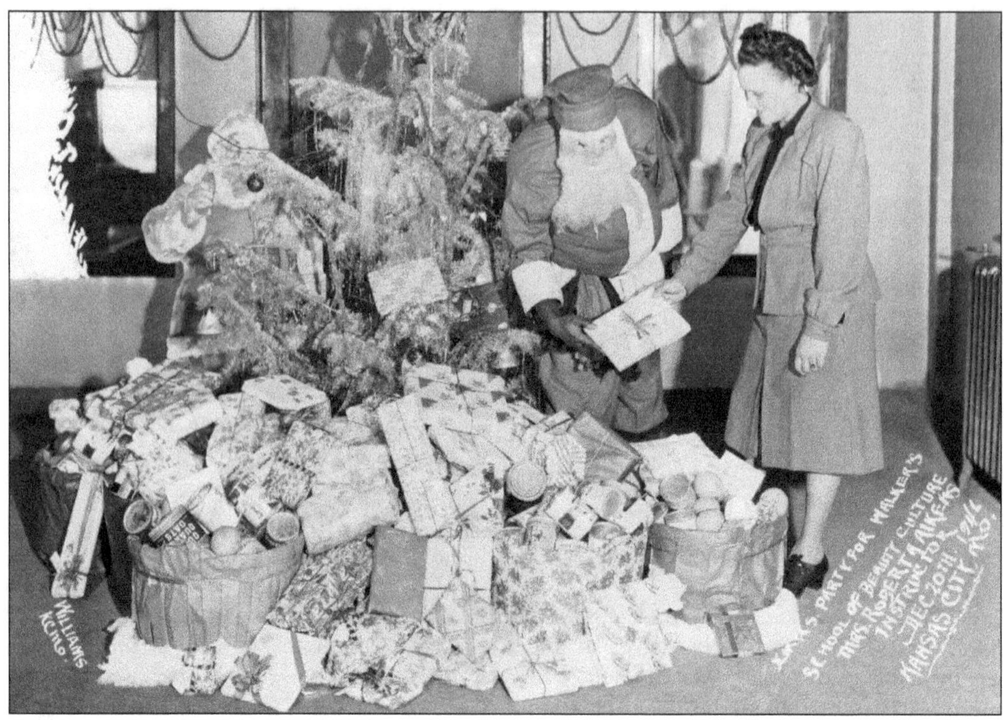

CHRISTMAS CHEER. In a tradition started by Madam Walker, all Walker schools collected food and toiletries to distribute to needy families at Christmas. Kansas City principal Roberta Nelson Aiken surveys the donations during a holiday party in December 1946. A close look reveals Quaker Oats, Palmolive soap, fresh oranges and canned pineapple, green beans, and spinach. (Courtesy of Madam Walker Family Archives.)

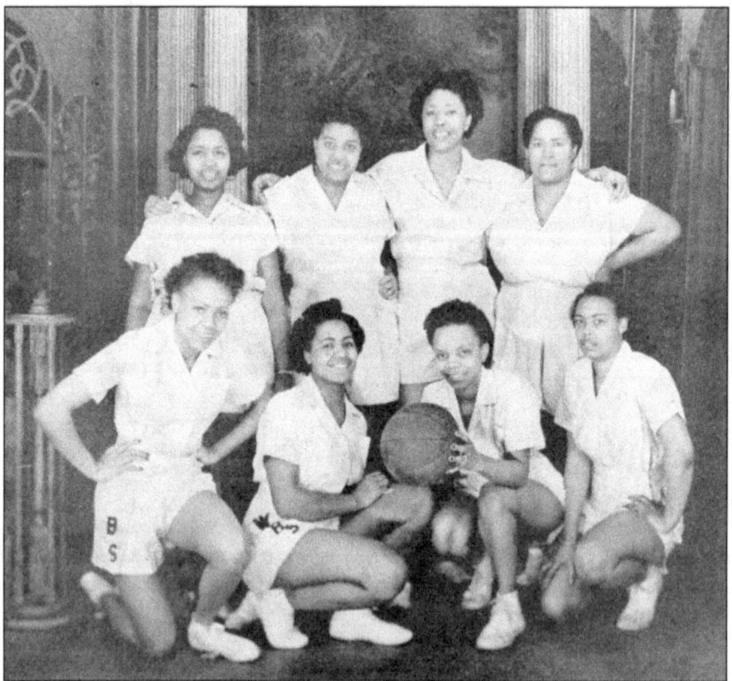

STAYING FIT. Overall attention to physical fitness was key to the Kansas City school's curriculum. Whether through a course in body massage or intramural competitive sports, students were encouraged to pursue a regimen that led to healthy minds and bodies. These Walker Beauty School basketball team members are ready to take on their opponents. (Courtesy of Madam Walker Family Archives.)

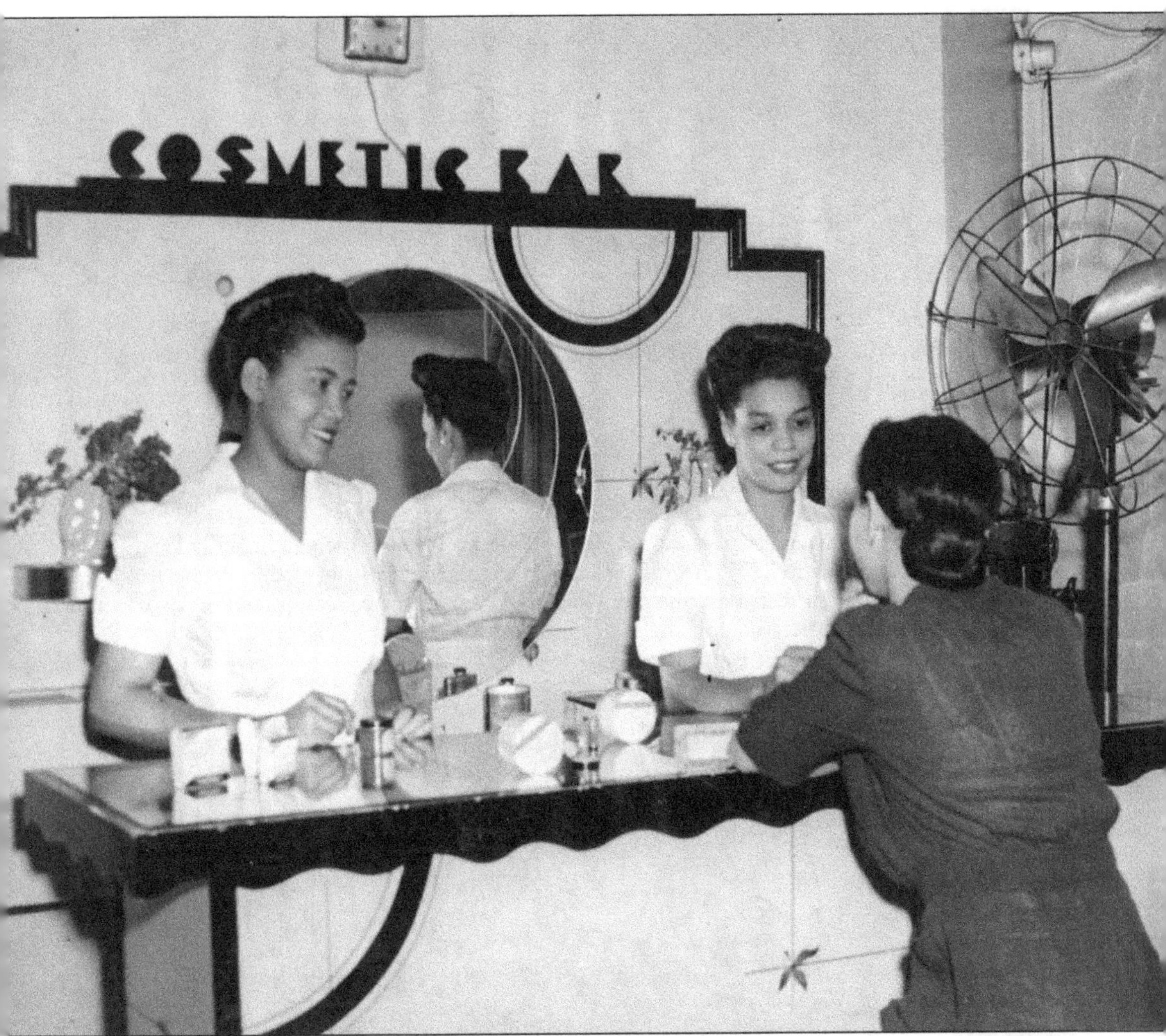

Ready for Their Close-up. Savonia Jarrett, left, and Frances Davidson Williams speak with a Walker Beauty Shoppe cosmetic bar customer in Indianapolis. A popular cosmetologist, Williams moved from Louisville in the late 1930s and later attended the Walker Beauty School. At one time, there were Walker salons operated by Walker graduates in most major American cities. Among the more well-known establishments were the Washington, DC, shop on Ninth Street near U Street and the Harlem beauty parlor at 2588 Seventh Avenue. In 1987, items from Marjorie Stewart Joyner's Chicago operation on Cottage Grove were moved to Washington, DC, to recreate her salon in the Smithsonian National Museum of American History's "Field to Factory" exhibition. Today, the Madam Walker Theatre Center is home to a Walker Beauty Salon operated by Elisabetta Goodall. (Courtesy of Madam C.J. Walker Collection, Indiana Historical Society.)

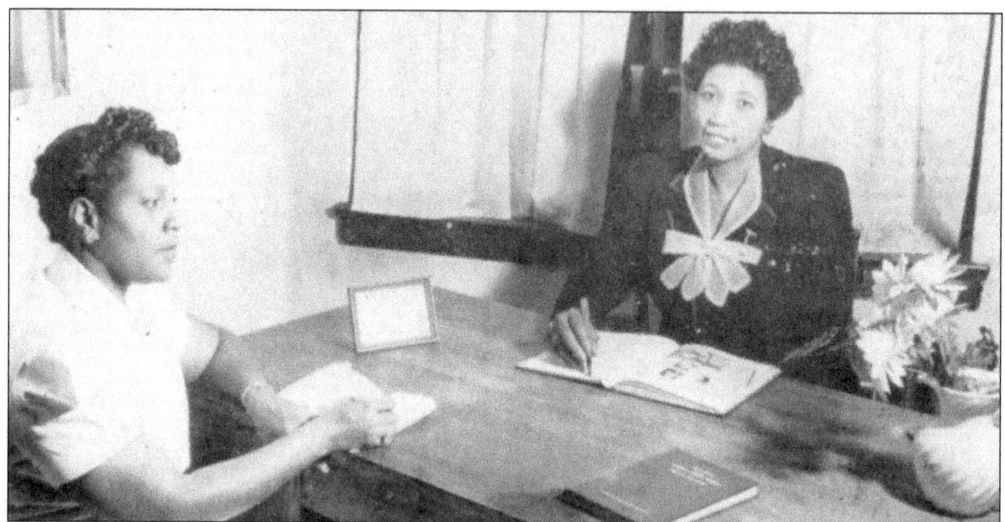

Leading the Way. After a stint as Kansas City's Walker school principal, Priscilla Dean Lewis moved to Indianapolis in 1935. A graduate of Chicago's Moler Beauty School, she studied at Columbia and Butler Universities. She was a local NAACP chapter president, secretary-treasurer of the Indiana Barber School, and the National Beauty Culturists League's dean of education. (Courtesy of Madam Walker Family Archives.)

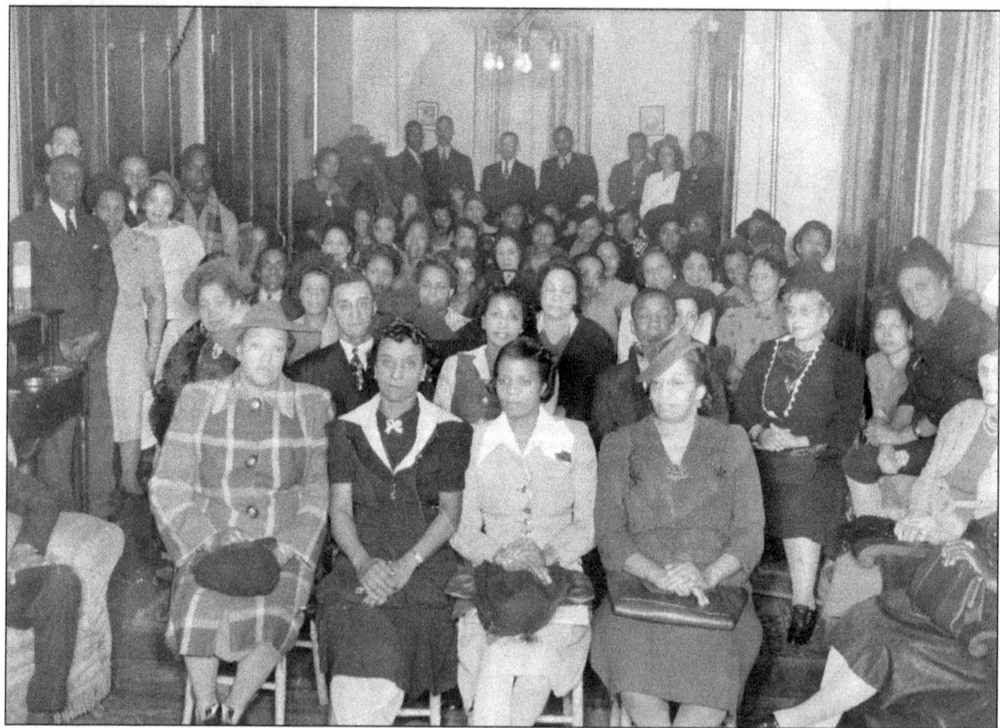

Community Activist. Walker school principals were selected for their leadership as well as cosmetology skills. Many were active in politics and voter registration drives as well as philanthropic activities. Priscilla Dean Lewis, in the second row wearing a vest, became the first woman member of the board of directors of Indianapolis's black YMCA and of its annual fundraising campaign. (Courtesy of Madam Walker Family Archives.)

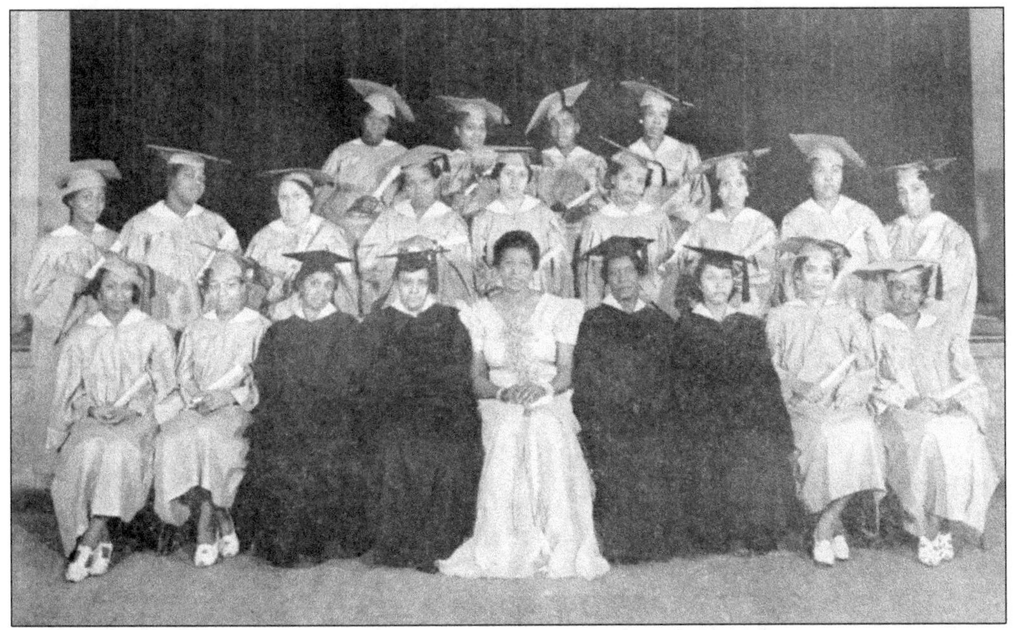

Commencement, 1938. When these Walker students graduated in 1938, America still was in the midst of the Great Depression. Struggling to find work and feed their families, many Americans found themselves relying on government assistance. That year, the federal Works Progress Administration employed more than three million people, but most of the jobs went to men. (Courtesy of Madam Walker Family Archives.)

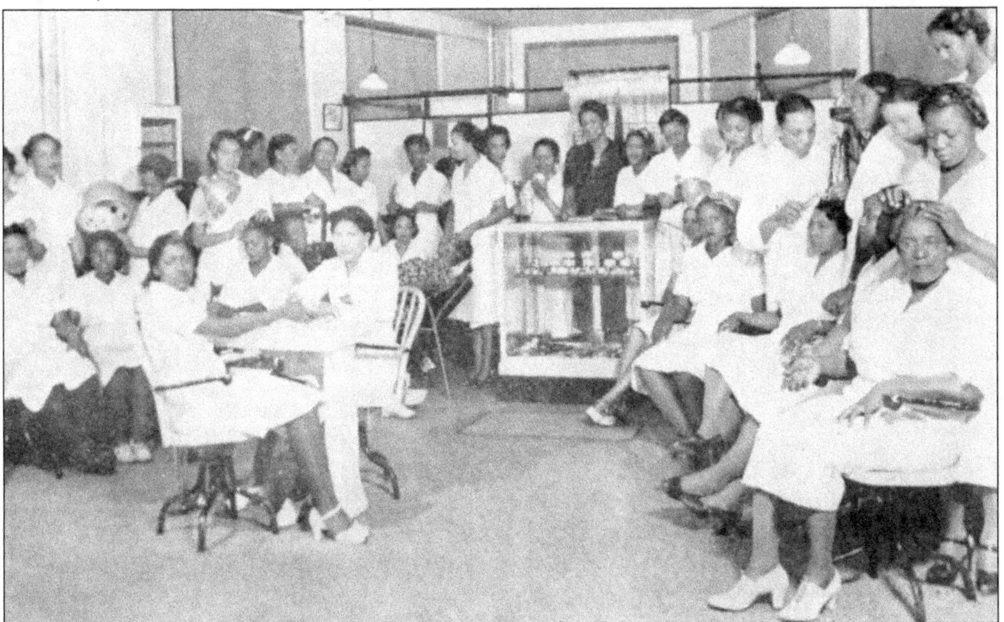

Beyond the Salon. For women willing to travel, the Walker schools offered courses tailored for maids of Pullman cars. Some also served as traveling companions and hairdressers for famous actresses. The curriculum available to these Indianapolis students included instruction on "marcel waving, manicuring, massaging, conversation and personal magnetism," presumably skills they would need when dealing with weary travelers. (Courtesy of Madam Walker Family Archives.)

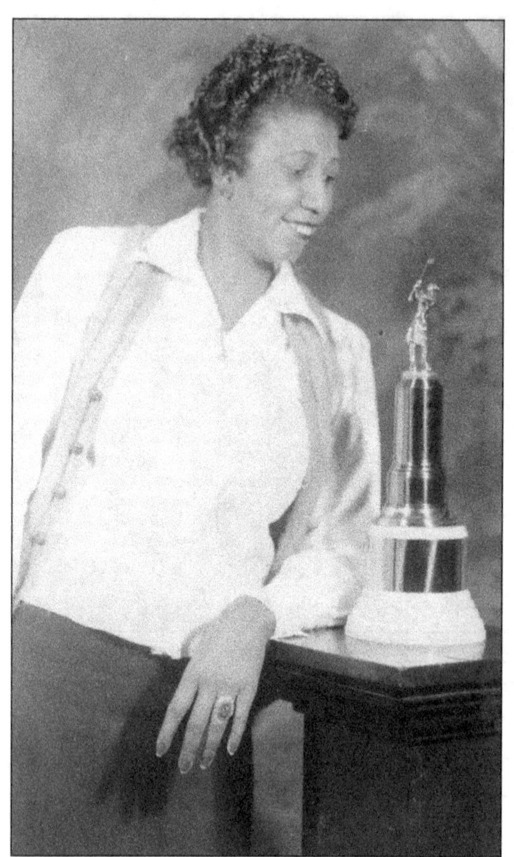

A Champion. When Priscilla Dean Lewis took over the Indianapolis school in 1935, enrollment had fallen to only eight students, a sign of the troubled economic times. The next year, she recruited 16 students and successfully guided them through the requirements of a new Indiana State licensing exam. Owner of her own large salon, Lewis went on to found the Fashionette Beauty and Barber School. (Courtesy of Madam Walker Family Archives.)

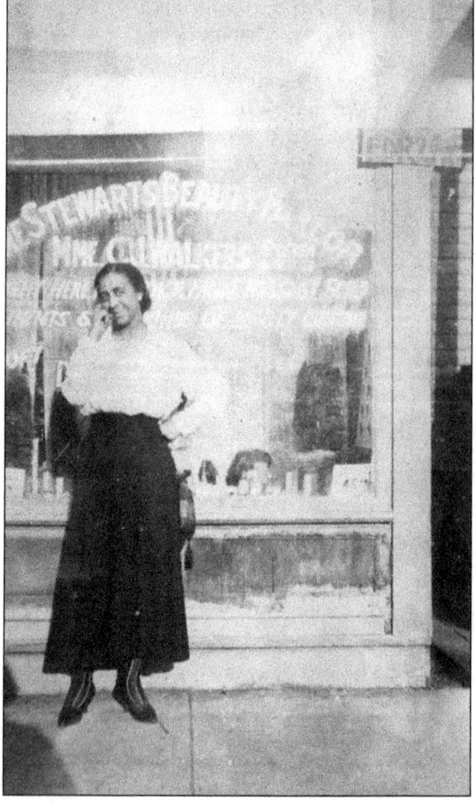

Independent Means. This Walker graduate exemplifies all the promises of the 1928 beauty school manual. It stated, "As a shop owner, you begin immediately to enjoy being your own boss, taking out, if you choose, whatever profits your shop may earn. Walker graduates all over the country are buying homes, automobiles, fine clothes, jewelry, rearing families, educating dependents all out of their earnings as a beauty culturist." (Courtesy of Madam Walker Family Archives.)

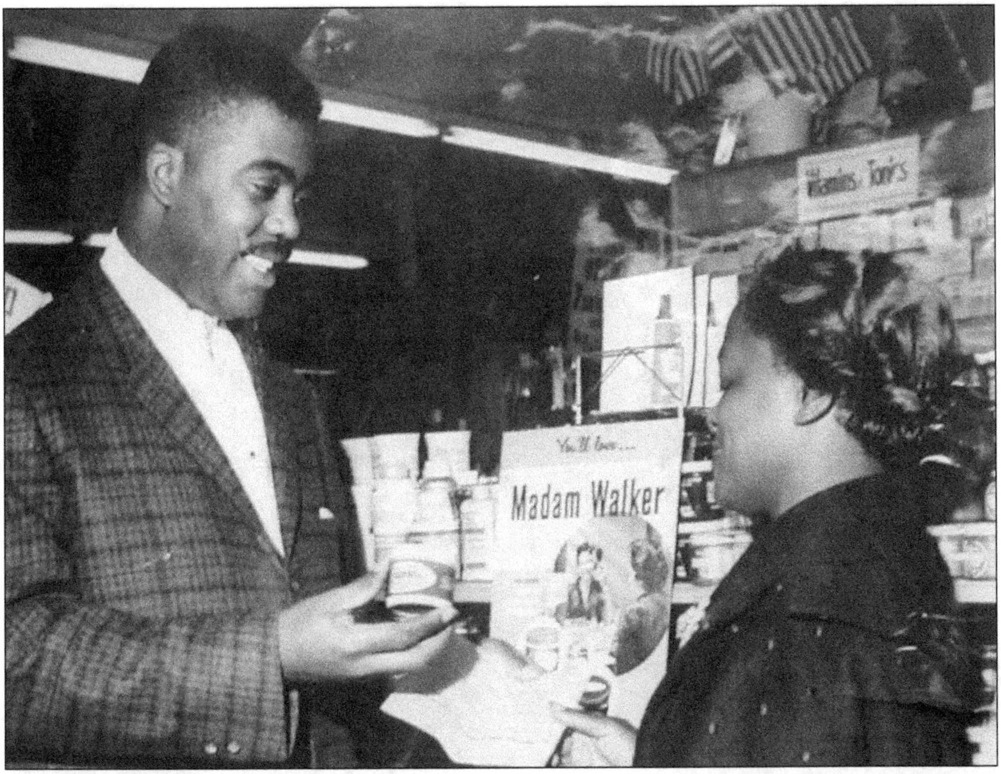

PERSONALITY PLUS. Neal Harris joined the Walker Company in the late 1950s as special sales representative traveling throughout the United States to trade shows, beauty supply stores, beauty salons, barbershops, and drugstores. His enthusiasm for the products and the legacy of Madam Walker was contagious. (Courtesy of Madam Walker Family Archives.)

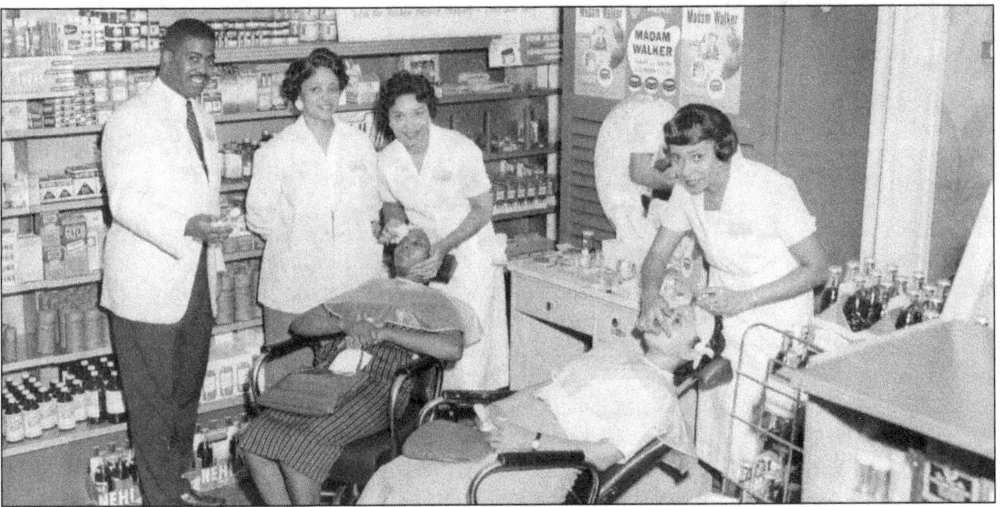

TEAMWORK. While beauty consultants demonstrated Walker skin and hair care products, special sales representative Neal Harris described the attributes of each item. Shelves behind them are stocked with Glossine, Brilliantine, Temple Salve, and Hair Conditioning Cream. Later, Harris would work for Johnson Products in Chicago, marketing Ultra Sheen and managing its international military base sales. (Courtesy of Madam Walker Family Archives.)

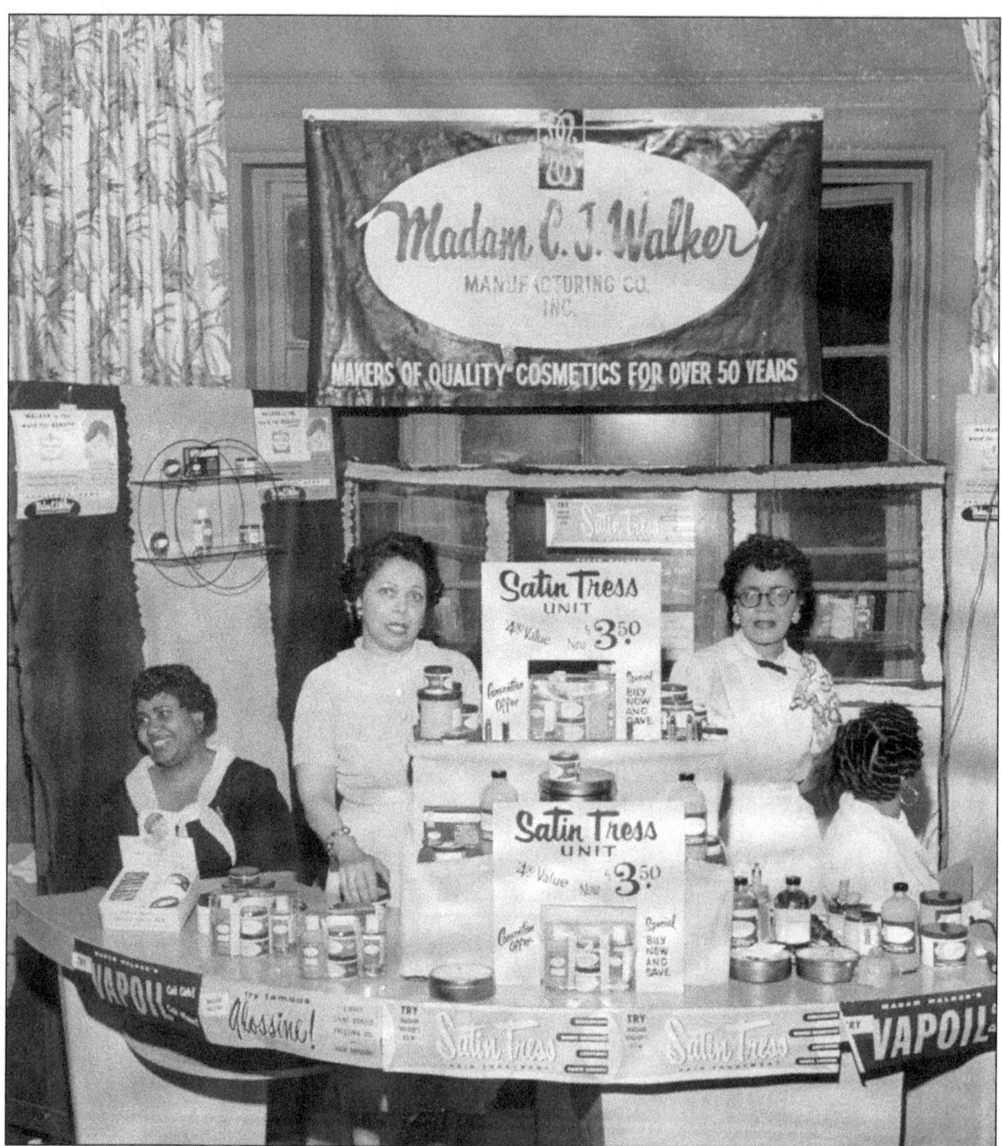

Something New. In 1949, the Walker Company introduced a product line called Satin Tress. A precursor to the chemical hair straighteners that would gain popularity among black women a few years later, Satin Tress avoided the harsh sodium hydroxide–based formulas and utilized what company literature described as an "oil-free," three-step process of a special shampoo, pressing lotion, and hair conditioning cream. Many Walker customers welcomed a less greasy, less waxy alternative to the original Walker ointments and to products like Vaseline, Royal Crown, and Dixie Peach, the cheaper options sold by white-owned companies. By the mid-1950s, the Walker Company—along with Annie Malone's Poro Company and Sarah Spencer Washington's Apex Company—remained among the top black-owned hair care firms in the country, but they were losing market share and actually controlled only a small percentage of the overall hair care product sales to black women. (Courtesy of Madam Walker Family Archives.)

Five

Good Times
The 1950s and 1960s

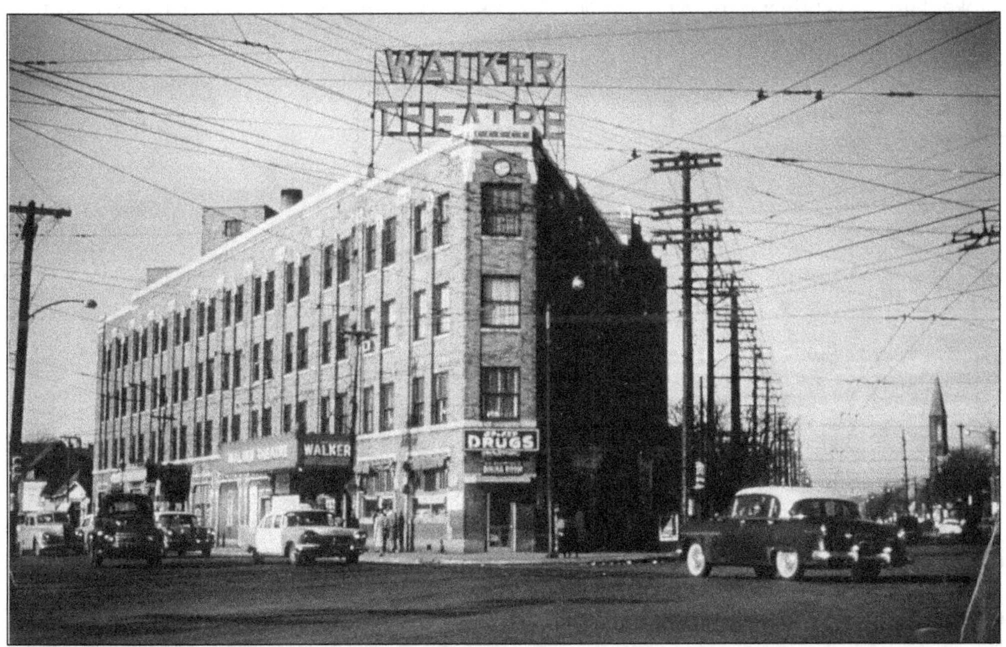

Good Times. Into the late 1950s, Indiana Avenue remained a vital hub for black business and social life. Bethel AME Church, the Phyllis Wheatley YWCA, the Fall Creek YMCA, Forrest Jones's Bar-B-Que Heaven, Baird's Hatters and Cleaners, Arlene's House of Music, Sea Ferguson's Bowling Alley, Denver and Sea Ferguson's Sunset Terrace Ballroom, and dozens of other small businesses were within walking distance of the Walker Building. (Courtesy of Madam Walker Family Archives.)

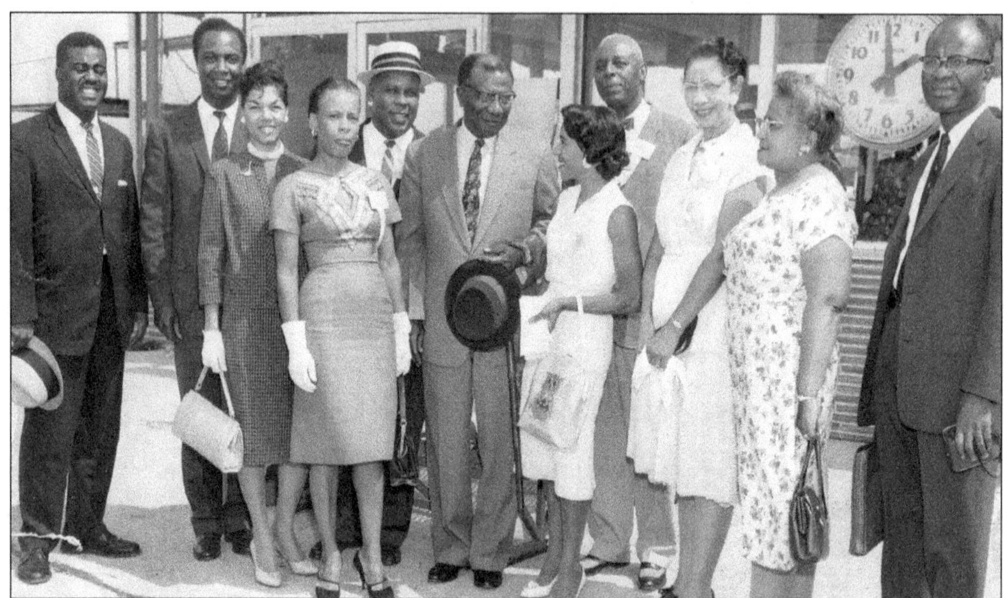

African Dignitaries. In August 1960, Ghanaian ambassador William M.Q. Halm, center front, was the Walker Company's diamond anniversary celebration keynote speaker. Greeting him at the Indianapolis airport are, from left to right, Neal Harris, William M.Q. Halm's son Albert Halm, Lois Reed, A'Lelia Ransom Nelson, Willard B. Ransom, A'Lelia Mae Perry Bundles, Robert L. Brokenburr, Violet Reynolds, Marie Brooks Overstreet, and press attaché C.B. Mensah. (Courtesy of Madam Walker Family Archives.)

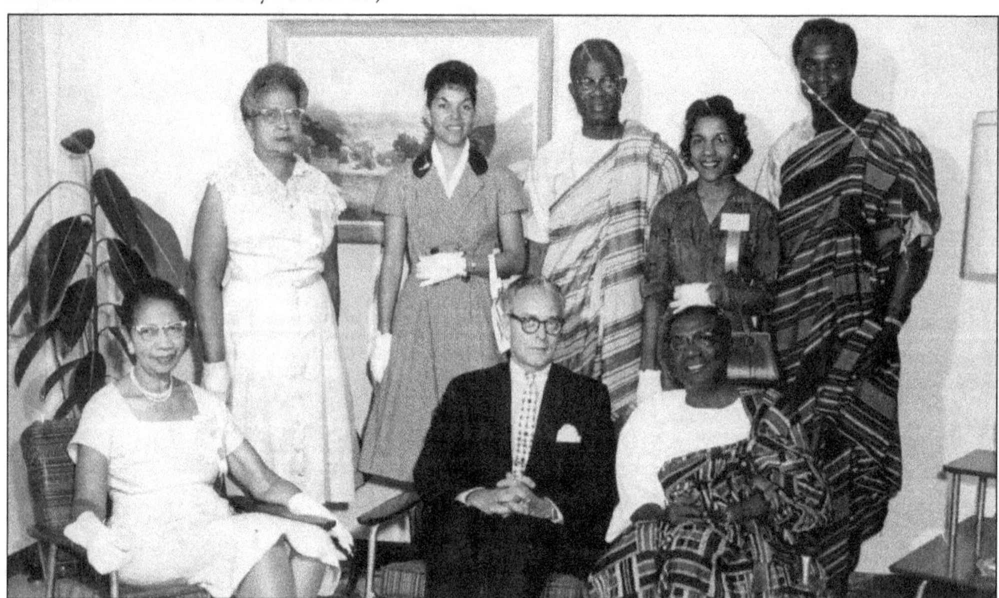

International Trade. As ambassador of Ghana, the West African nation that had won its independence from British colonial rule in 1957, William M.Q. Halm, sitting on the far right, cultivated relationships with black-owned American businesses as part of his strategy to develop trade opportunities. Walker Company officials welcomed his visit because they, too, hoped to expand sales in Ghana, Liberia, Ethiopia, and other African countries. (Courtesy of Madam Walker Family Archives.)

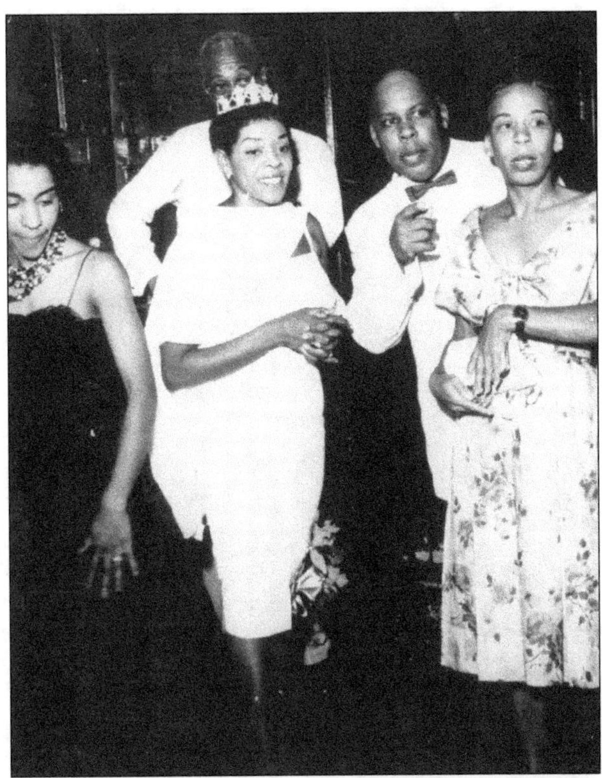

The Queen. "Queen of the Blues" Dinah Washington, center, was riding high from her Grammy Award–winning "What a Difference a Day Makes" when she headlined the Walker's August 1960 anniversary concert. She was a favorite of Walker vice president A'Lelia Mae Perry Bundles, left, and Walker president A'Lelia Ransom Nelson, right, who are joined by attorney Robert L. Brokenburr, left, and Walker general manager Willard Ransom, right. (Courtesy of Madam Walker Family Archives.)

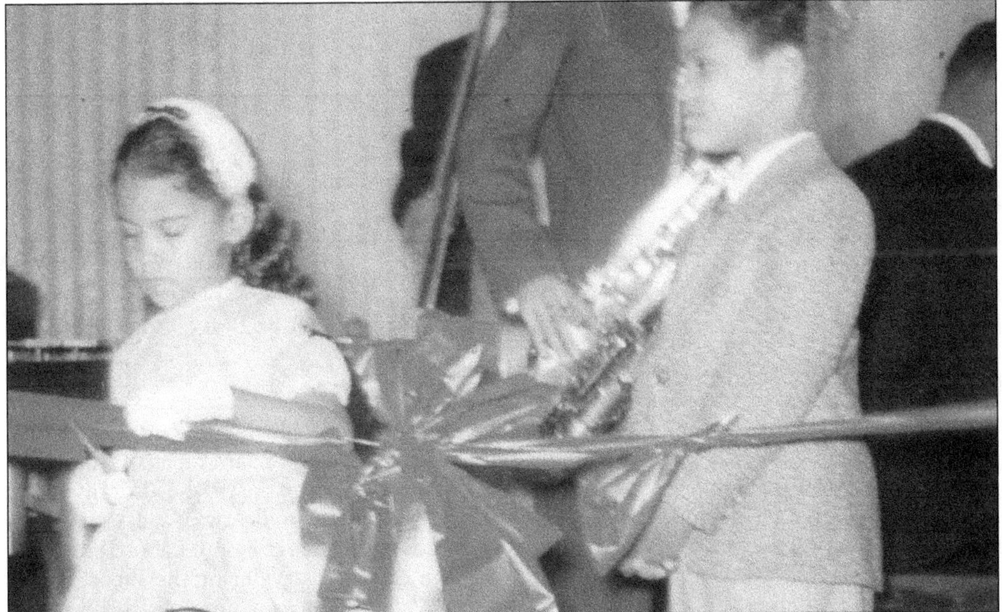

Grand Opening. As part of yearlong anniversary celebration in 1960—really its 54th year in business rather than 60th as company news releases announced—the Walker Company remodeled its Grand Casino Ballroom. Cutting the ribbon are A'Lelia Perry Bundles, great-great-granddaughter of Madam C.J. Walker and daughter of Walker vice president A'Lelia Mae Perry Bundles. Her young escort is Stewart Hawkins. (Courtesy of Madam Walker Family Archives.)

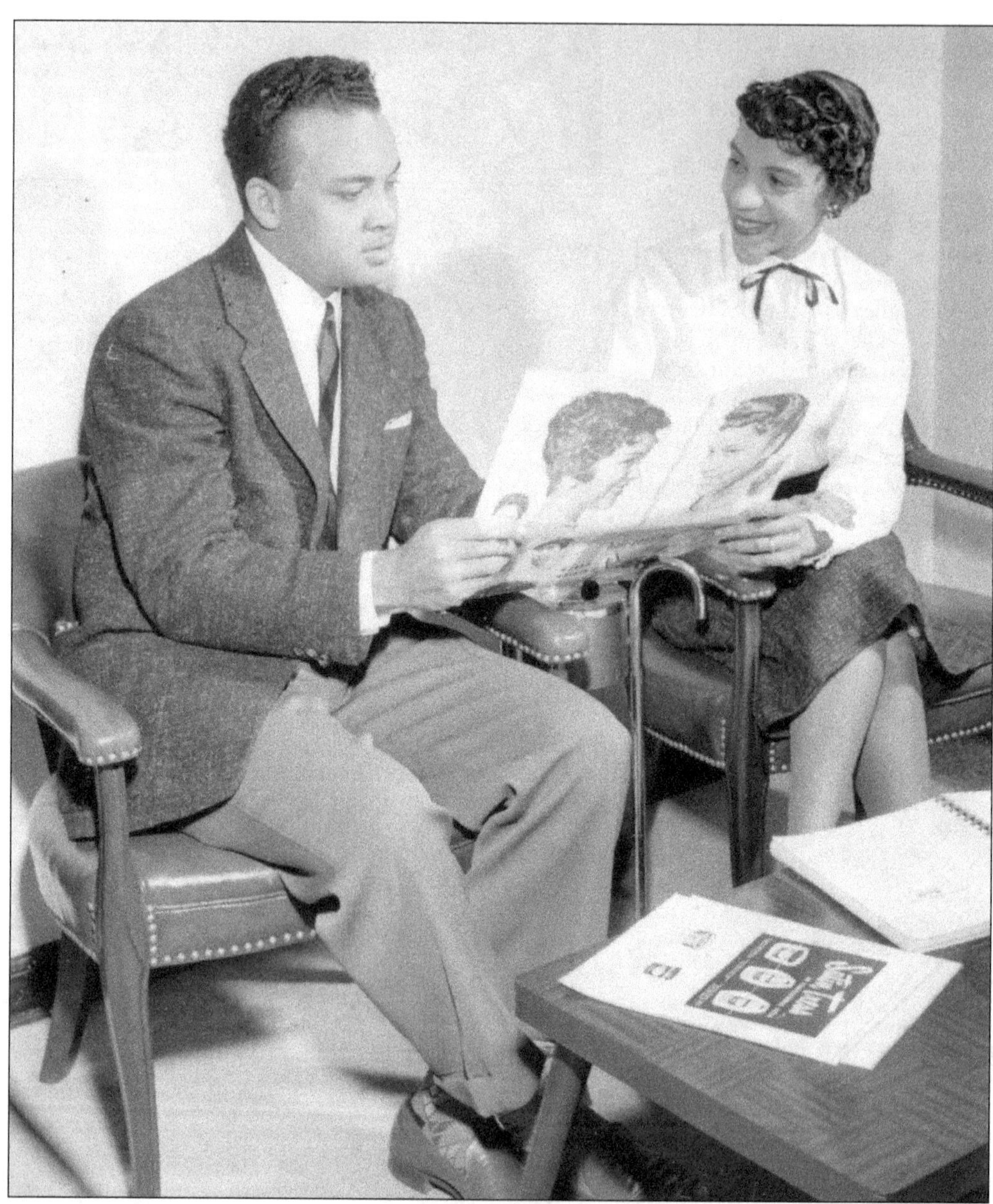

Partners. A'Lelia Mae Perry Bundles, Madam Walker's great-granddaughter and Howard University chemistry and business major, was a Walker Company executive and board member from 1945 until her death in 1976. A member of Washington Township's School Board, she also was active in local and national Democratic politics. Her husband, S. Henry Bundles, was Walker national sales manager during the mid-1950s until being recruited as president of Summit Laboratories, one of the new firms that would come to lead the black hair care industry during the 1960s. Along with its primary competitors—Poro and Apex—the Walker Company dominated the black-owned beauty companies during the first half of the 20th century, but it continued to lose steam as Johnson Products, Summit, and others entered the marketplace. To promote their chemical relaxers, these firms developed aggressive marketing campaigns, presenting their approach as more modern than hot combs and curling irons. As Summit Labs president, Bundles led his company to the *Black Enterprise* 100. (Courtesy of Madam Walker Family Archives.)

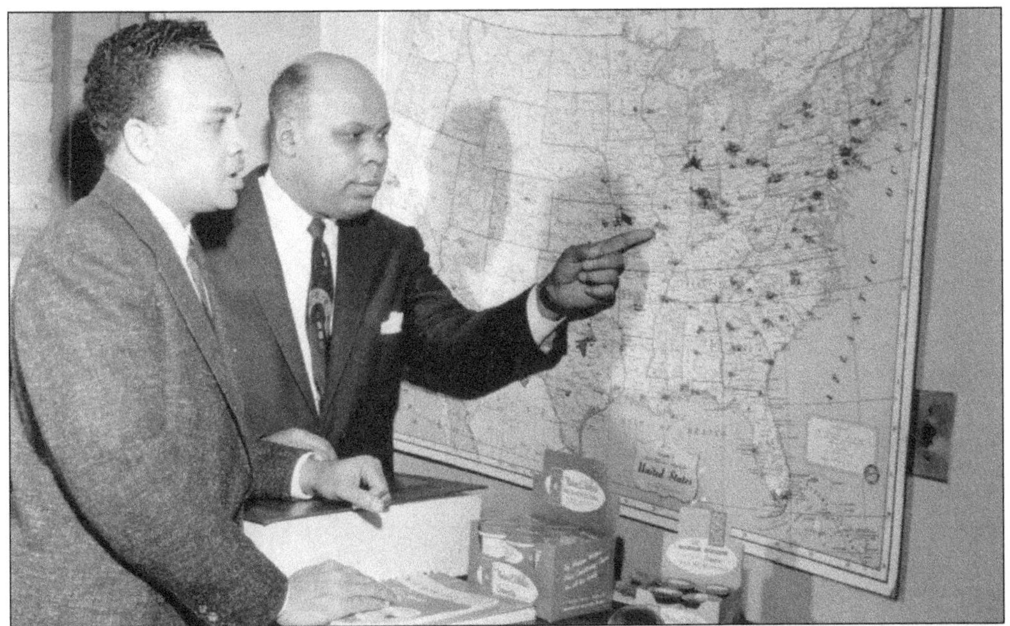

Mapping Strategy, 1957. Walker national sales manager S. Henry Bundles, left, discusses an upcoming sales trip with general manager Willard B. Ransom, son of F.B. Ransom, Walker Company general manager until his death in 1947. A graduate of Talladega College and Harvard Law School, Willard Ransom helped organize Indiana's state NAACP chapter and pushed civil rights legislation in the state's general assembly. (Courtesy of Madam Walker Family Archives.)

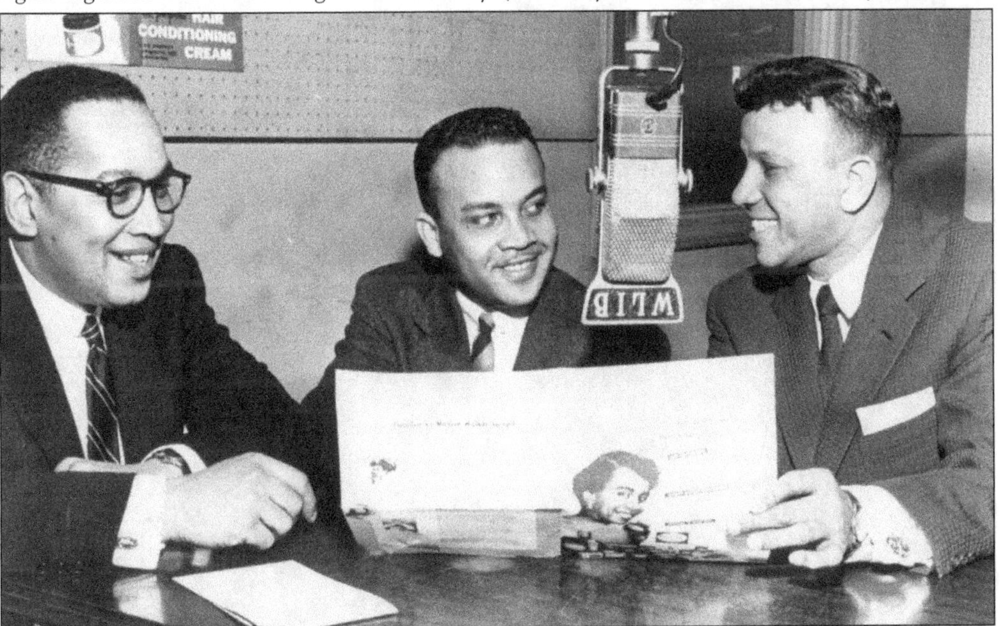

On the Airwaves, 1957. S. Henry Bundles, center, joins legendary broadcaster Hal Jackson, right, in WLIB's New York studios. During his two years as national sales manager, Bundles boosted Walker product sales to their highest levels in 20 years. An Indiana University journalism major, he was a *Pittsburgh Courier* Chicago edition staff writer and an Apex regional sales manager before joining the Walker Company in 1955. (Courtesy of Madam Walker Family Archives.)

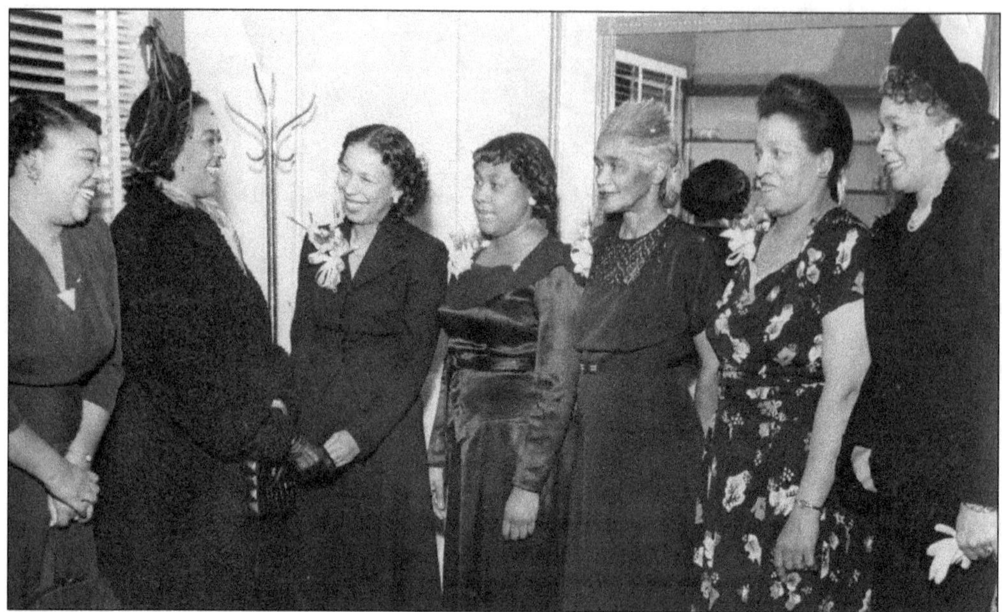

A Walker Welcome. A'Lelia Ransom Nelson, third from left, daughter of Walker attorney F.B. Ransom, was named Walker Company president in 1951. A graduate of Talladega College and Columbia University's graduate program in library science, she moved in 1948 to New York, where she was a librarian for the City College of New York from 1969 to 1996. (Courtesy of Madam Walker Family Archives.)

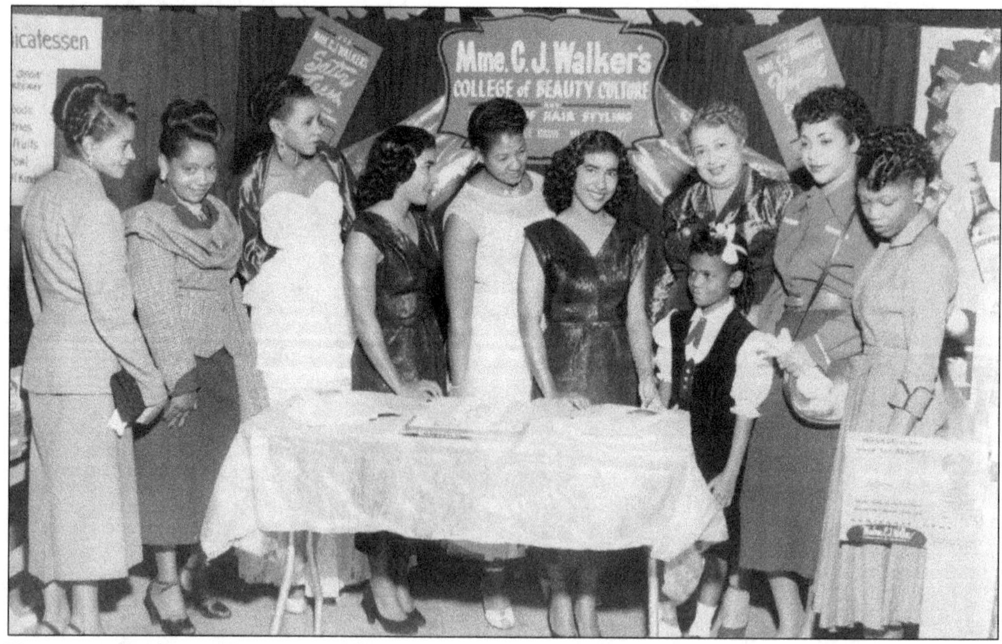

Beauty at Its Best. To create public appeal, Walker featured attractive local models at hairstyling demonstrations. Identical twins and talented musicians, Xernona, left, and Xenobia Brewster appear at this Chicago event during the mid-1950s. Xernona Brewster would marry Edward Clayton, a speechwriter for Martin Luther King Jr., and go on to become the first black woman to host her own television program in the South. (Courtesy of Madam Walker Family Archives.)

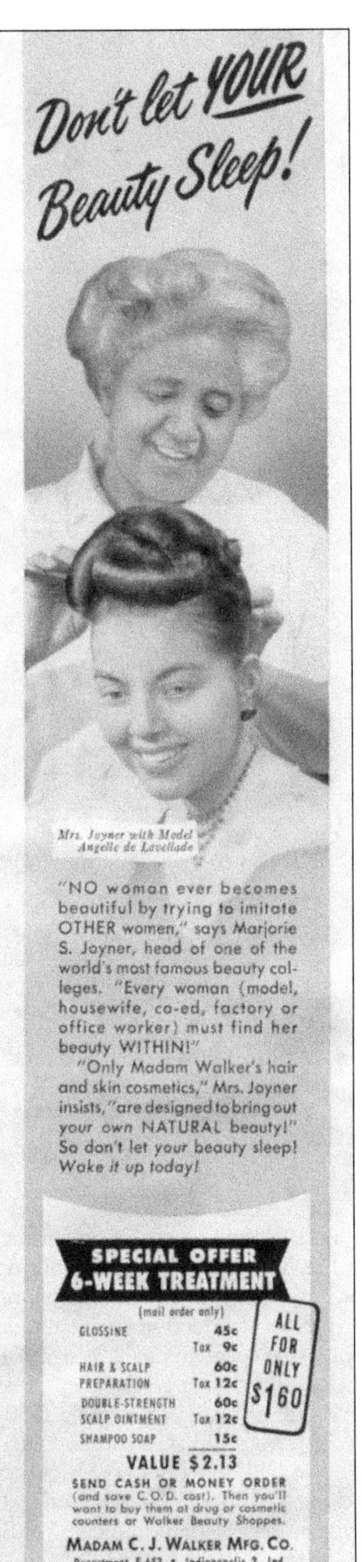

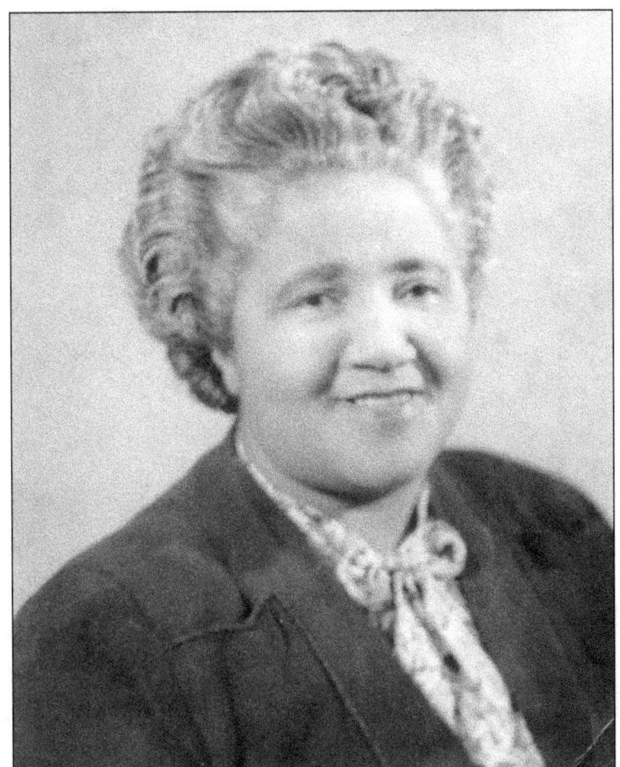

Chance Meeting. Marjorie Stewart Joyner met Madam Walker in Chicago in 1916 when her mother-in-law insisted she take a class Walker was teaching. Stewart had learned to style white women's hair at Chicago's Moler Beauty School but lacked skills to style black women's hair. On their chance encounter, Joyner's public presence was so impressive that Walker trained and hired her to teach other students. (Courtesy of Madam Walker Family Archives.)

A Flair for Glamour. Marjorie Joyner had an instinct for promotion and publicity. Aware that well-known celebrities who endorsed and used Walker products could attract customers, she developed friendships with models and entertainers. In this Walker advertisement, she styles the hair of Angelle de Lavallade, a popular Los Angeles model, who had appeared on the cover of *Jet* in November 1951. (Courtesy of Madam Walker Family Archives.)

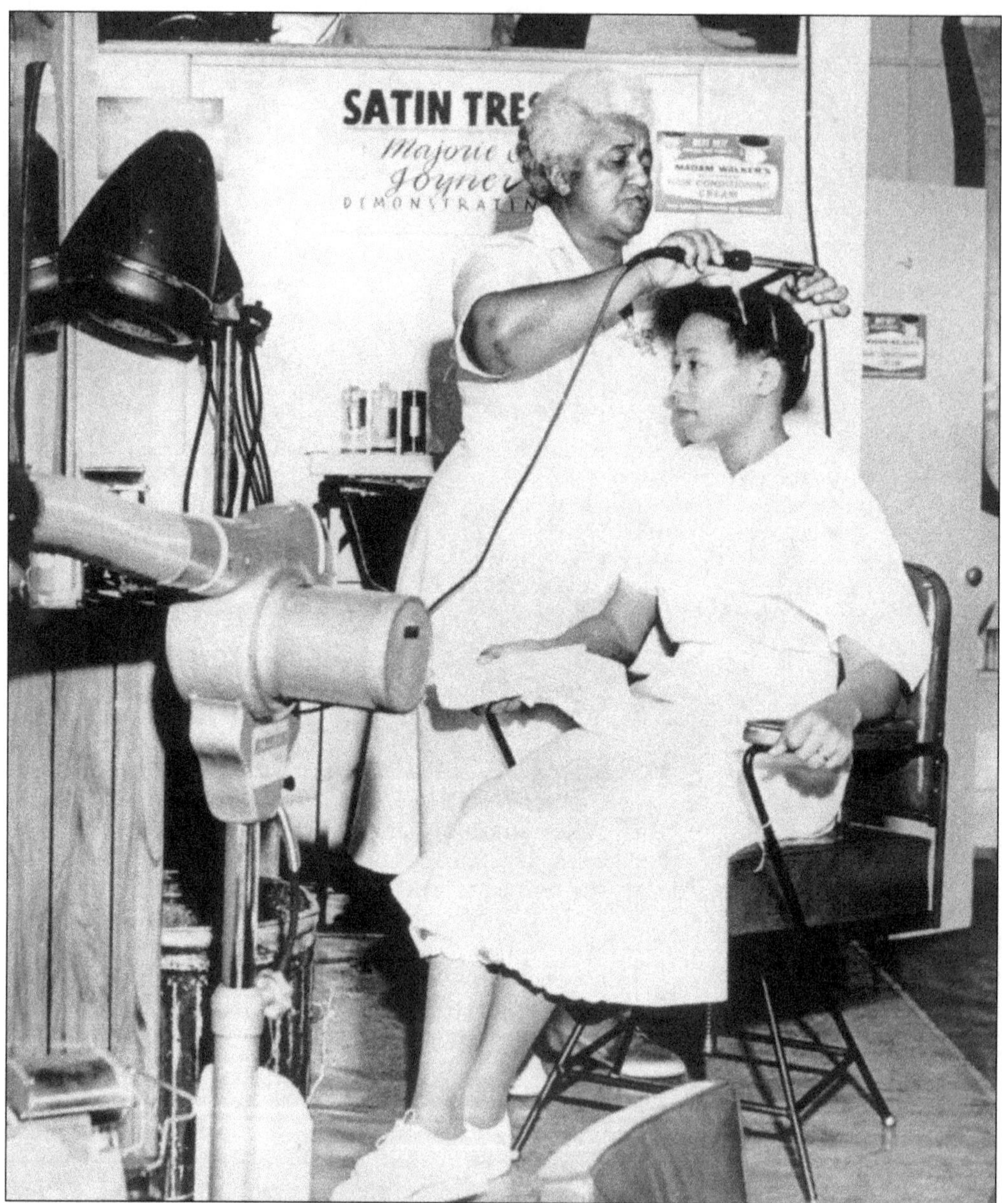

INNOVATOR. Born in 1896 in Monterey, Virginia, Marjorie Joyner was the daughter of a schoolteacher. When her parents divorced, she moved to Illinois with her mother. Within a few years of joining the Walker Company, she assumed leadership positions in the Chicago school, eventually becoming national supervisor of 12 Walker schools. Perhaps the company's most effective and dynamic spokesperson other than Walker herself, she helped write Illinois's first cosmetology laws in 1924. She also created the formula for Satin Tress, a product and process that updated the oily "press and curl" regimen of the early Walker System, though some Walker officials of the early 1950s prevented her from claiming ownership to the patent. Joyner's interests and activism extended well beyond the Walker Company. Through Madam Walker, she had met Dr. Mary McLeod Bethune, founder of Daytona Normal and Industrial Institute (later Bethune Cookman College), with whom she developed a lifelong friendship. She supported Bethune as a founding member of the National Council of Negro Women. (Courtesy of Madam Walker Family Archives.)

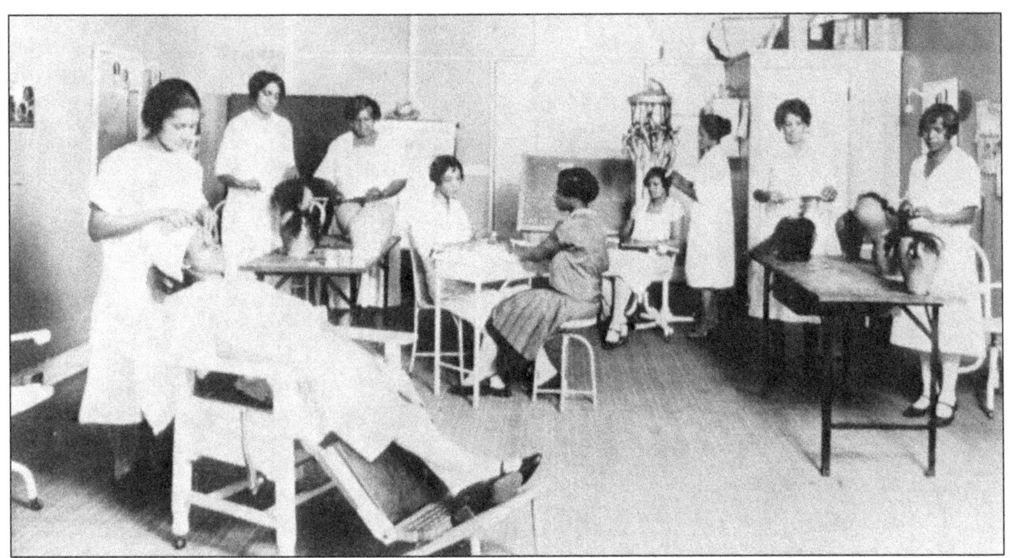

Inventor. In 1928, Marjorie Joyner, third from right, received a patent for a permanent-wave machine—a contraption of cords and heated metal rods—that was designed to create a smoothly curled hairstyle with a longer lasting set. In this 1920s photograph, she is shown administering the process, while other Walker technicians demonstrate facials and manicures and practice hairstyling on mannequins. (Courtesy of Madam Walker Family Archives.)

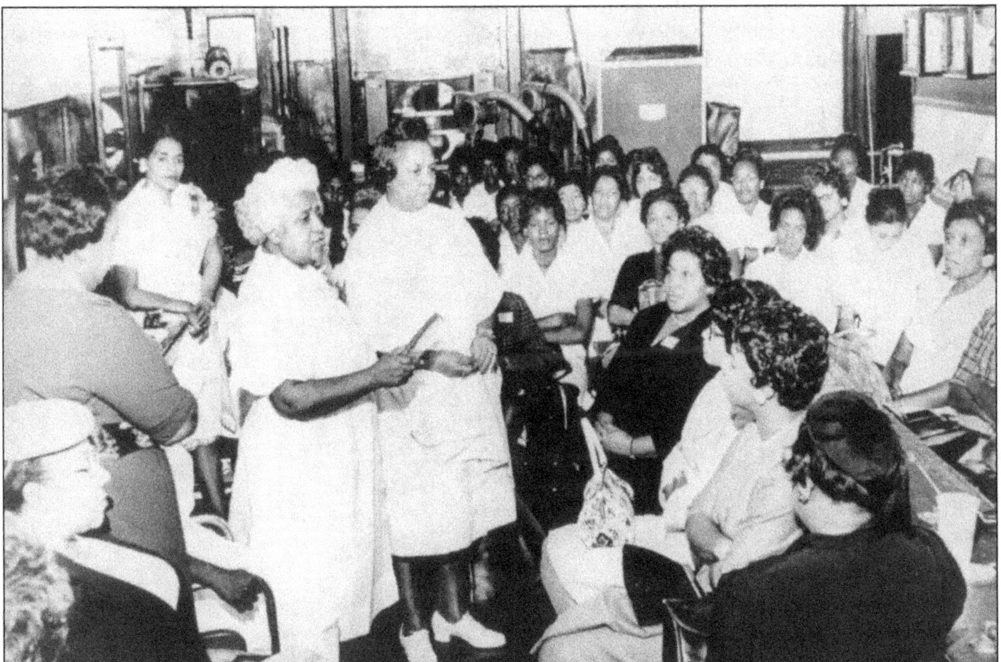

Master Instructor. Joyner was the first black graduate of Chicago's Moler Beauty School. Her clientele in her first salon was mostly white. But her true calling was teaching other black women to become successful beauticians and entrepreneurs. She was the National Beauty Culturists League's president during the 1930s. She founded Alpha Chi Pi Omega fraternal society and the United Beauty School Owners and Teachers Association in 1945. (Courtesy of Madam Walker Family Archives.)

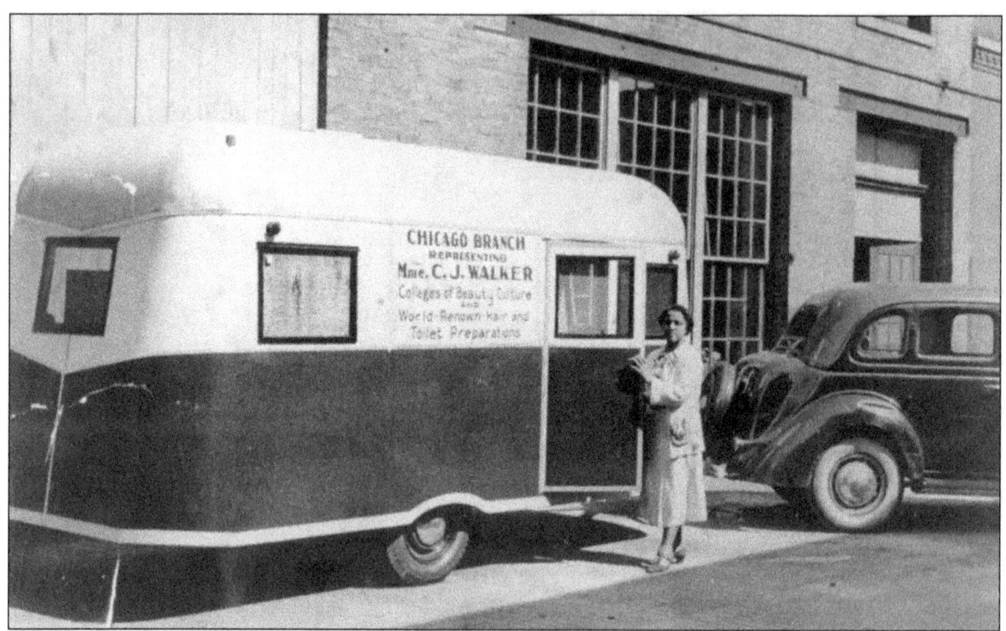

READY TO ROLL. Marjorie Joyner spent much time on the road promoting Walker products. This mobile salon allowed her to avoid the indignities of Jim Crow restrictions when she traveled to demonstrate the Walker System to women in small towns. In 1938, Joyner settled a lawsuit against the Burlington-Rock Island Railroad after she was forced to ride in a baggage car with a corpse. (Courtesy of Madam Walker Family Archives.)

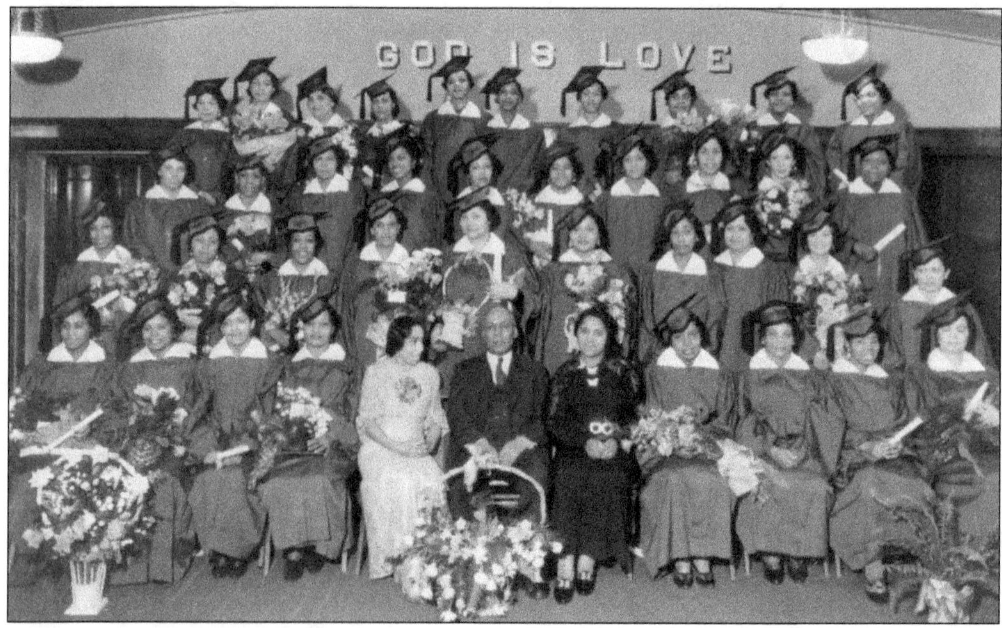

LAUNCHED. Walker Company president Mae Walker Perry, center in the light-colored dress, and attorney F.B. Ransom join Marjorie Joyner at the 1936 Chicago graduation. A decade later in the midst of the post–World War II boom, 600 men and women would graduate with the 1946 Walker class. Joyner retired from the Walker Company in 1963 after nearly 50 years as an employee. (Courtesy of Madam Walker Family Archives.)

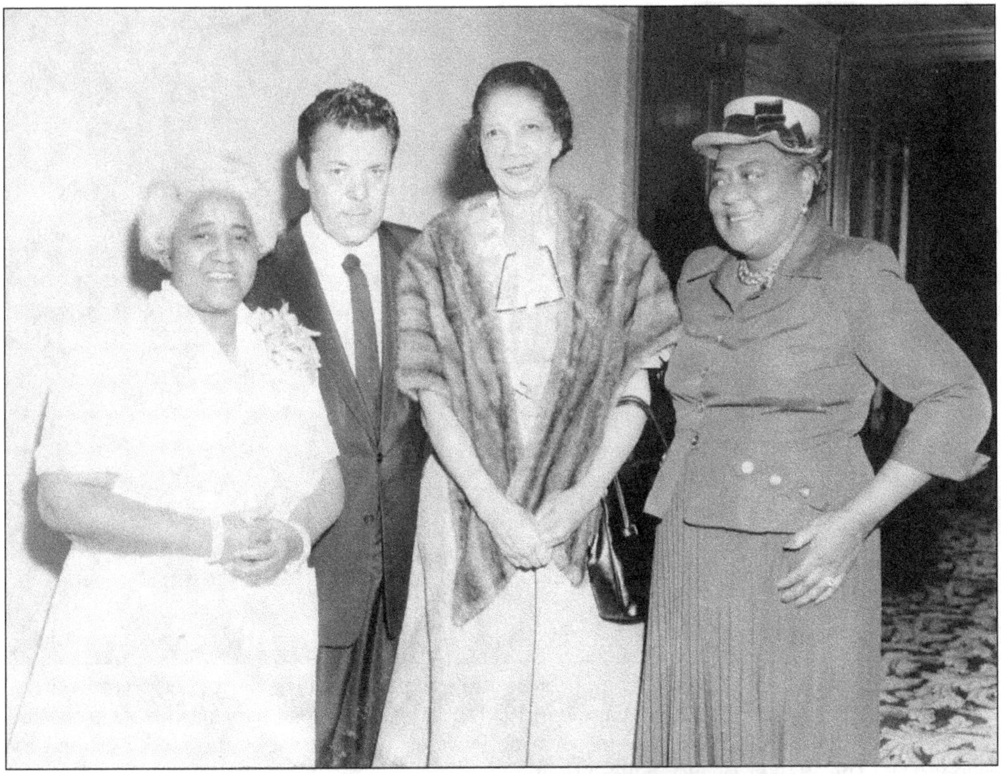

Hollywood Connections. With Chicago as her base—and the world as her oyster—Marjorie Joyner actively engaged popular celebrities to garner publicity for Walker events. On this evening, she is joined by an unidentified man and Walker secretary Violet Reynolds, as she hosts actress Louise Beavers, far right, who was most well known for her starring role as Delilah Johnson in the 1934 movie *Imitation of Life.* (Courtesy of Madam Walker Family Archives.)

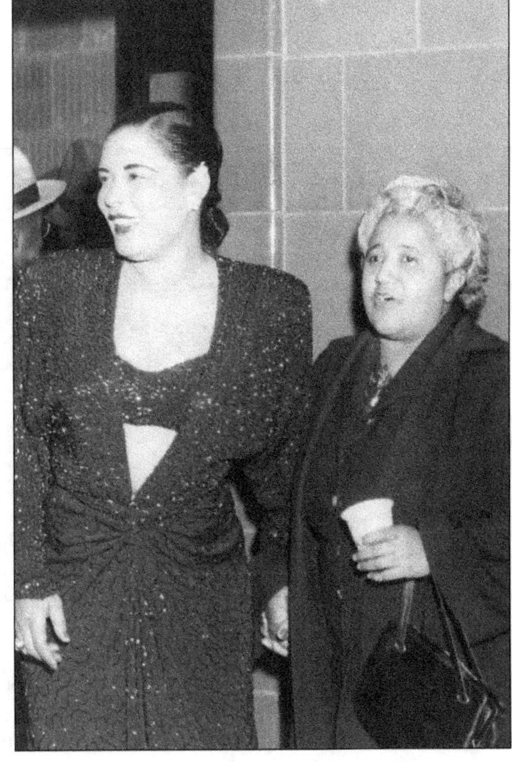

Star Struck. During World War II, Marjorie Joyner hosted several United Service Organization-Walker Beauty School events for black soldiers. Among the entertainers was jazz songstress Billie Holiday, who was at her peak during the 1940s when she recorded "God Bless the Child" and "Lover Man." Another USO-Walker event featured actors Eddie "Rochester" Anderson, Jack Benny, and Lena Horne, who appeared in Walker advertisements. (Courtesy of Madam C.J. Walker Collection, Indiana Historical Society.)

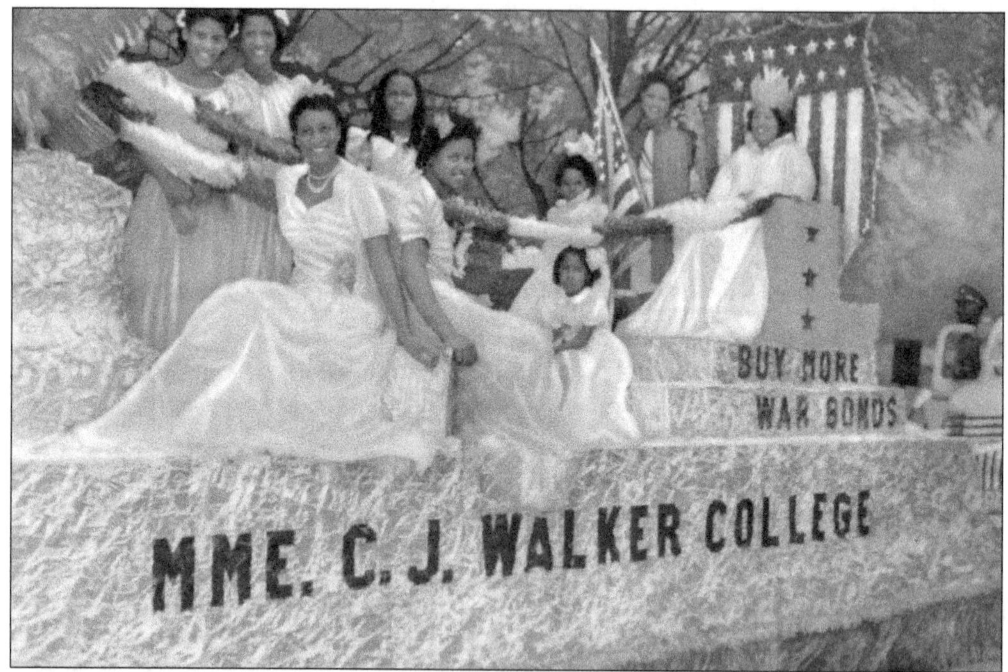

EVERYBODY LOVES A PARADE. A woman of boundless energy, Marjorie Joyner organized the *Chicago Defender*'s first Bud Billiken parade in 1929 to raise money for needy families. She chaired the parade committee until she was in her nineties. Her involvement guaranteed a prime spot each year for the Walker Beauty School float and its well-coiffed court of beauties. (Courtesy of Madam Walker Family Archives.)

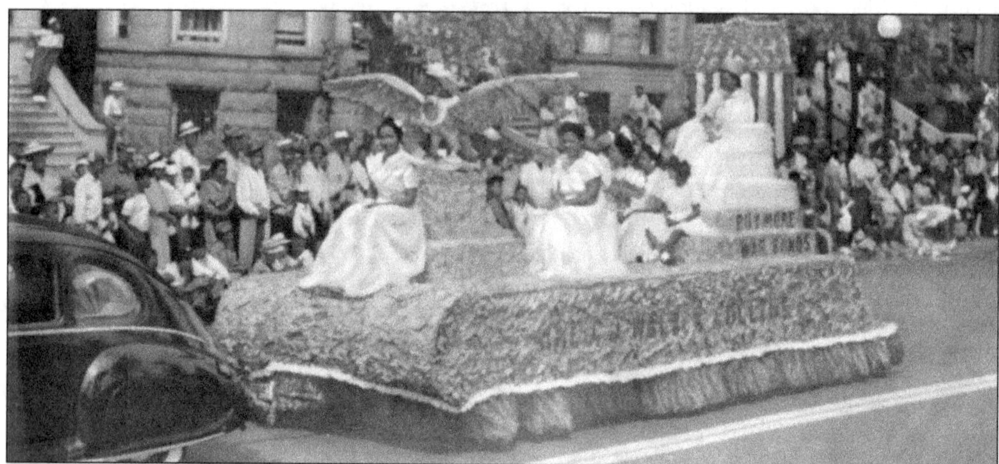

SUPPORTING THE WAR, 1945. During the final year of World War II, the Walker Beauty School adopted a patriotic theme for its Billiken parade float. Marjorie Joyner, longtime director of the *Chicago Defender* Charities, used her network of Walker graduates and beauticians to sell war bonds. During the war, First Lady Eleanor Roosevelt appointed Joyner to a leadership position with the Democratic National Committee. (Courtesy of Madam Walker Family Archives.)

Six

Crowning Glory
Vintage Walker

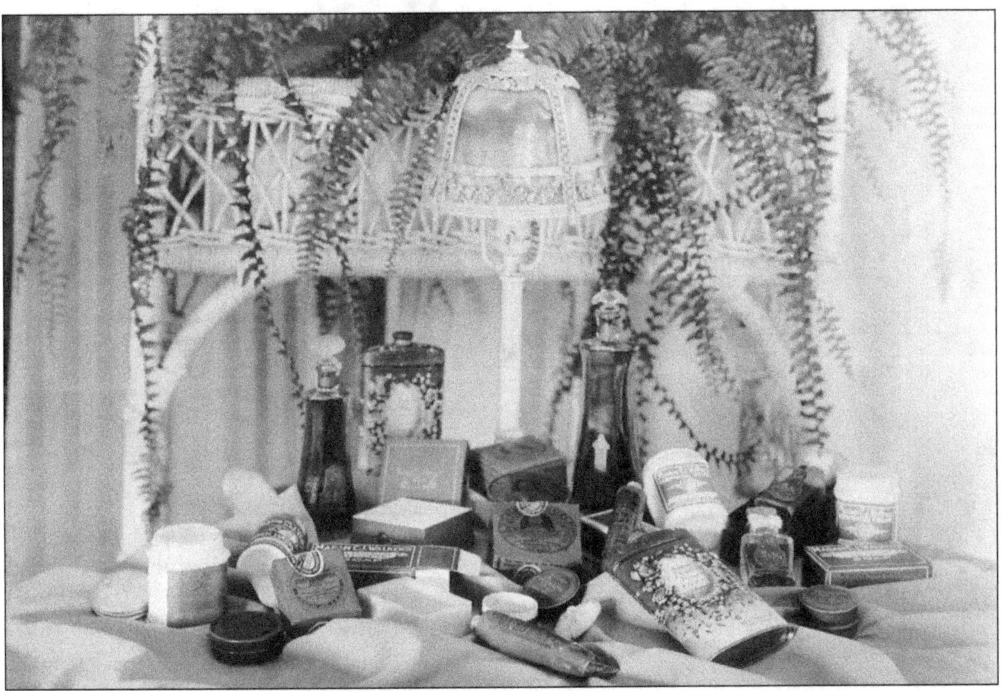

Crowning Glory. From Madam Walker's initial five products—Wonderful Hair Grower, Vegetable Shampoo, Glossine, Temple Salve, and Tetter Salve—the line grew to include face powder, rouge, lipstick, talcum powder, perfumes, soap, lotion, witch hazel, cold cream, dental cream, and men's hair pomade. Always widely advertised, Walker products initially were sold only by authorized Walker agents. By the 1940s, they were available in retail outlets. (Courtesy of Madam Walker Family Archives.)

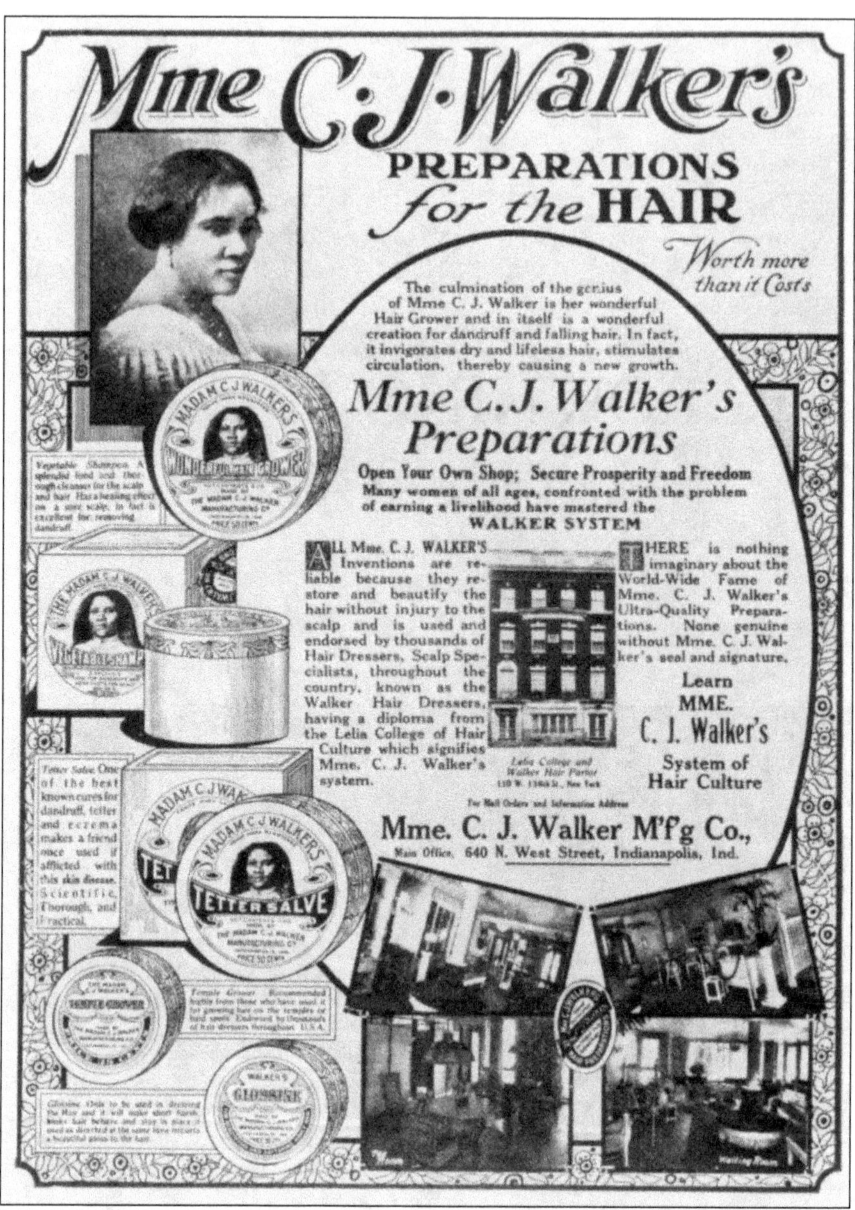

I Promoted Myself. In 1912, Madam Walker told an audience that she had had to "promote herself" into the hair care business to move beyond the drudgery of laundry work. That philosophy carried into this 1917 advertisement. "Own your own shop. Secure Prosperity and Freedom. Many women of all ages, confronted with the problem of earning a livelihood have mastered the WALKER SYSTEM." Created shortly after A'Lelia Walker remodeled her Harlem salon on 136th Street between Seventh Avenue and Lenox Avenue (now Malcolm X Boulevard), this advertisement included images of the salon that likely were commissioned by the Walkers and taken by the well-known Byron commercial photography firm of New York. It ran several times in A. Philip Randolph's *The Messenger* and a number of other black publications. Randolph, who would go on to organize the Brotherhood of Sleeping Car Porters, later said his wife Lucille Green's earnings as a Walker-trained cosmetologist allowed him to be a political activist. The revenue from Walker advertisements also aided his cause. (Courtesy of Madam Walker Family Archives.)

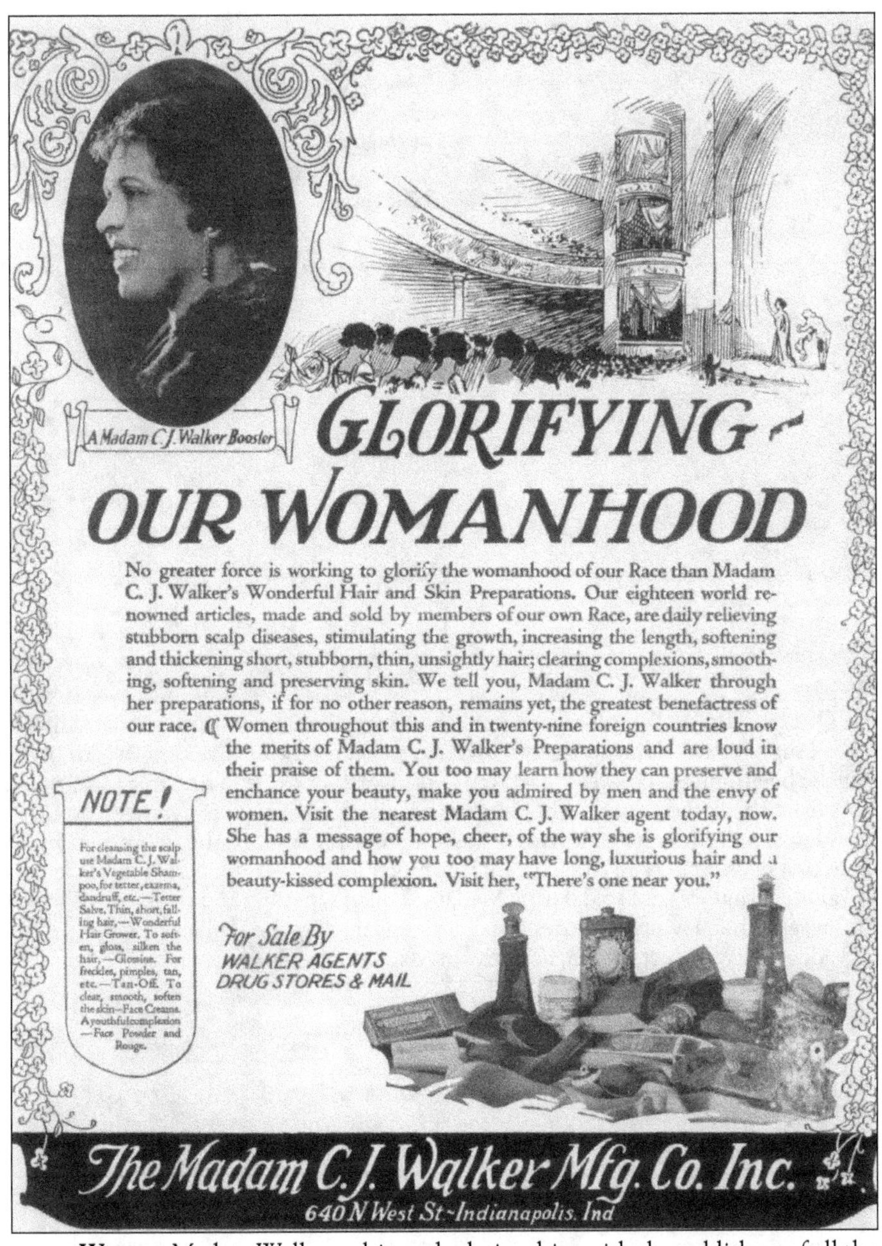

Glorifying Women. Madam Walker cultivated relationships with the publishers of all the major black newspapers including the *Pittsburgh Courier*'s Robert Vann, the *New York Amsterdam News*'s Fred Moore, and the *Chicago Defender*'s Robert Sengstacke Abbott. This early-1920s advertisement boasted of customers in 29 foreign countries and made a direct appeal to racial pride during an era when most professional and educational doors were closed to African Americans. It stated, "No greater force is working to glorify the womanhood of our Race than Madam C.J. Walker's Wonderful Hair and Skin Preparations. Our eighteen world renowned articles, made and sold by members of our own Race, are daily relieving stubborn scalp diseases, stimulating growth and increasing length. Visit the nearest Madam Walker agent today. She has a message of hope, cheer, of the way she is glorifying our womanhood and how you too many have long, luxurious hair and a beauty-kissed complexion." (Courtesy of Madam Walker Family Archives.)

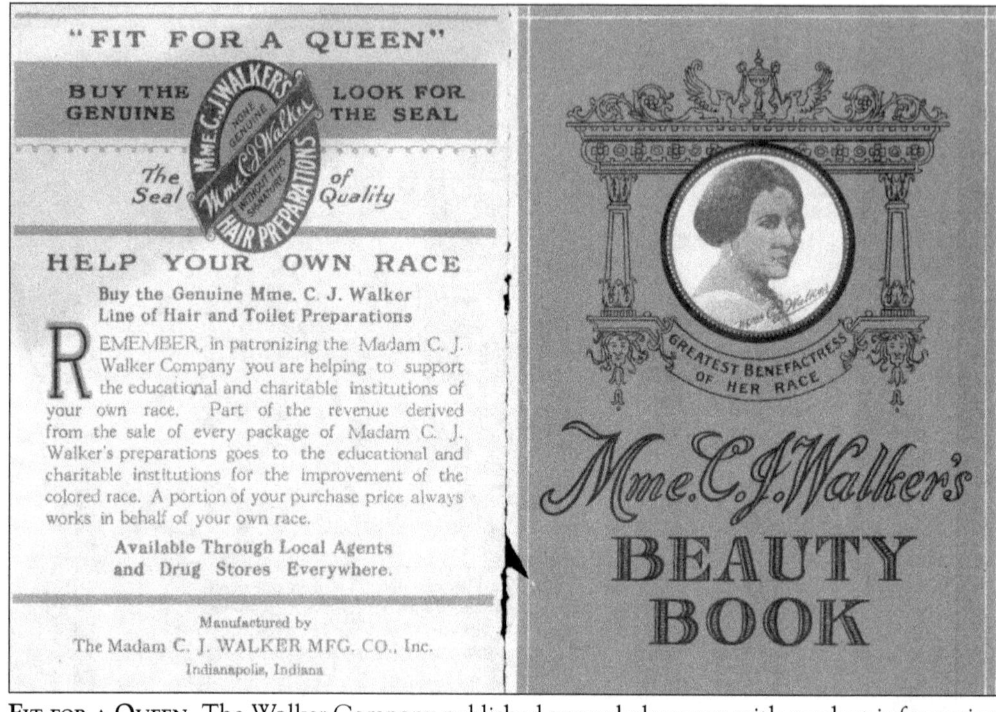

Fit for a Queen. The Walker Company published annual almanacs with product information and practical suggestions. "Hints to agents" advised the purchase of "five cents worth of mints in order that the breath might be sweet" and "ten cents worth of oxide of zinc in a little bag to keep away odors from the body." Another hygiene tip addressed personal appearance. "See that your hair always looks well. In order to interest others you must first make the impression by keeping your hair in first-class condition." Included in this brochure is a description of a skin bleach called "Tan-off," an item that was not sold during Madam Walker's lifetime and something she opposed. Research suggests that a white toiletries distributor engaged by the Walker Company during the late 1920s added this product. (Both, courtesy of Madam Walker Family Archives.)

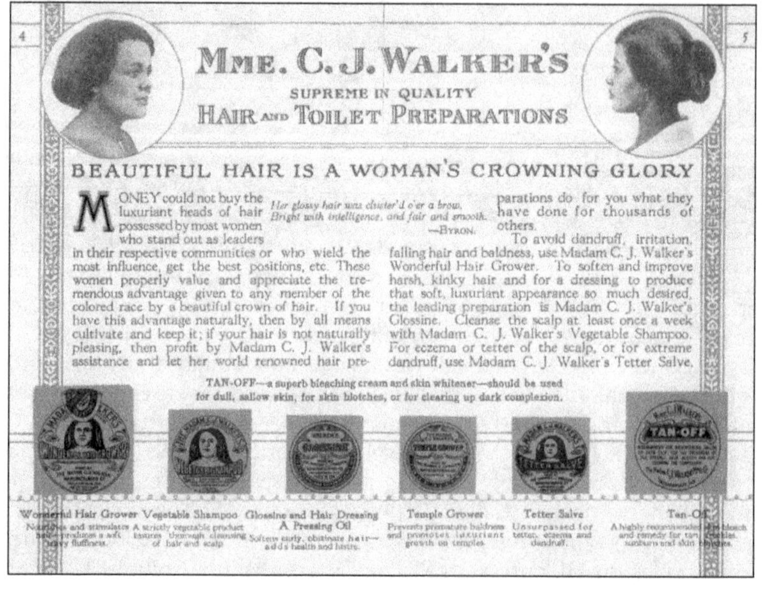

Roaring Twenties. With the popularity of the Marcel waves and bobbed cuts of the 1920s, the Walker Company adapted its advertisements to reflect the changing times. Walker agents, of course, straightened hair with heated steel combs, but Walker literature avoided the words "straight" and "straightening," aware that African Americans sometimes were mocked for removing the natural kinkiness from their tresses. (Courtesy of Madam Walker Family Archives.)

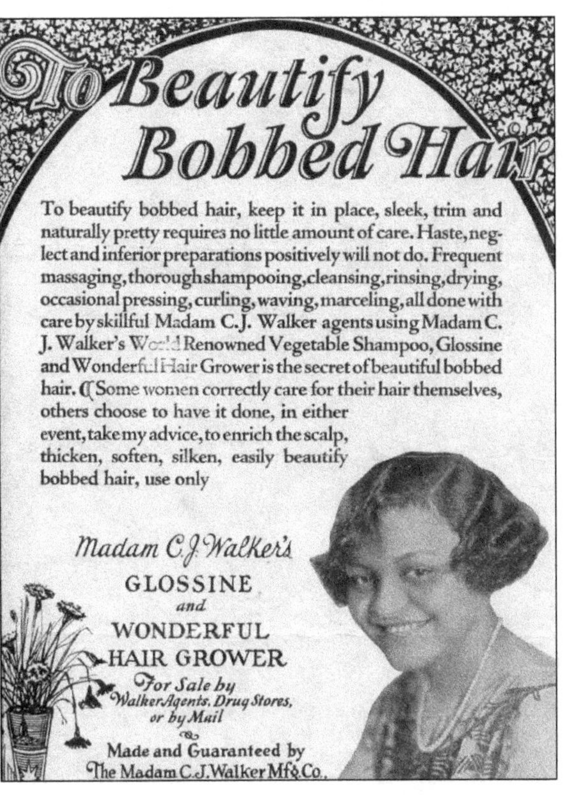

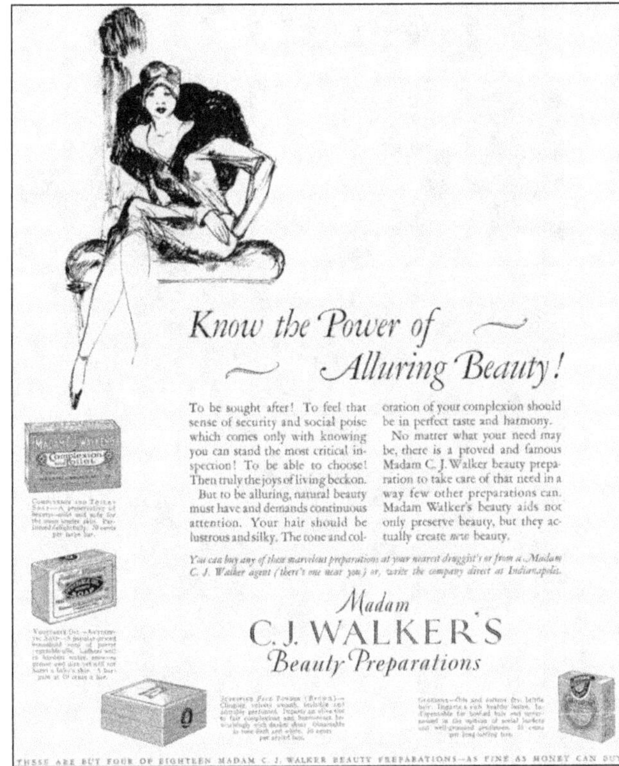

New Era. Almost devoid of African facial features, this flapper in a 1920s Walker advertisement bears no resemblance to original promotional materials that almost-always included Madam Walker's photograph. At this time, the advertising manager was a man whose selection of images reflected what his own idea of female attractiveness rather than what the founder had envisioned. (Courtesy of Madam Walker Family Archives.)

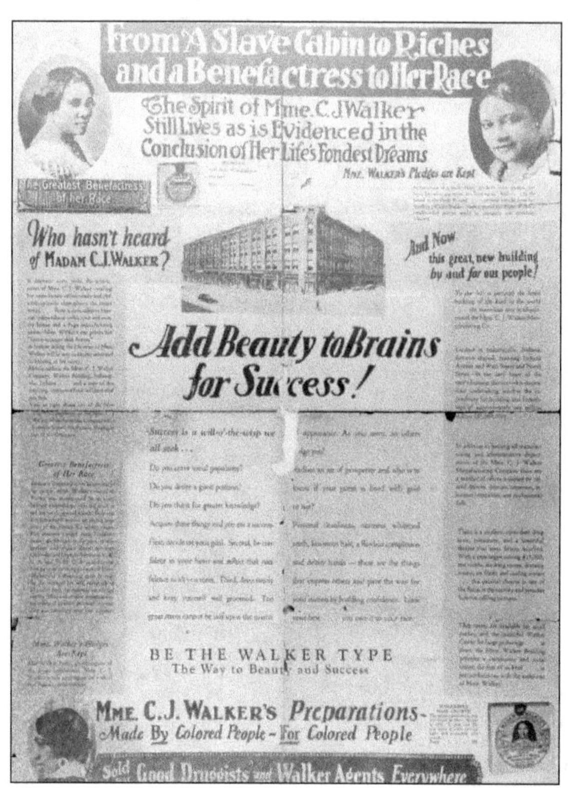

Benefactress. Over time, as other concerns—including white cosmetics firms—developed products that were similar to the original Walker line, the company pushed the legacy of Madam Walker's philanthropy and black ownership as a way to distinguish itself. "Made by Colored People for Colored People," the tag line read. (Courtesy of Madam Walker Family Archives.)

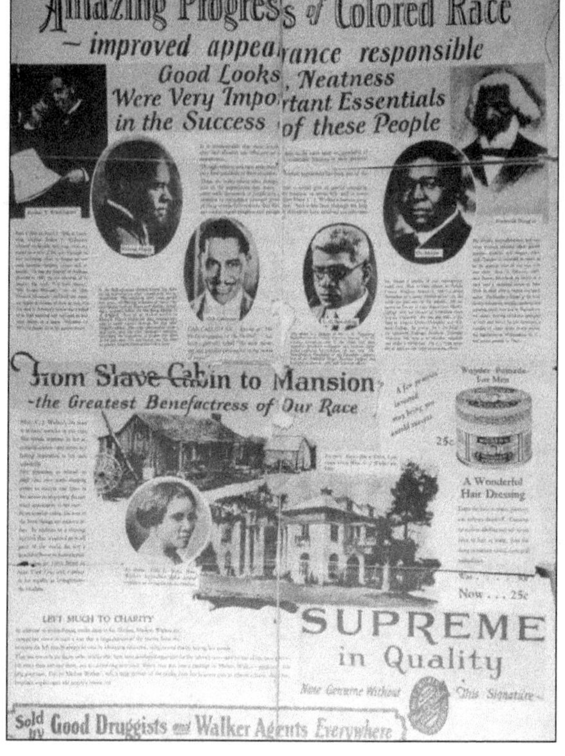

Amazing Progress. As a manufacturer of cosmetics and hair care products, the Walker Company emphasized the role of grooming and appearance in achieving professional success. This panel—part of a four-page newspaper supplement—promotes Walker's Wonder Pomade for Men and features six accomplished African American men from the fields of education, insurance, politics, and music. (Courtesy of Madam Walker Family Archives.)

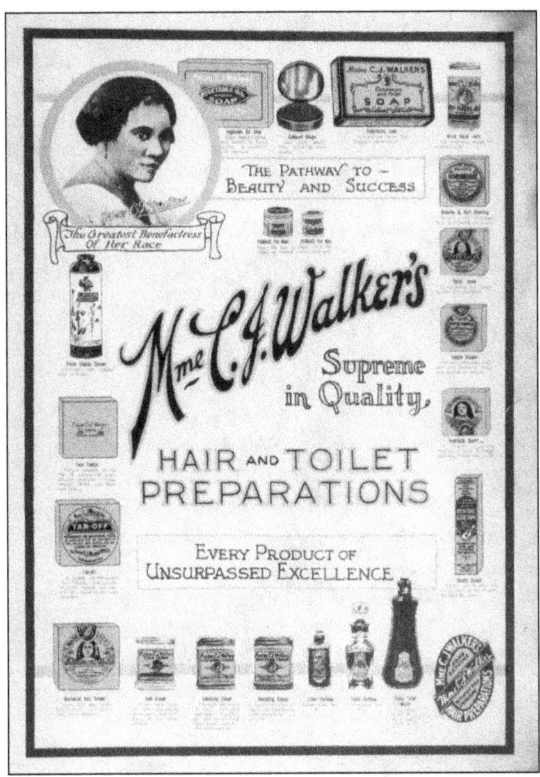

SUPREME IN QUALITY. Widespread advertising—touting the high quality of Walker products—was part of a strategy designed to assist Walker sales agents who often found themselves competing with a range of cheaper items that began flooding the market in the 1930s. The Walker marketing department hoped to persuade customers that the prestige of Walker products was worth the premium price. (Courtesy of Madam Walker Family Archives.)

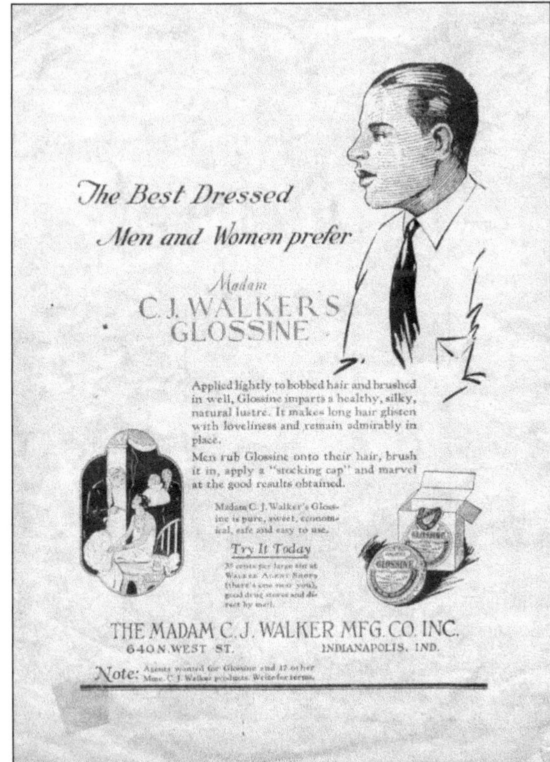

STANDARDS OF BEAUTY. Throughout history, American cosmetics advertising generally has idealized European standards of beauty. Straight hair, thin lips, and small noses were considered more desirable by the society at large than kinky hair and full features. By featuring her own image, Madam Walker challenged those notions. (Courtesy of Madam Walker Family Archives.)

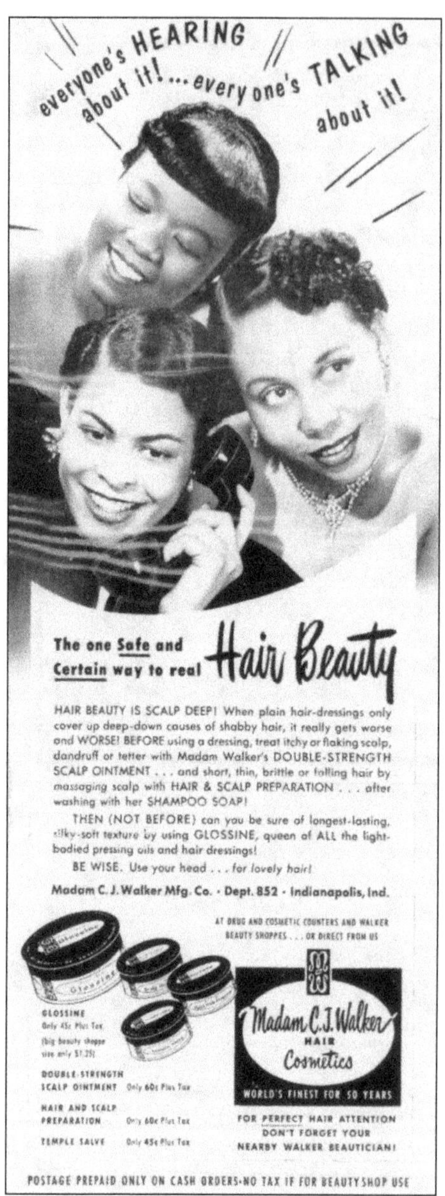

Everyone's Talking. African American women's complexions range from very dark to very light, each reflecting its own unique beauty. While the text of this 1950s advertisement features hair products, the image returns to Madam Walker's desire to celebrate the range of black women's attractiveness. To avoid accusations of "false advertising" from the Food and Drug Administration, Walker's Wonderful Hair Grower had been renamed Walker's Scalp Ointment. (Courtesy of Madam Walker Family Archives.)

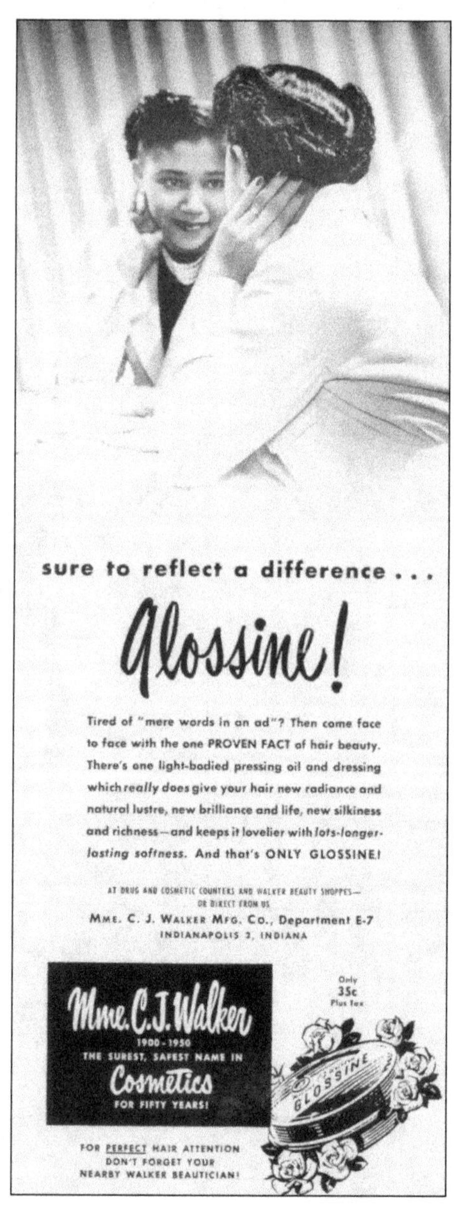

Reflecting a Difference. Hairstyles of the 1950s, with their high sheen and intricate designs, required the skills of trained cosmetologists. For most African American women, whose hair was not naturally straight or glossy, achieving this look required a couple of hours in a beauty salon. With words like "radiance," "luster," "brilliance," and "silkiness," the Walker Company hoped to steer customers to Walker Beauty School graduates. (Courtesy of Madam Walker Family Archives.)

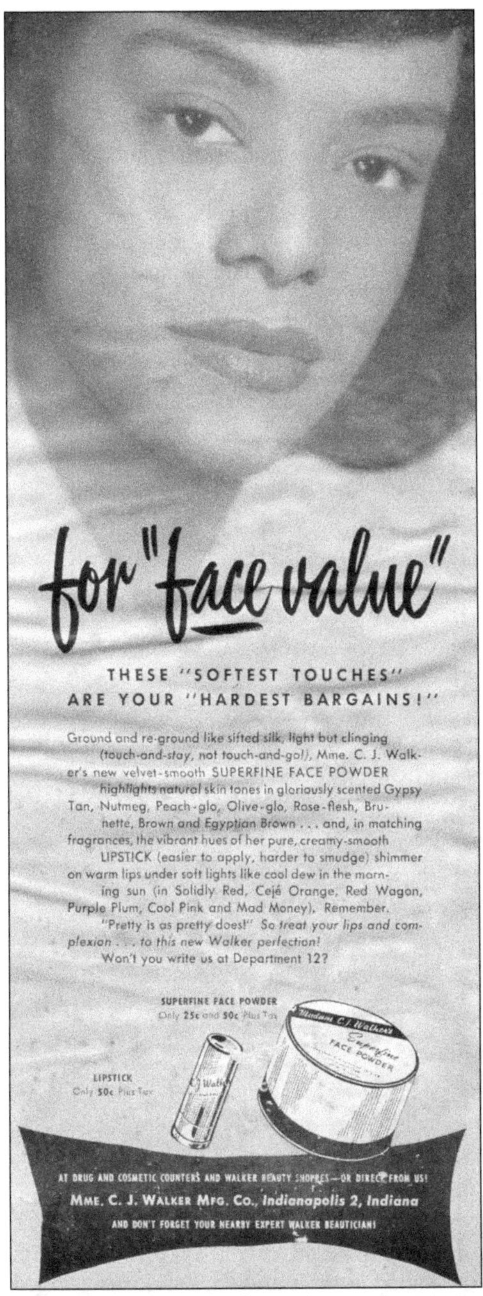

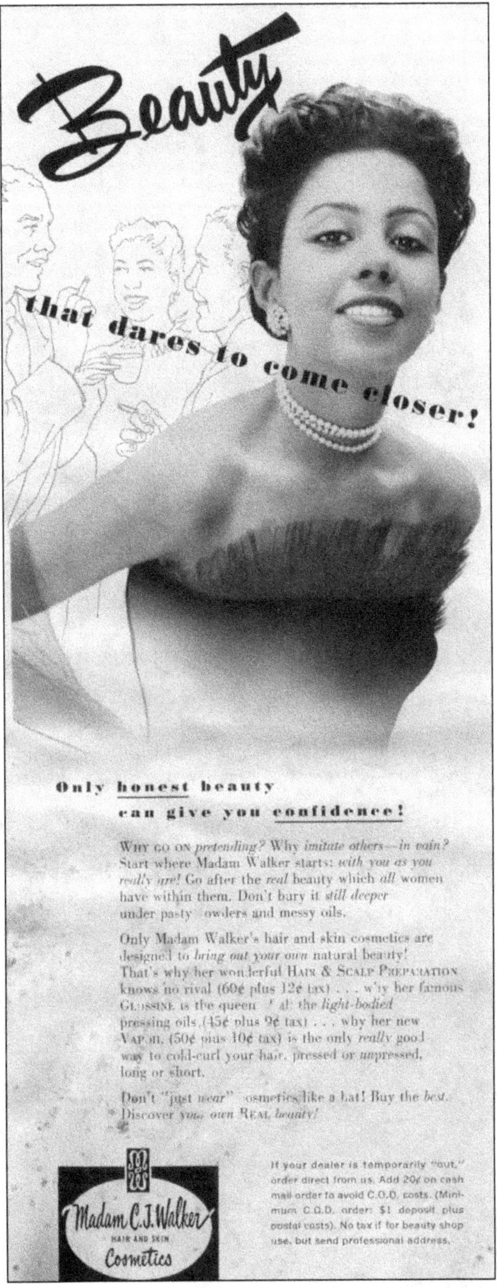

HONEST BEAUTY. By the 1950s, with a new advertising agency on board, the Walker Company again showed black women with full lips and noses. The Afro hairstyles of the late 1960s still were more than a decade away, but the notion of enhancing one's "natural beauty" was embedded in these messages. "Only honest beauty can give one confidence," read the copy, which urged black women not to "imitate others" and to seek their own "real" beauty. "Don't bury it all still deeper under pasty powders and messy oils," it advised. Powder shades with names like Tan, Nutmeg, Olive-glo, Egyptian Brown, Brunette, Rose, and Peach-glo reflected the range of skin tones. Lipstick shades were playfully called Solidly Red, CeJé Orange, Red Wagon, Purple Plum, Cool Pink, and Mad Money. (Both, courtesy of Madam Walker Family Archives.)

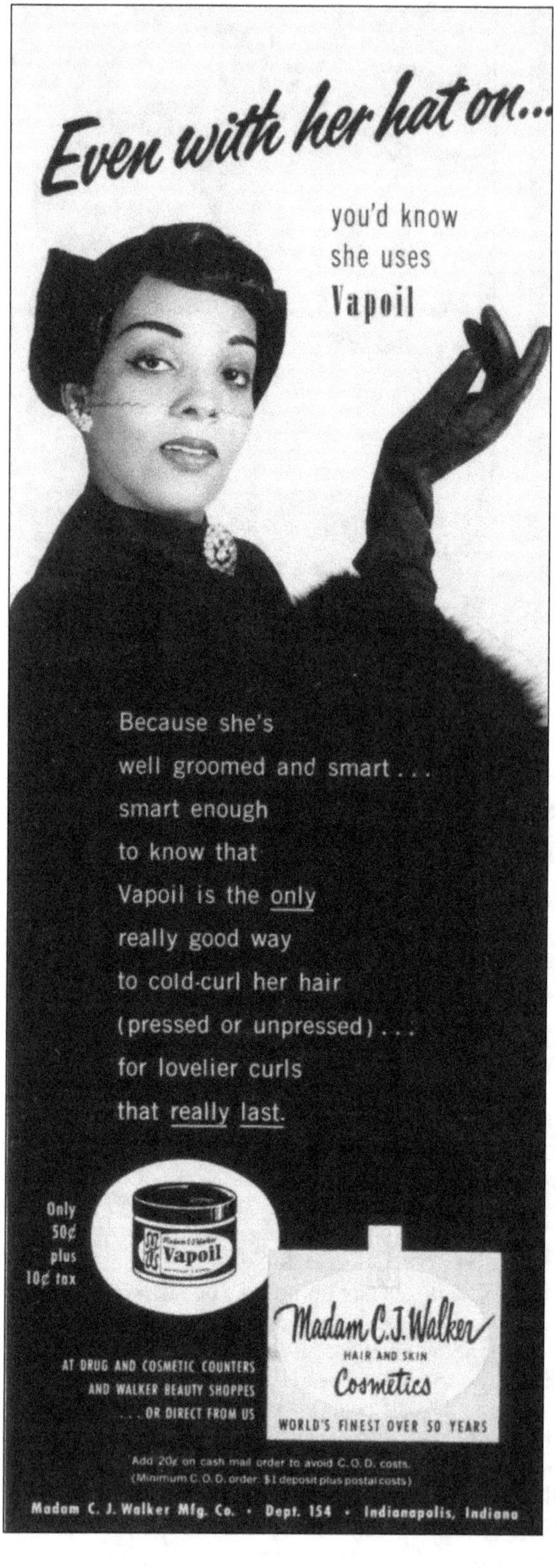

Even with her hat on...

you'd know
she uses
Vapoil

Because she's
well groomed and smart . . .
smart enough
to know that
Vapoil is the only
really good way
to cold-curl her hair
(pressed or unpressed) . . .
for lovelier curls
that really last.

Only
50¢
plus
10¢ tax

Vapoil

Madam C.J. Walker
HAIR AND SKIN
Cosmetics
WORLD'S FINEST OVER 50 YEARS

AT DRUG AND COSMETIC COUNTERS
AND WALKER BEAUTY SHOPPES
. . . OR DIRECT FROM US

Add 20¢ on cash mail order to avoid C.O.D. costs.
(Minimum C.O.D. order: $1 deposit plus postal costs)

Madam C. J. Walker Mfg. Co. · Dept. 154 · Indianapolis, Indiana

GLAMOROUS. The original Wonderful Hair Grower was a heavy ointment containing petrolatum, beeswax, and sulfur. In the absence of other options in the 1910s, women welcomed it, but they were less than pleased with the oily residue it left. The phrase "even with her hat on" alerted customers that Vapoil—the Walker Company's new cold-curl setting gel—was relatively grease-free and would not stain women's Sunday hats. (Courtesy of Madam Walker Family Archives.)

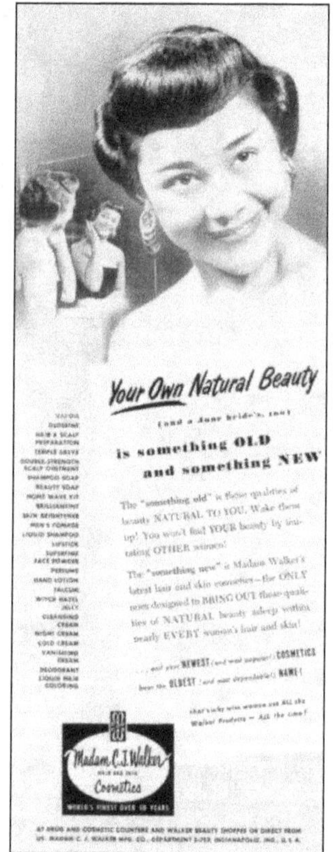

NATURAL BEAUTY. Like many of its competitors, the Walker Company honed in on a message of "natural beauty." As Susannah Walker notes in her book *Style and Status*, "Walker had no exclusive or original claim to the use of natural beauty as an advertising hook; 'natural' was an unusually common adjective in black beauty culture advertising in the post-war period." (Courtesy of Madam Walker Family Archives.)

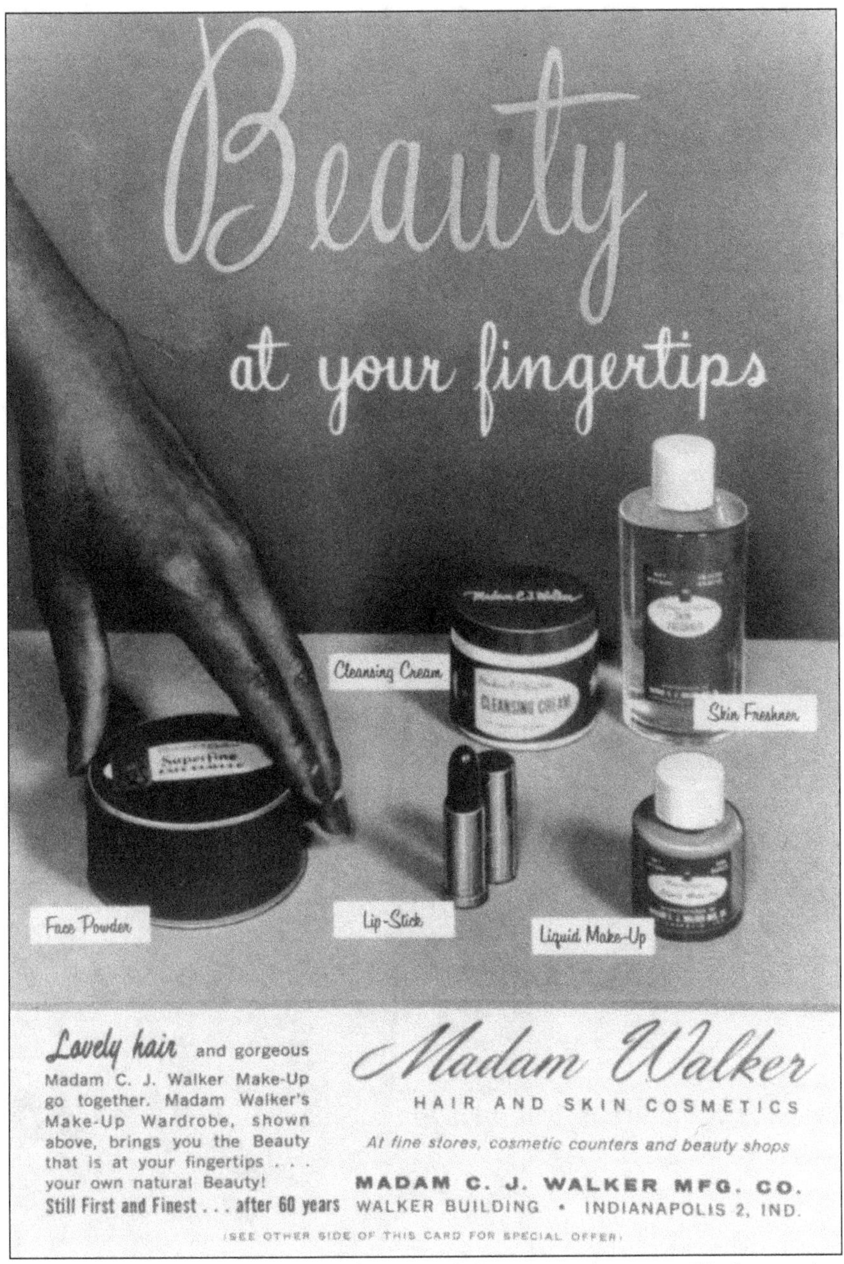

Beauty at Your Fingertips. The Mark Gross Advertising Agency of Indianapolis created attractive advertisements in the late 1950s and 1960s as the Walker Company sought to tout its reliable reputation and extend its brand with a wider line of cosmetics. "Still First and Finest" was its motto. In addition to the cleansing cream, face powder, and lipstick it had marketed for decades, the company added a skin freshening astringent and liquid makeup in shades to match the powder. This full-color postcard was mailed to thousands of Walker agents and customers. It offered a "make-up wardrobe" of five products valued at $4.17 for "only $3.00 plus 30 cents tax." Powder and foundation came in "light," "medium," or "dark." Additional free samples and a booklet with makeup tips were included in a reusable plastic kit with each order. (Courtesy of Madam Walker Family Archives.)

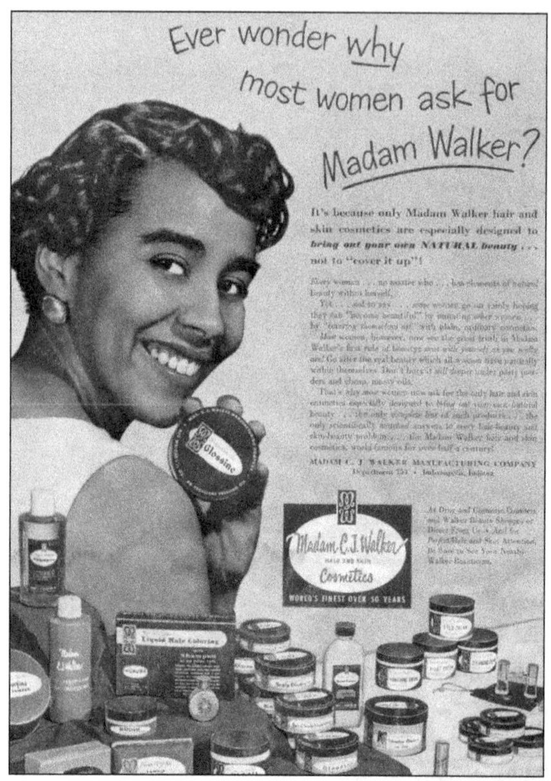

A New Look. Walker packaging was completely redesigned by the Mark Gross Advertising Company in 1958 with a distinctive "MW" logo and oval nameplates. The color scheme for tin containers was brown and goldenrod. Labels on glass jars and soap wrappers were brick red. A deodorant, liquid shampoo, lotion, and hair coloring were added to the product line. (Courtesy of Madam Walker Family Archives.)

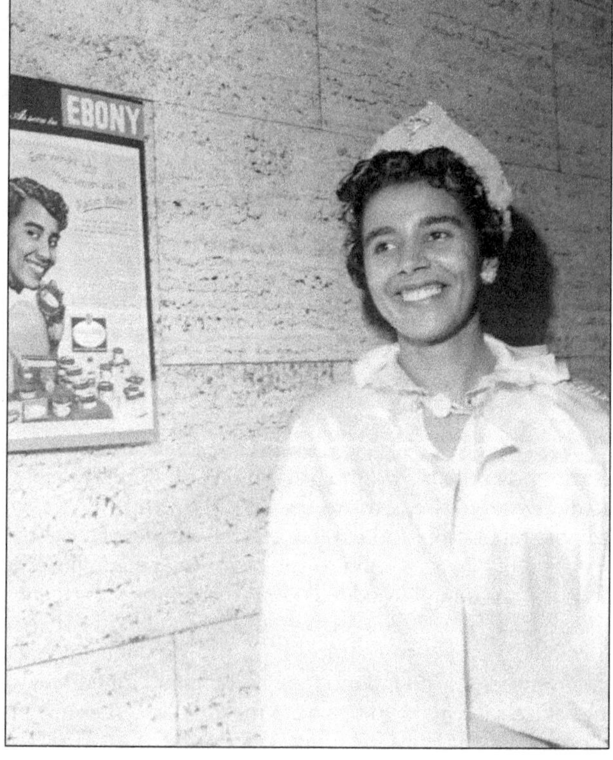

Local Beauty. The model who posed for this full-page color *Ebony* magazine advertisement, visits the lobby of the Walker Building in Indianapolis where her photograph is displayed. Her name is not known, but she lived in Indianapolis and may have been a Walker Beauty School graduate. (Courtesy of Madam Walker Family Archives.)

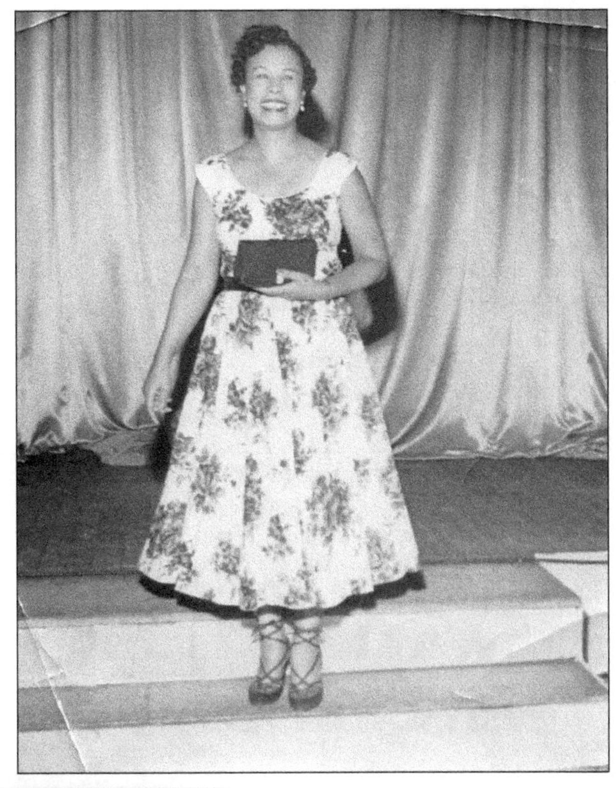

In the Public Eye. Bernice Kent represented the Walker Company at trade shows and served as grand basileus of Alphi Chi Pi Omega, the barbers and beauticians organization founded by Marjorie Joyner. Kent and Joyner led members on trips to France, Haiti, and Mexico where they learned hairstyling techniques from world-renowned hairdressers. (Courtesy of Madam Walker Family Archives.)

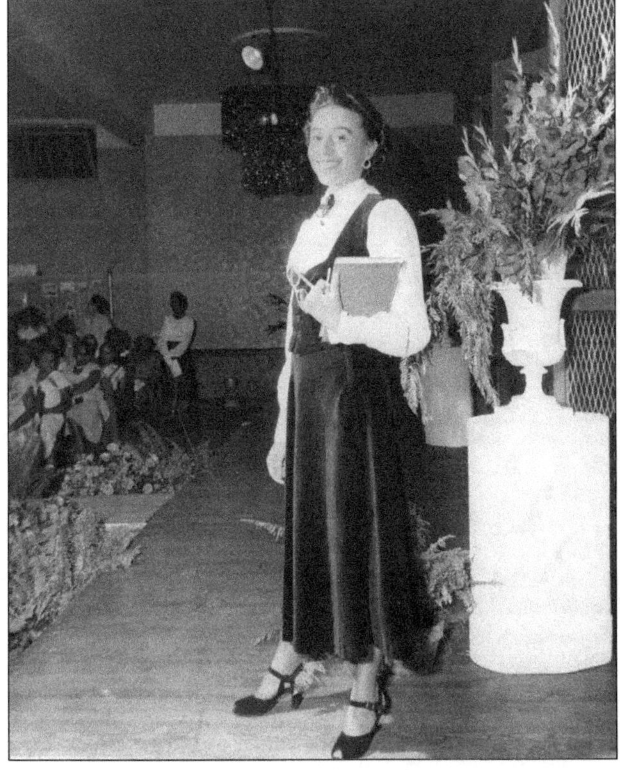

On the Runway. Many of the women who modeled at Walker hair shows were Walker staff members or relatives of employees. Ready to walk across the stage in the Walker Casino in this early-1960s photograph is Betty Taylor Ransom, wife of Clifford Ransom and daughter-in-law of Walker attorney F.B. Ransom. She was a secretary and administrative assistant for the Indianapolis Public Schools. (Courtesy of Madam Walker Family Archives.)

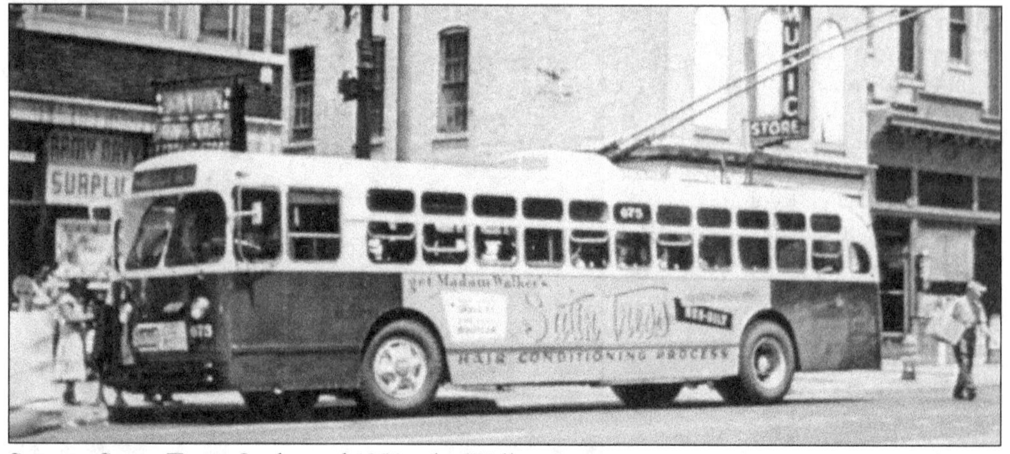

Selling Satin Tress. In the mid-1950s, the Walker Company mounted an aggressive marketing campaign as Walker schools' national supervisor Marjorie Joyner embarked on a 27-city tour from Florida to Texas to teach beauticians to administer the Satin Tress process she had developed. The banners appeared on buses with routes in black neighborhoods in major American cities. (Courtesy of Madam Walker Family Archives.)

WALKER is the
word for BEAUTY!

Madam C.J. Walker
Cosmetics
WORLD'S FINEST FOR 50 YEARS

Lipsticks • Powders • Rouges
Skin Brightener • Shampoo
Soaps • Perfumes • Deodorants
Cold Creams • Cleansing Creams
Hand Creams • Night Creams

Glossine • Double-Strength Scalp Ointment
Hair and Scalp Preparation • Temple Salve

AVAILABLE HERE!

Madam C.J. Walker
MANUFACTURING CO., INDIANAPOLIS 2

FOR PERFECT BEAUTY ATTENTION
SEE YOUR WALKER BEAUTICIAN!

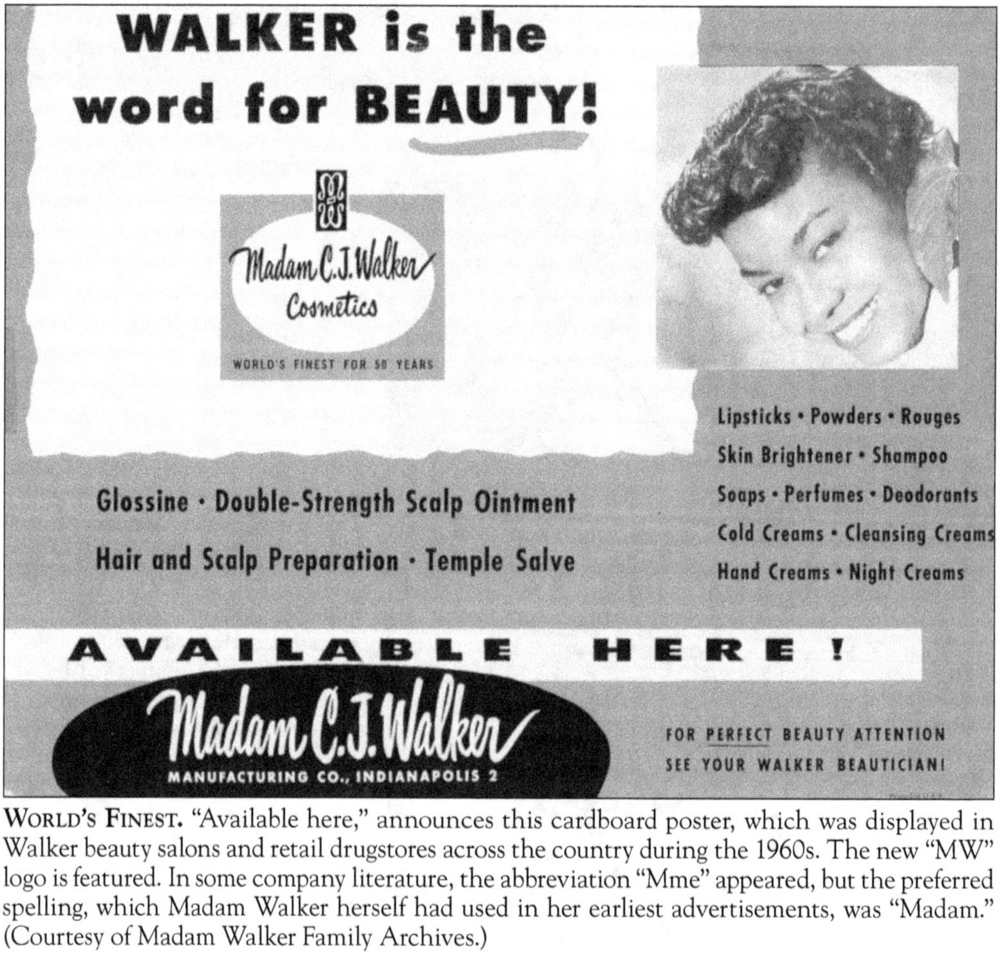

World's Finest. "Available here," announces this cardboard poster, which was displayed in Walker beauty salons and retail drugstores across the country during the 1960s. The new "MW" logo is featured. In some company literature, the abbreviation "Mme" appeared, but the preferred spelling, which Madam Walker herself had used in her earliest advertisements, was "Madam." (Courtesy of Madam Walker Family Archives.)

Seven

Decline and Renewal
Making a Comeback

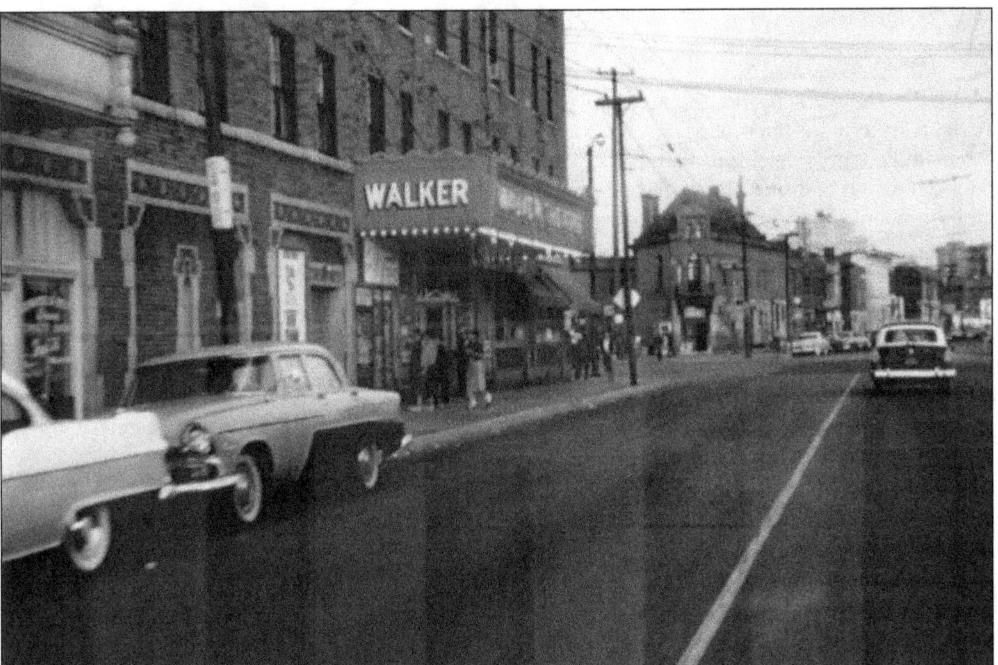

Moving On. In 1956, when O. James Fox accepted a volunteer photography assignment from the American Friends Service Committee to document the black neighborhood on the northwest edge of downtown Indianapolis, much of the single-family housing near the Walker Building was deteriorating. As formerly segregated areas of the city began integrating, many black families and businesses relocated. (Courtesy of O. James Fox Collection, Indiana Historical Society.)

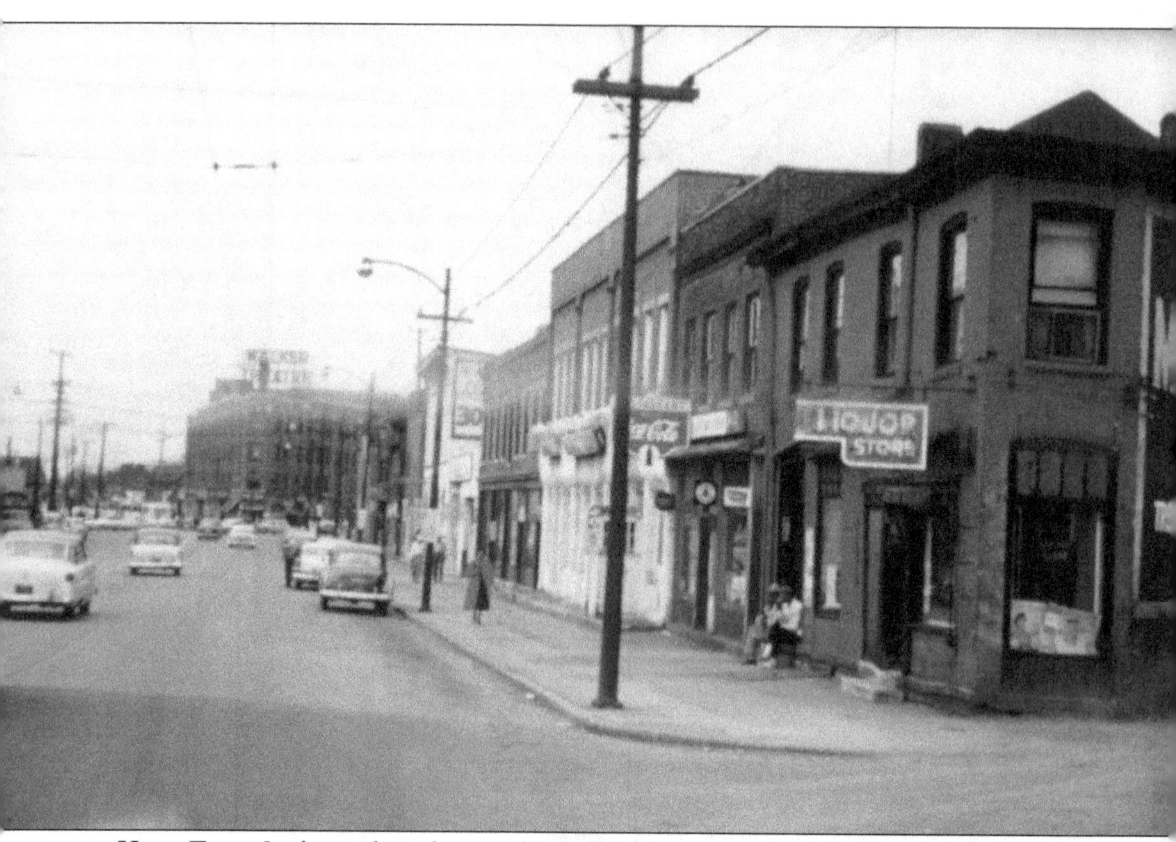

HARD TIMES. In the residential areas adjacent to the Walker Building (visible at the rear center), African Americans had raised families for more than a century in Queen Anne–style houses and other single-family dwellings. When Lockefield Gardens opened nearby in 1938, as the city's first public housing complex, its prized apartments became home to many hardworking families of modest means. Among the houses of worship that enriched the lives of the area's black residents was Bethel AME Church. Located just two blocks from the Walker Building, it became Madam Walker's church when she arrived in 1910. But the neighborhood also had a less exemplary side. Throughout much of its history, legitimate businesses like the *Indianapolis Recorder* and Willis Mortuary coexisted with prostitution, gambling, and bootleg liquor operations in their midst. During Prohibition and after, city leaders looked the other way as illicit activities flourished. By the late 1950s, when O. James Fox photographed the 500 block of Indiana Avenue, a liquor store dominated the corner. (Courtesy of O. James Fox Collection, Indiana Historical Society.)

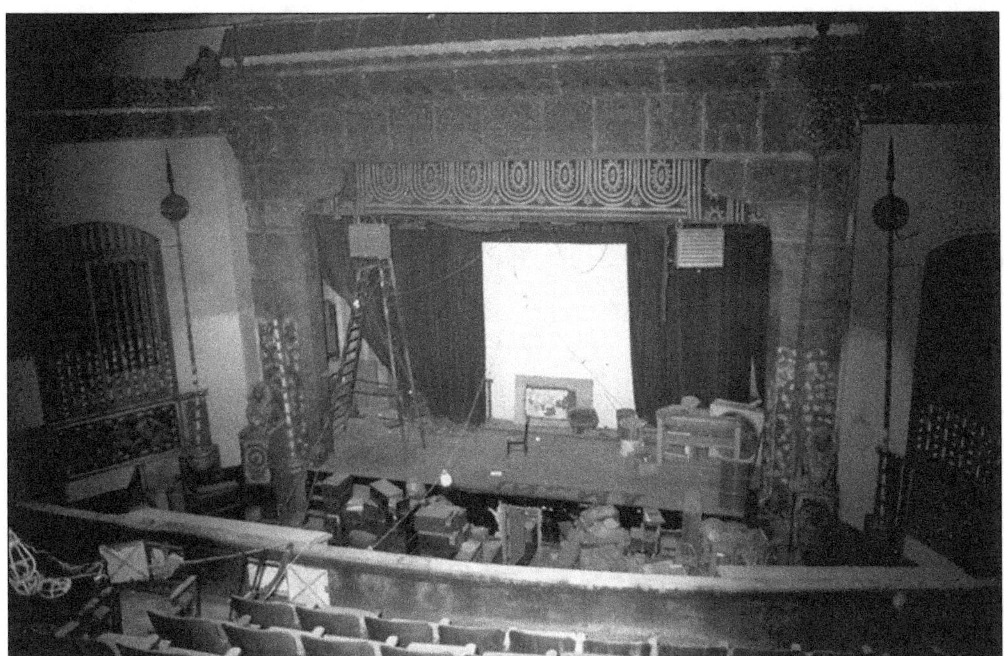

The Music Stops. By the late 1970s, the Walker Building, too, was in disrepair. Its once-beautiful theater was abandoned as integration no longer barred black audiences from downtown movie theaters. The original Barton Organ—one of only 250 built by the Amherst, Wisconsin, manufacturer between 1918 and 1931—long had been removed. (Courtesy of William Rasdell.)

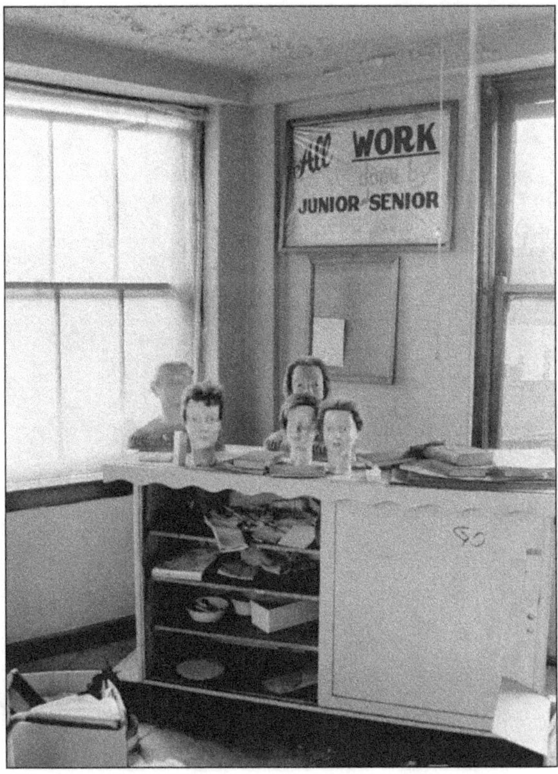

Losing Ground. One by one Walker schools in Chicago, Kansas City, Dallas, Washington, DC, and Indianapolis closed. The Walker Company no longer dominated black hair care as Johnson Products, Summit Laboratories, and others gained market share, and as Revlon, Clairol, and L'Oreal developed lines for black customers. The company was sold in 1985. Today, dozens of firms vie in the multibillion-dollar market Madam Walker helped create. (Courtesy of William Rasdell.)

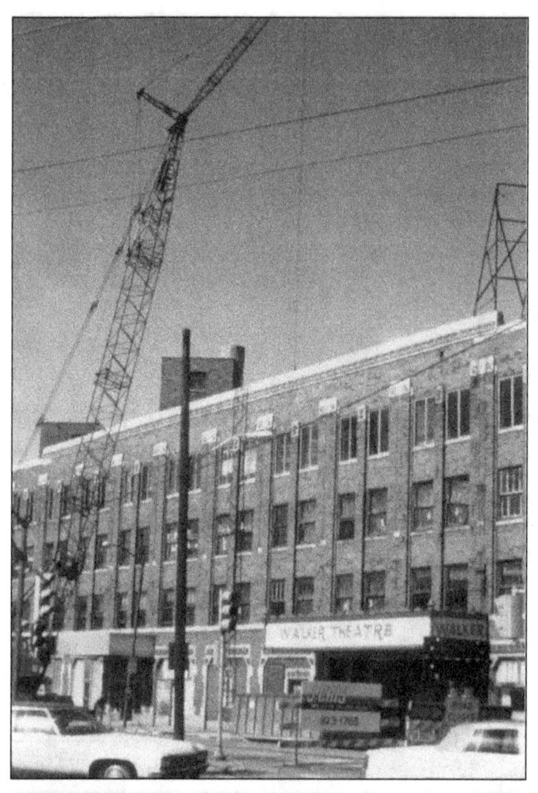

To the Rescue. In 1979, a group of concerned Indianapolis citizens formed a nonprofit partnership to explore strategies to save the Walker Building from demolition. Robert Ransom Jr., grandson of Walker Company general manager F.B. Ransom, proposed revitalizing the building in a meeting with Lilly Endowment senior program officer Charles Blair. To further explore the concept, Ransom, Blair, and Reuben Hill, visited Brooklyn's Billie Holiday Theater and Bed-Stuy Restoration Corporation. They also enlisted the support and advocacy of S. Henry Bundles and Willard Ransom, Walker Company board members with connections to the original founding families, who both held leadership roles in Indianapolis civic and business organizations. As the Madam Walker Urban Life Center, the group purchased the Walker Building with funds from the Lilly Endowment, the US Commerce Department's Economic Development Administration, and other sources. (Both, courtesy of Jimmy Beard.)

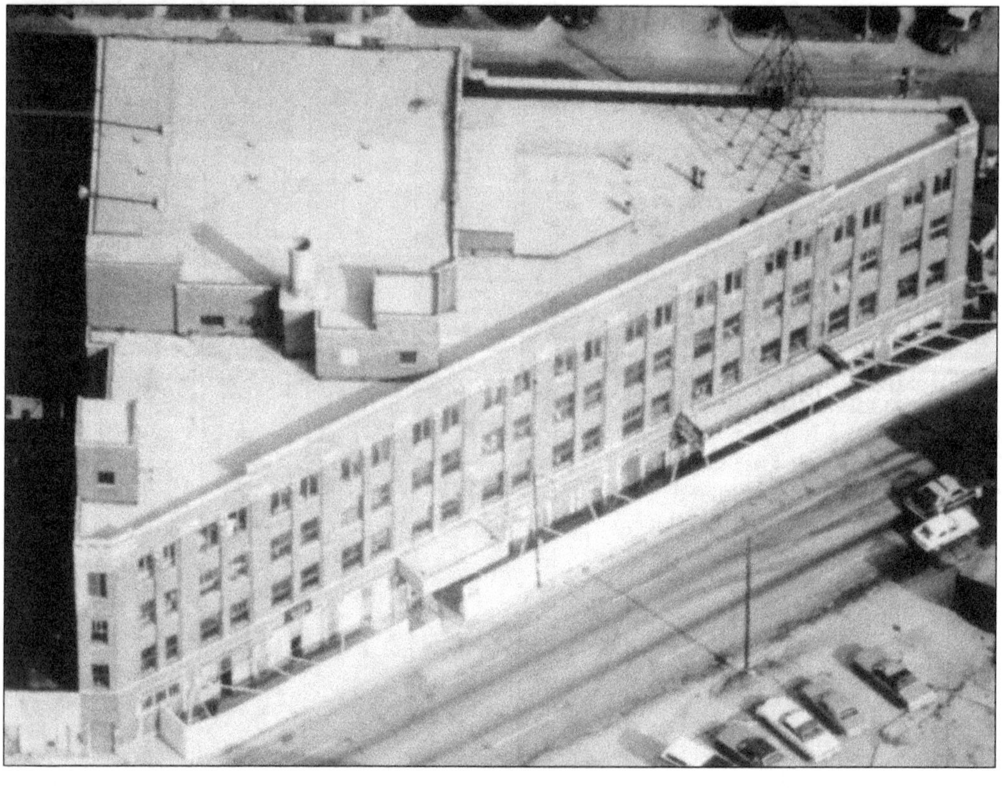

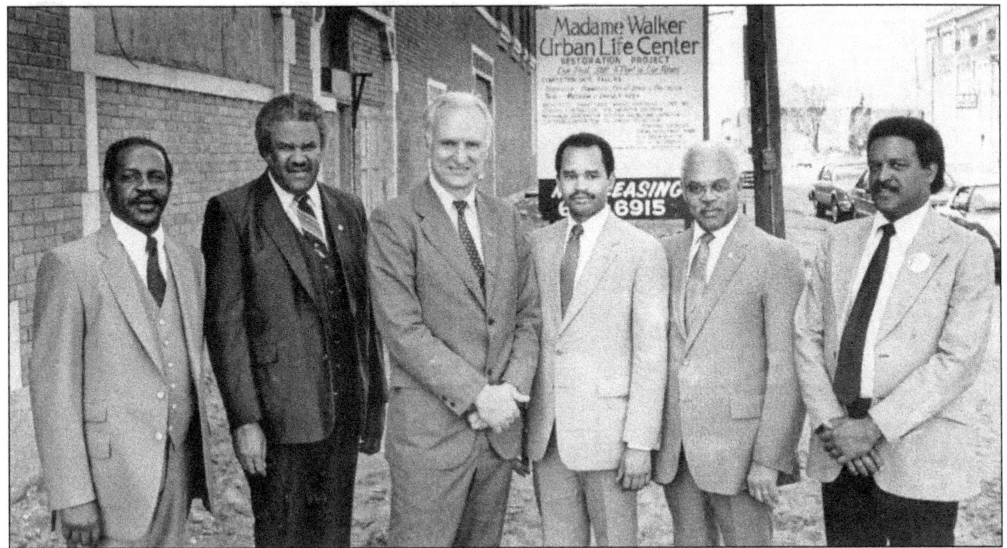

PRESERVATION AND PROGRESS. The restoration project was designed to spur economic redevelopment on Indiana Avenue. Mayor William H. Hudnut, third from left, joins community leaders and elected officials John F. Martin, Stanley Strader, Cary Davis, Ray Crowe, and Julius Shaw. Dr. Joseph Taylor, not pictured, served as the first Madam Walker Urban Life Center (MWULC) board chairman after retiring as dean of IUPUI's School of Liberal Arts. (Indianapolis Recorder Collection, Indiana Historical Society.)

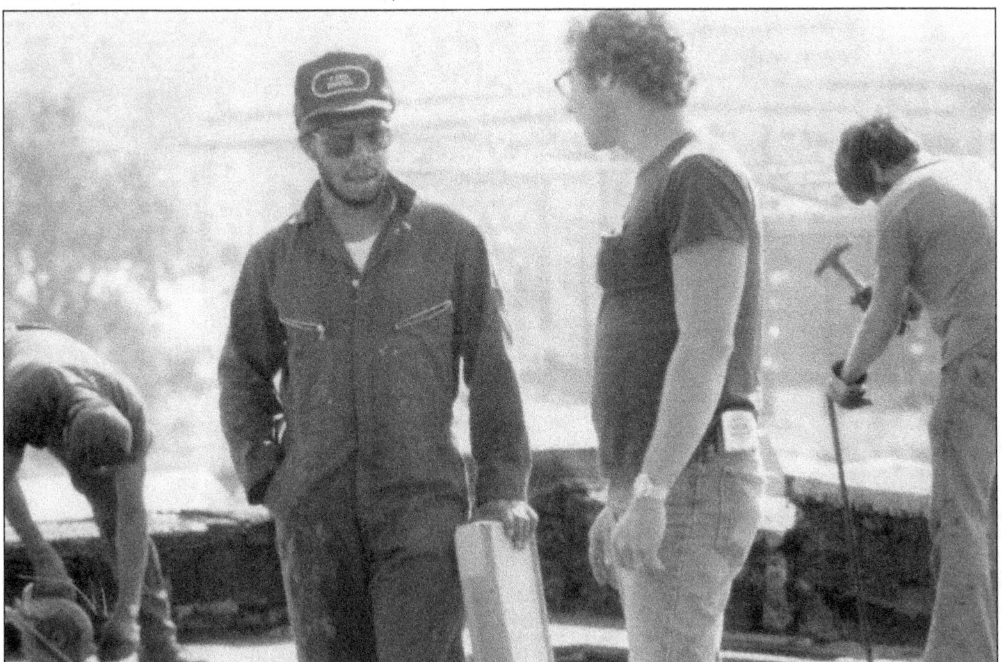

RAISING THE ROOF. Jimmy Beard, left, president of J. Beard Management, was the contractor for the massive overhaul of the roof. He remembers removing a patchwork of seven or eight layers of tar and paper before reaching rotted wood, evidence of decades of deferred maintenance. Plumbing contractor Jeff Kirkoff, right, created custom drains. With a lucky string of sunny days, the work was finished in one month. (Courtesy of Jimmy Beard.)

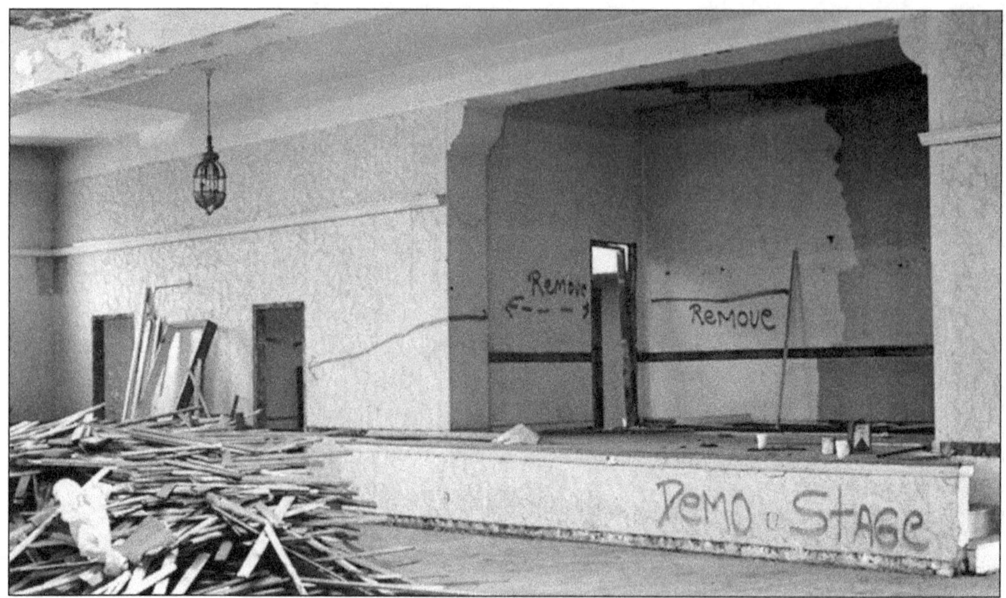

Demolition. After emergency structural and roof repairs, an extensive $2.6 million interior renovation began. Leo Stenz Corporation served as general contractor. Robert LaRue of Wright Porteous & Lowe was lead architect. The Grand Casino Ballroom stage, where so many early-20th-century orchestras and bands had played and where hundreds of Walker Beauty School graduates had received their diplomas, was demolished to enlarge the room. (Courtesy of William Rasdell.)

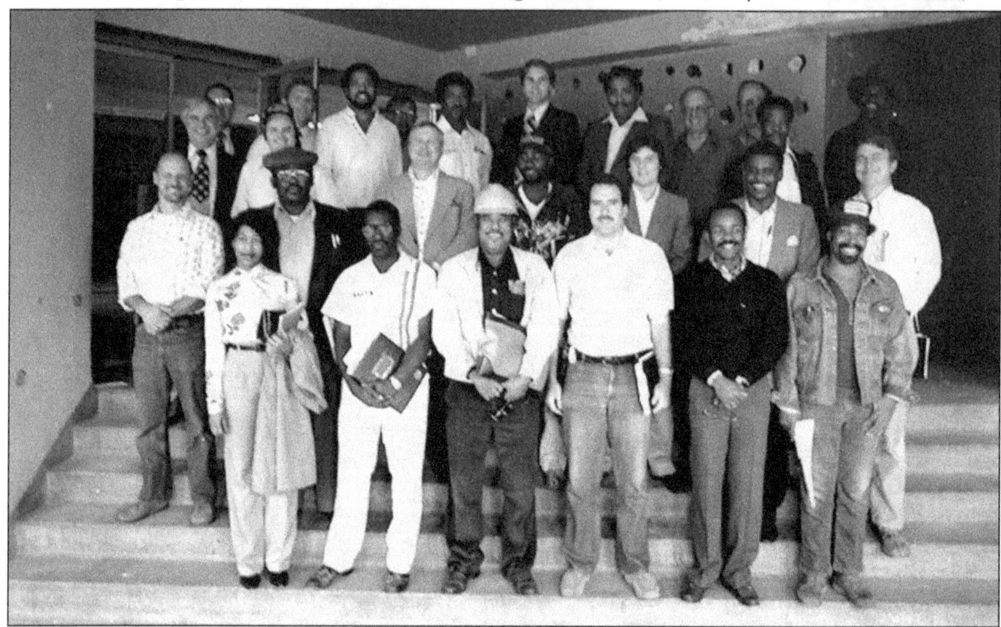

Bringing the Walker Back. By December 1983, restoration of the four-story, yellow tapestry-patterned brick and terra-cotta trimmed facade was complete, as was much of the interior office space. Twenty-five percent of the construction and design work went to minority contractors. Sadly, though, as the Walker Building restoration progressed, many of the other commercial buildings that had given the neighborhood its visual identity were being razed. (Courtesy of William Rasdell.)

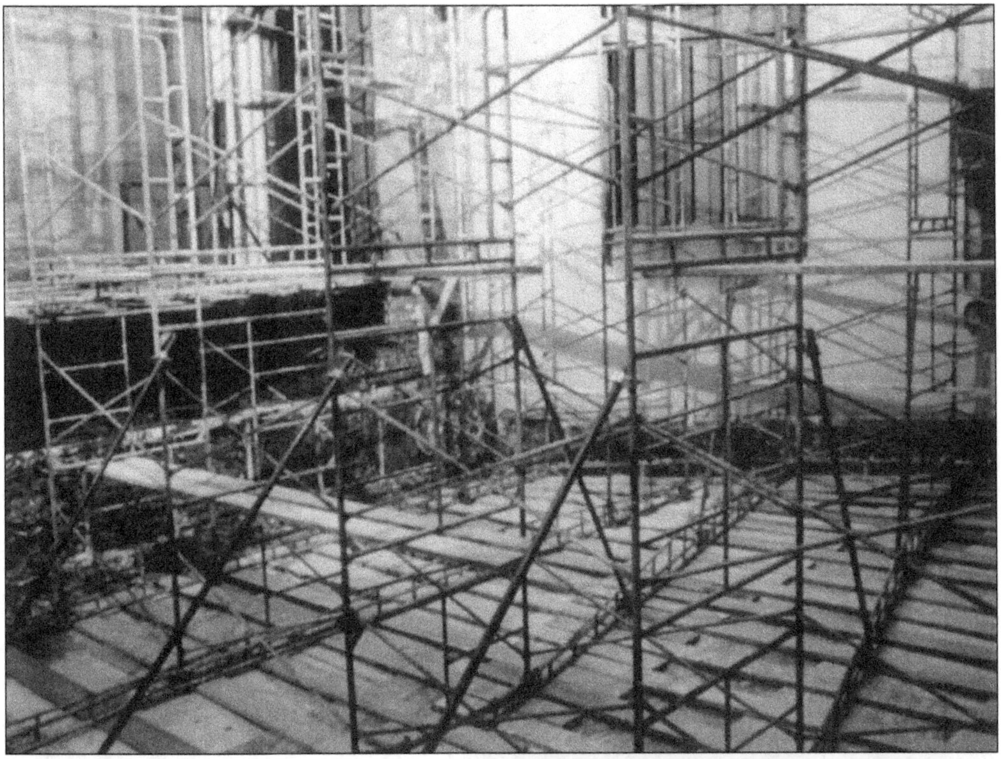

CRAFTED WITH CARE. Having completed the roof in 1982, Jimmy Beard returned five years later as general contractor for the Walker Theatre restoration. Beneath the floor, he discovered an elaborate system of vents, pipes, and cones that had cooled the theater in an early version of air-conditioning. Throughout the project he marveled at the craftsmanship, care, and quality materials of the original construction 55 years earlier. (Courtesy of Jimmy Beard.)

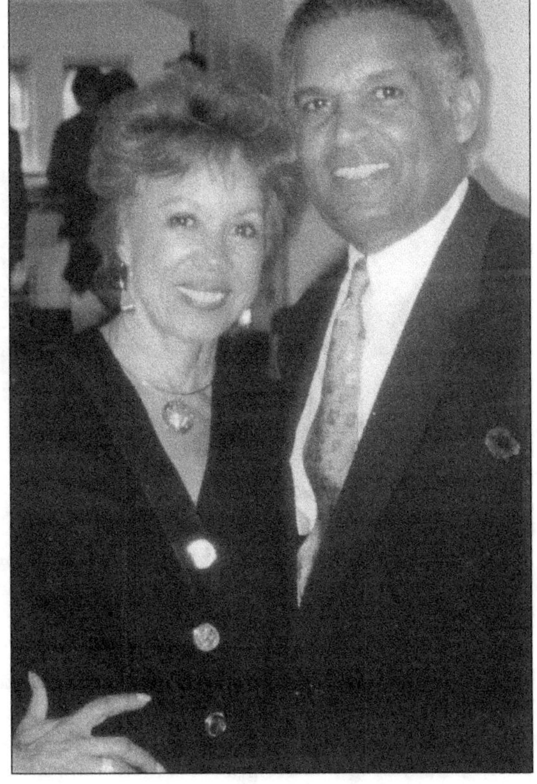

DRAMATIC DESIGN. "We felt a part of history," says Blackburn Architects CEO Alpha Blackburn of the role she and her husband, Walter S. Blackburn, a Fellow of the American Institute of Architects (FAIA), played in the building's renaissance. For a more luxurious appearance—as she believes Madam would have wished "for her people"—Blackburn insisted the theater seats' mohair velvet upholstery be applied with the nap up. The Walker has honored the couple's architecture and design careers. (Courtesy of Alpha Blackburn.)

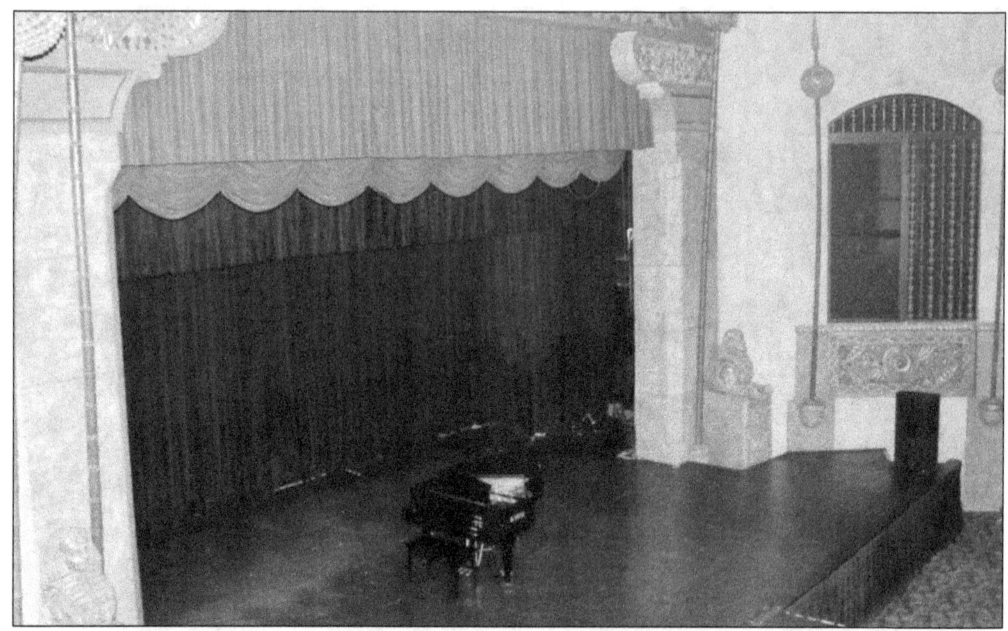

Vibrant Vision. Led by contractor Jimmy Beard, Local Color, a team of 15 custom painters, brought the theater's African Art Deco interior back to life. Years of accumulated soot from the antiquated coal heating system had covered intricate geometric patterns, Yoruba symbols, and vibrant colors. "When we first sprayed the walls with water, it was like peeling away a thick sheet of black paper," Beard remembers. (Courtesy of Carl Black.)

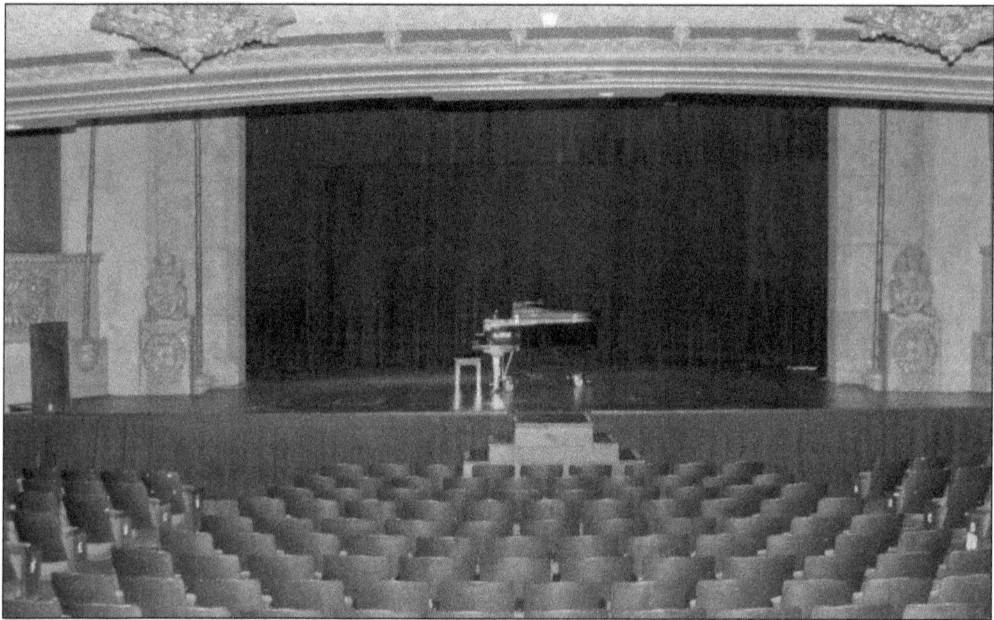

Curtains Up. The Walker Theatre reopened in October 1988 with a gala featuring the Jimmy Coe Orchestra, actors Roscoe Lee Brown and Rosalind Cash, entertainers Isaac Hayes and Gregory Hines, and *Roots* author Alex Haley. Initially called the Madam Walker Urban Life Center, it was renamed the Madam Walker Theatre Center to reflect the organization's artistic mission. In 1991, the building was designated a National Historic Landmark. (Courtesy of Carl Black.)

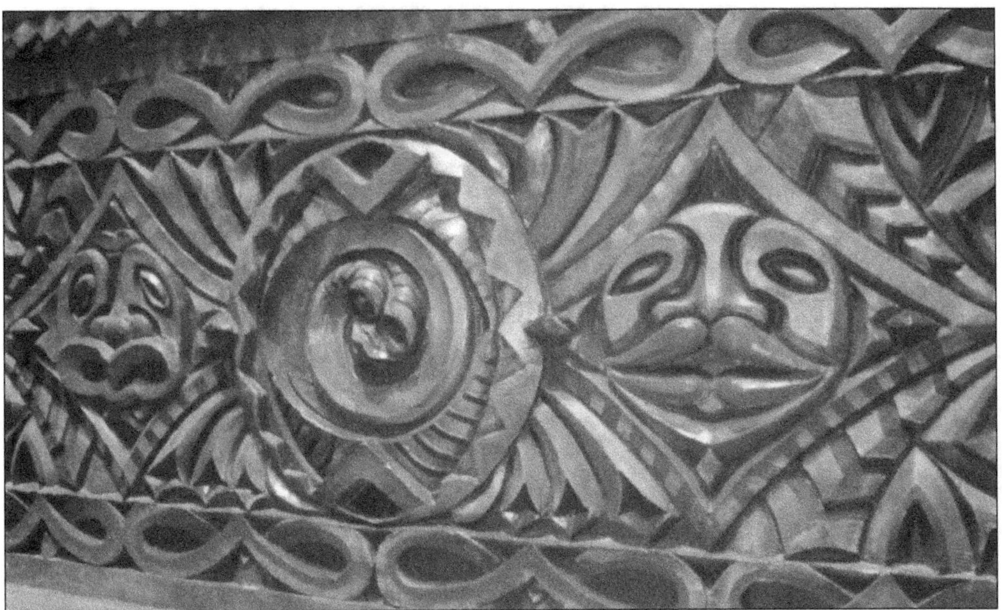

Master Sculptor. For the Walker Building's exterior terra-cotta designs, architects Rubush and Hunter engaged Alexander Sangernebo, a Russian Estonia immigrant and master sculptor for the American Terra Cotta and Ceramic (ATC&C) Company. During the post–World War I construction boom, ATC&C created facades for nearly 1,500 buildings. The plaster artist who crafted these African-featured tragedy-comedy masks is not known. (Courtesy of Madam Walker Family Archives.)

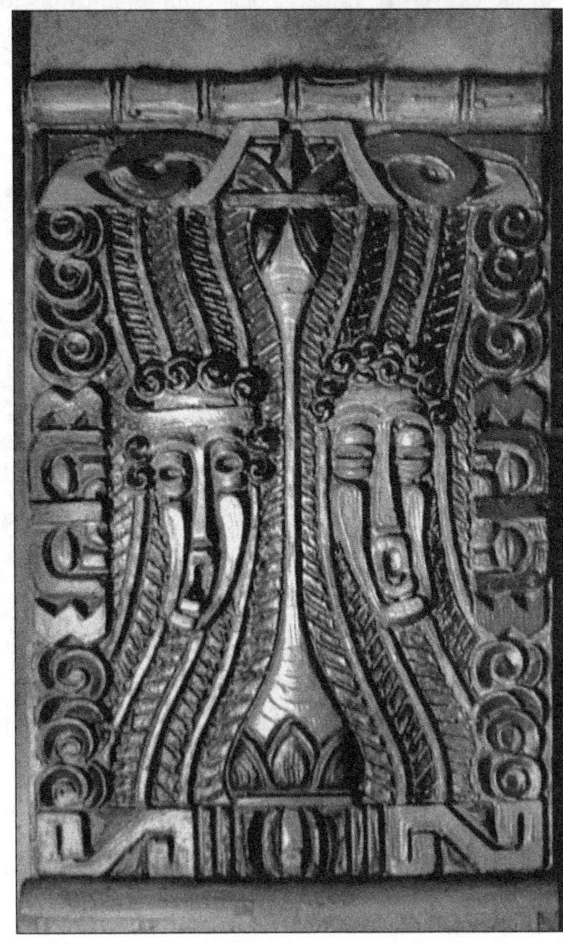

African Art Deco. Throughout the Walker Theatre are dozens of woodcarvings and plaster moldings of African faces, animals, sphinxes, spears, and tribal symbols. Artists who evaluated the original designs discovered 110 shades of color on the masks, medallions, doorways, and frames of the lobby, balcony, theater, and stage. This African couple, distinguished by their coiled hairstyles and elongated faces, are painted red, yellow, and green. (Courtesy of William Rasdell.)

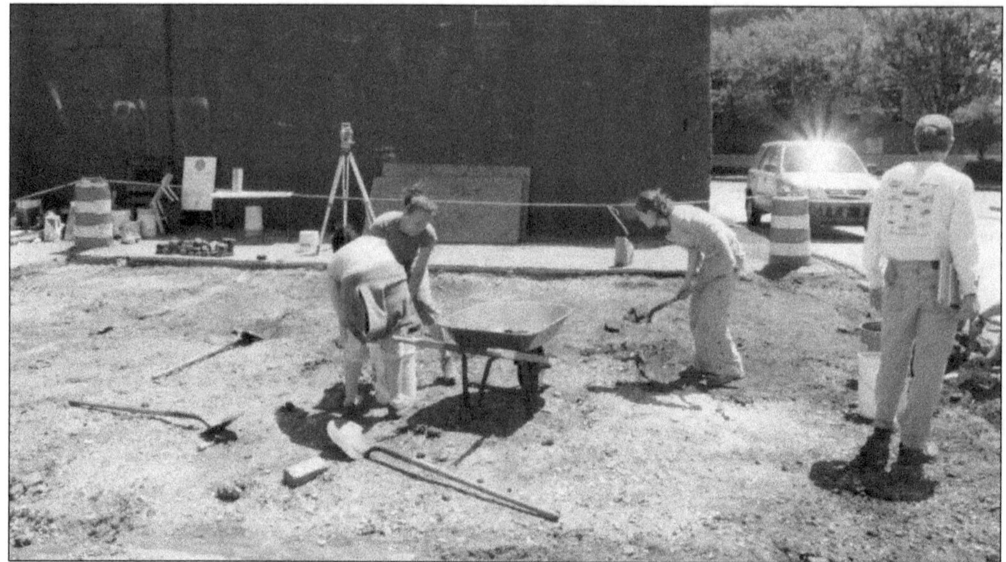

Archaeological Dig. With the Walker Building located just north of the Indiana University-Purdue University, Indianapolis, campus, anthropology department chair Paul Mullins, right with his back to the camera, has made the surrounding neighborhood a working laboratory. In the parking lot behind the building, students search for everyday material culture from a black community that thrived from the mid-19th century until the mid-20th century. (Courtesy of Paul Mullins and Lewis Jones.)

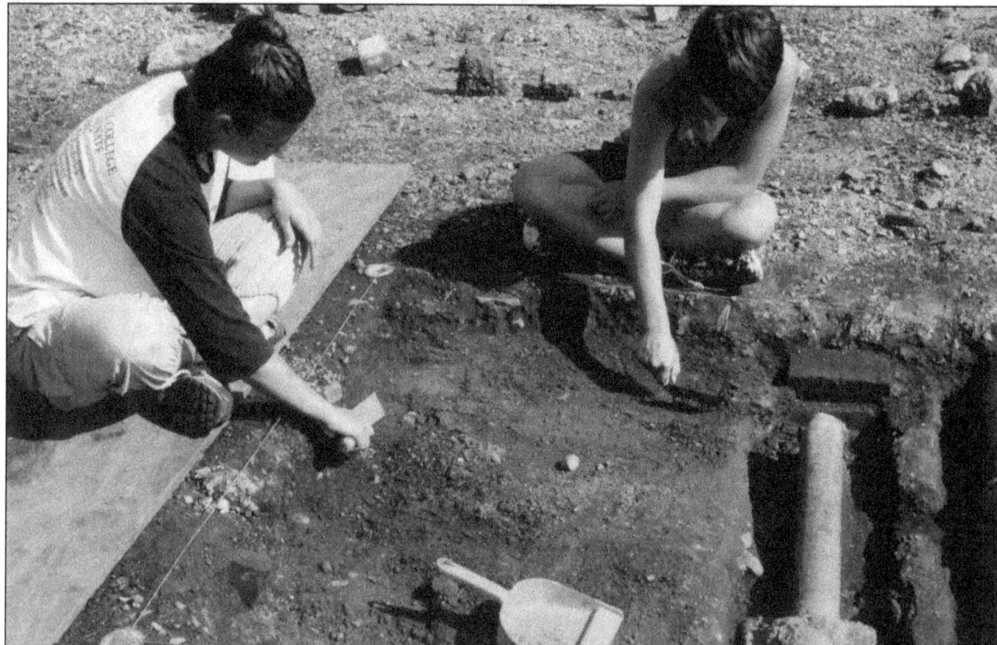

Sifting and Searching. Since arriving at IUPUI in 1999, Professor Mullins has used archaeology and anthropology to study the 19th-century transition of a mixed-race neighborhood into the racially segregated black neighborhood that existed when Madam Walker arrived in 1910. Mullins and his students also have examined the impact of IUPUI's development and expansion on that neighborhood during the last quarter of the 20th century. (Courtesy of Paul Mullins and Lewis Jones.)

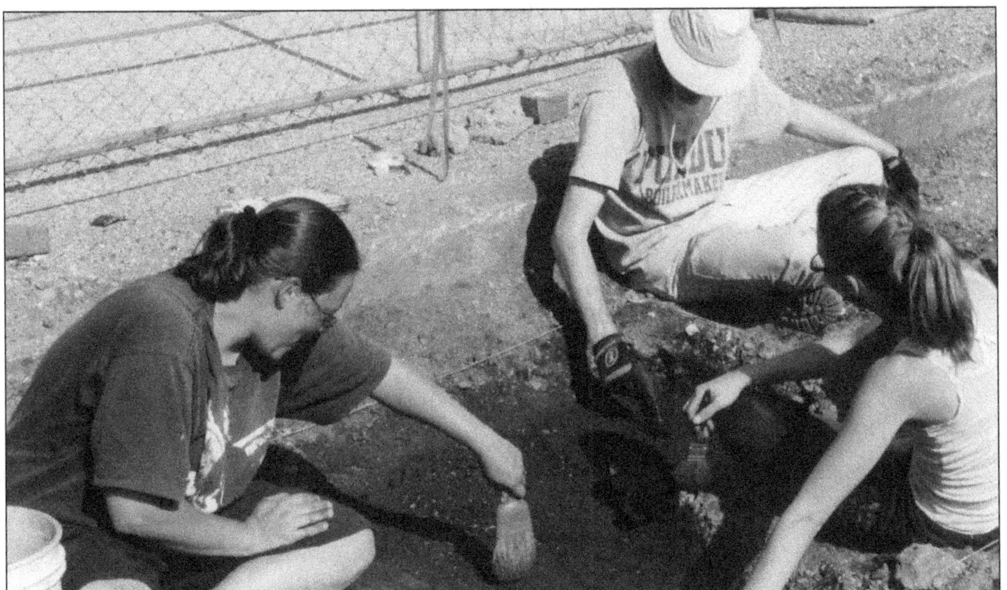

Discovering the Past. During the 2009 summer semester, IUPUI anthropology professor Paul Mullins and Indiana University, Bloomington, graduate student Lewis Jones led students and neighborhood volunteers in an excavation of the property where Madam Walker's home once stood at 640 North West Street not far from the existing Walker Theatre Center. Students received training in field excavation methodology, public interpretation, laboratory analysis, and archaeological theory. (Courtesy of Paul Mullins and Lewis Jones.)

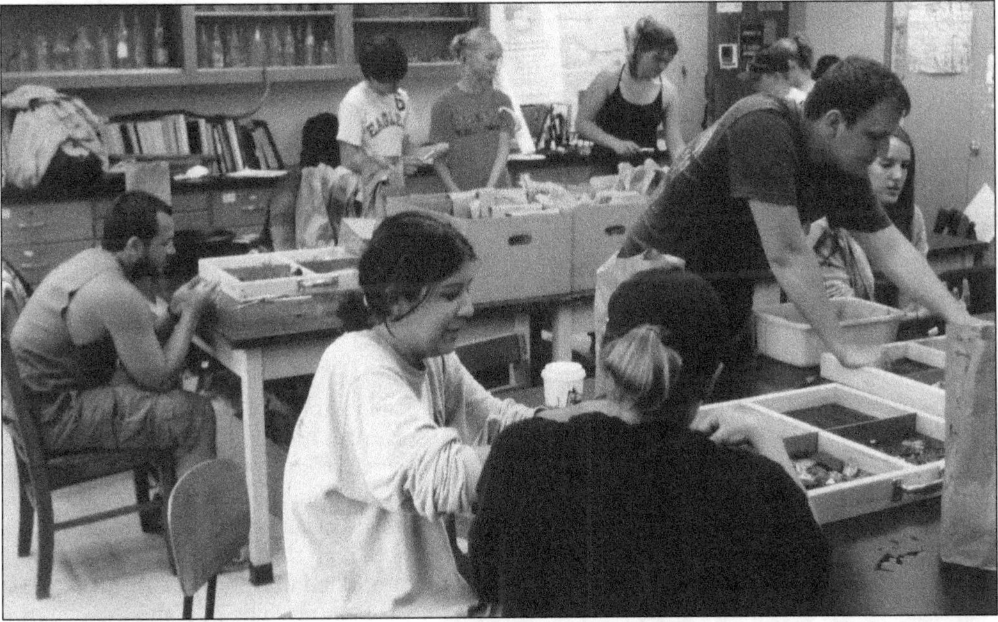

Artifact Analysis. In the IUPUI archaeology field school lab, students analyze and catalog their discoveries. While they found no original Walker product containers or personal household items that belonged to Madam Walker during their six-week dig, they uncovered broken dishes, medicine containers, beer bottles, and cutlery from as early as the 1870s and 1880s. (Courtesy of Paul Mullins and Lewis Jones.)

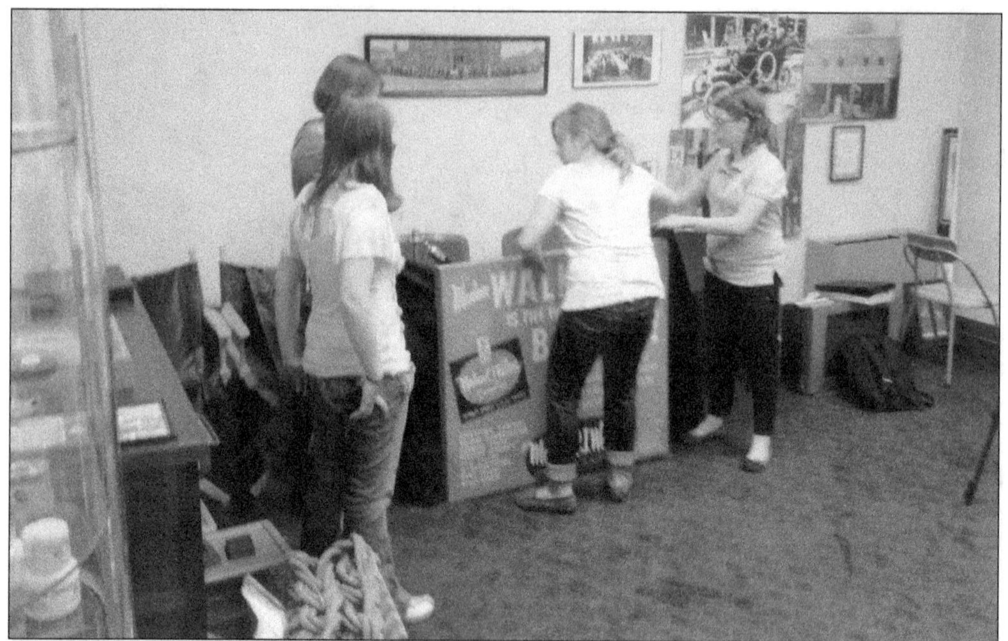

Preserving the Legacy. Richard McCoy, an art conservator based in Indianapolis and IUPUI adjunct instructor of museum studies, led 13 graduate students in a semester-long course focused on the documentation and preservation of historic artifacts and ephemera in the Madam Walker Theatre Center in 2012. In the Walker Museum, students hang a 1960s-era Walker advertising sign. (Courtesy of Richard McCoy.)

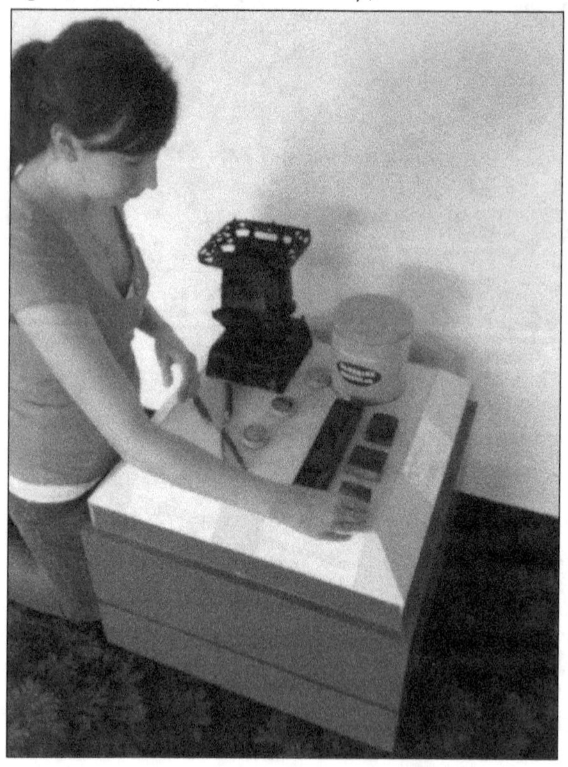

History on Display. IUPUI museum studies graduate student Megan Geurts arranges historic Walker Company materials in an exhibition case in the Walker Theatre Center Museum. She and 12 classmates catalogued materials already in the museum as well as items discovered in storage areas throughout the building. Their database of descriptions, condition assessments, recommendations for future care, and high-quality digital photographs will assist future researchers. (Courtesy of Richard McCoy.)

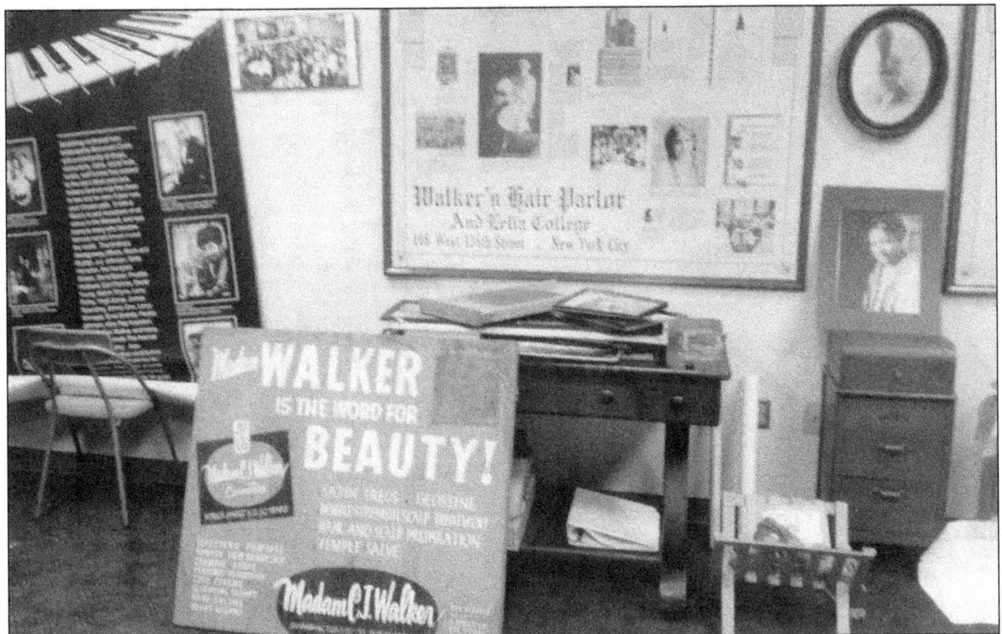

Work in Progress. To create historical context, the IUPUI museum studies class spent many hours learning about Madam Walker, early years of the Walker Company, and the Indiana Avenue neighborhood. While reorganizing this museum display, students established the provenance of several items including rotogravure printing blocks, a Baldwin upright piano, and the 1940s Hobart industrial mixer used to process the thick ointments sold by the Walker Company. (Courtesy of Richard McCoy.)

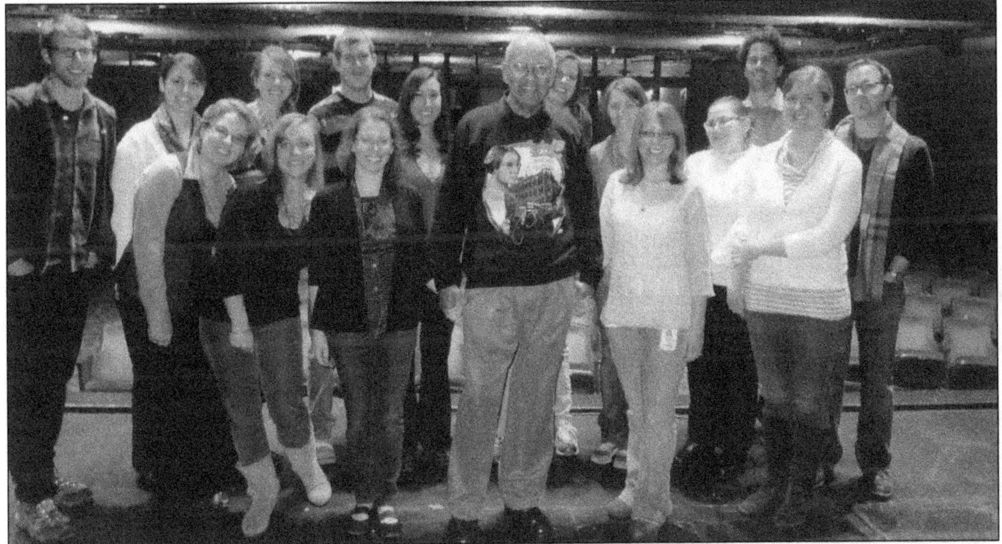

Mission Accomplished. By semester's end, Richard McCoy's class had explored the Walker Building from basement to roof. With Walker Theatre Center docent Thomas Ridley, center, are McCoy, rear third from right, graduate assistant Deanna Cundiff, and the class members Ariel Aurbach, Michael Barclay, Stephen Borden, Alex Carrier, Allison Cosby, Megan Geurts, Ashley Hays, Stephanie Hebda, Lauren Lucchesi, Kate Massman, Stephanie Michaels, Jenny Rigsby, and Jake Sheff. (Courtesy of Malina Jeffers.)

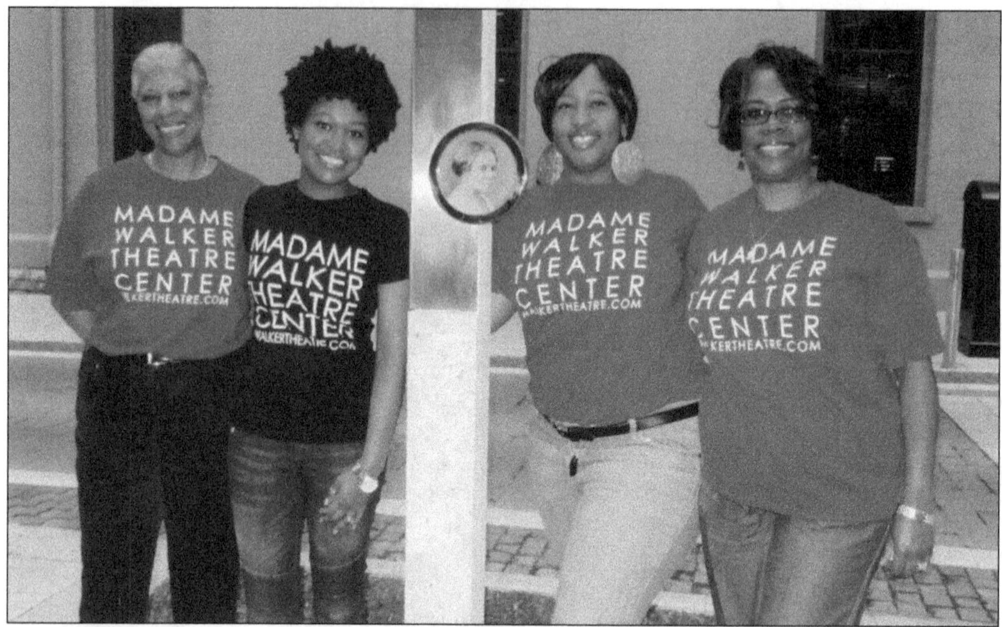

On the Case. In March 2012, Madam Walker was in the inaugural class of 10 famous Hoosiers whose likenesses were placed on pillars along Georgia Street near the Indianapolis Convention Center and Lucas Oil Stadium. On hand to celebrate were four Walker Theatre staff members: office manager Mary Kelley, marketing and programs director Malina Jeffers, project coordinator Sherrell Robinson, and rentals and events director Sherri Brown Webster. (Courtesy of A'Lelia Bundles.)

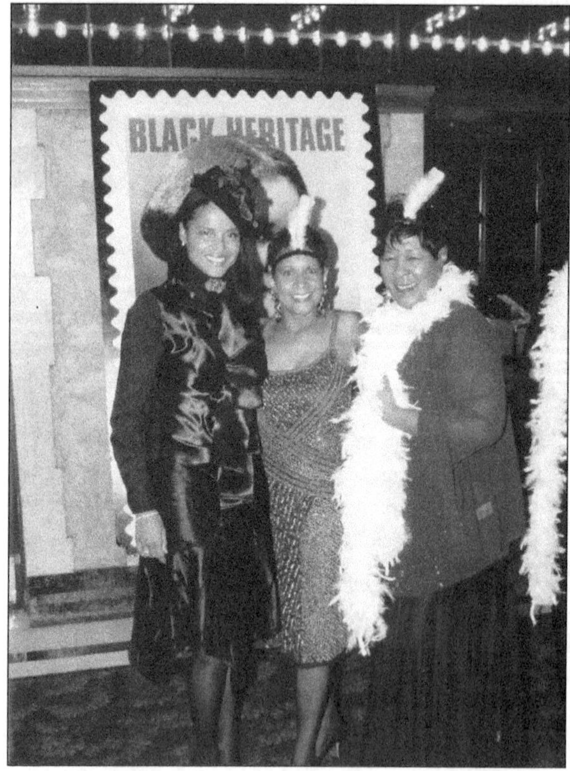

Walker Anniversary. Cynthia Bates (right), Walker Theatre Center president from 2005 until 2009, injected new energy into its performing arts programs and enhanced community and youth engagement. A former telecommunications executive and accomplished pianist-organist, she enlivened the theater with internationally known artists. During the Walker's 80th anniversary, she celebrates with actress and author Victoria Rowell (left) and A'Lelia Bundles (center), Walker's great-great-granddaughter and board member emerita. (Courtesy of Carl Black.)

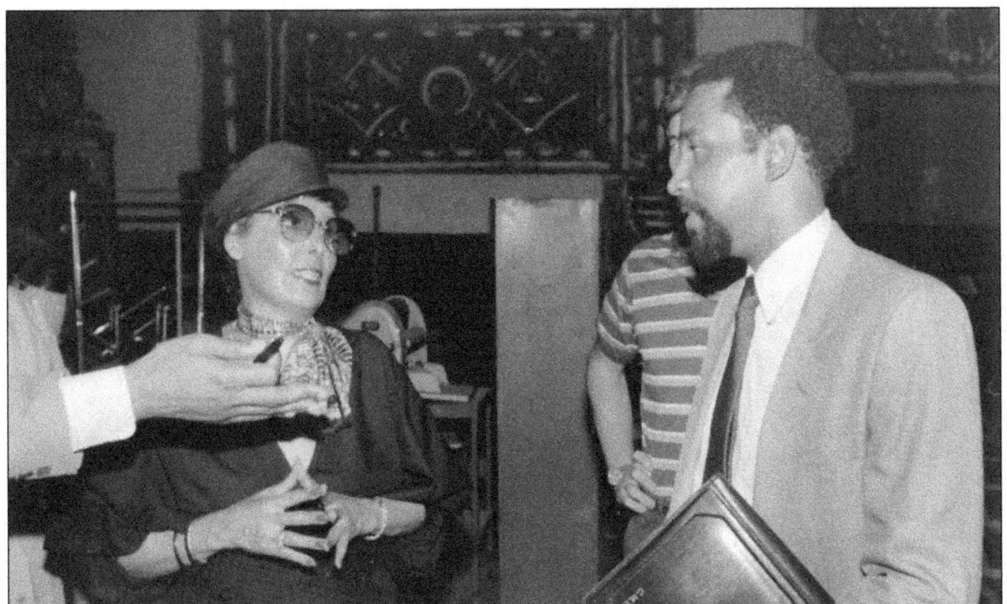

Diamond Celebration. Charles Blair, president of the Walker Theatre Center during the early 2000s, greets entertainment legend Lena Horne, who headlined the Walker's 75th anniversary celebration concert in 2002. A senior program officer with the Lilly Endowment during the early 1980s, Blair was among the Indianapolis citizens who helped lead the campaign for the building's restoration. He also was a board member during the 1990s. (Courtesy of William Rasdell.)

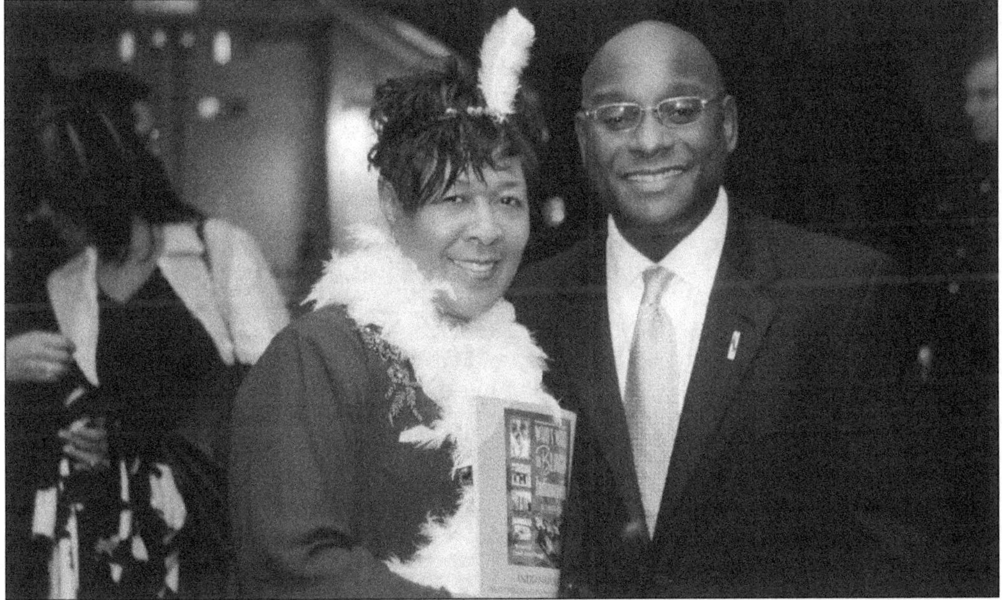

Above and Beyond. Former Walker Theatre Center president Cynthia Bates and former board chairman Orson Mason, who is a health care industry executive, kick off the Walker's 80th anniversary. During his tenure, Mason raised more than $250,000 for the organization acquiring a grand piano, computers, office equipment, HVAC repairs, a security assessment, and legal services through the support of Clarian Health (now IU Health) and his own personal outreach. (Courtesy of Carl Black.)

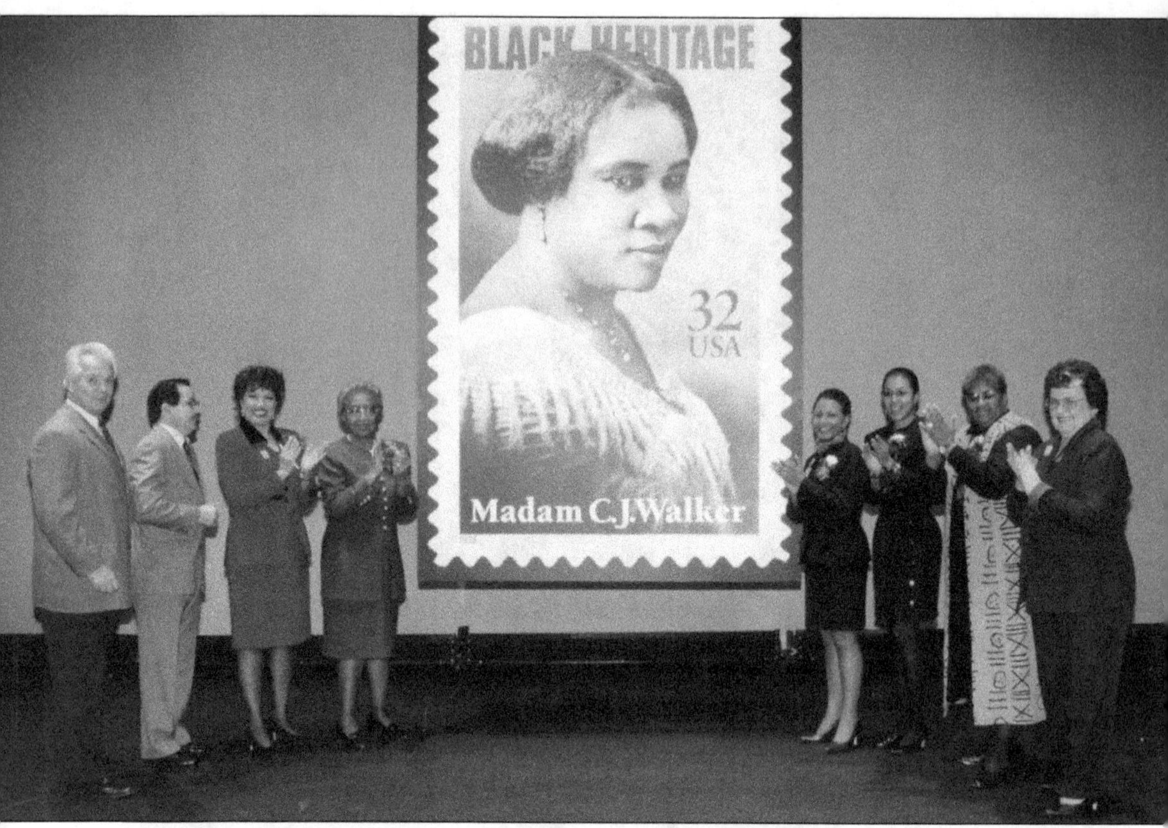

Stamp of Approval. In January 1998, Madam C.J. Walker became the 21st historical figure to be featured in the US Postal Service's Black Heritage Series. Walker's great-great-granddaughter A'Lelia Bundles (fourth from right) and Ambassador Harold Doley, an investment banker who owns Walker's home in Irvington, New York, worked together to persuade the Citizens' Stamp Advisory Committee to select Walker as only the sixth black woman to appear on a US stamp. After Doley introduced Bundles to US Postal Service governor LeGree Daniels, fourth from left, Bundles enlisted the support of Network, an organization of black women postmasters. She collected more than 50,000 signatures from cosmetologists, community groups and national organizations and endorsement letters from US senators Richard Lugar (R-IN) and Carol Moseley Braun (D-IL). First-day-of-issue keynote speaker was ABC News anchor Carole Simpson, third from left. Standing to the right of the enlarged stamp are Bundles; attorney Karen Lloyd, the then-Walker board chairman; Rev. Anne Henning Byfield; and an unidentified postal service official. The two men, left, also are postal service employees. (Courtesy of Walt Thomas.)

Eight

CAPTURING THE FUTURE
JAZZ ON THE AVENUE

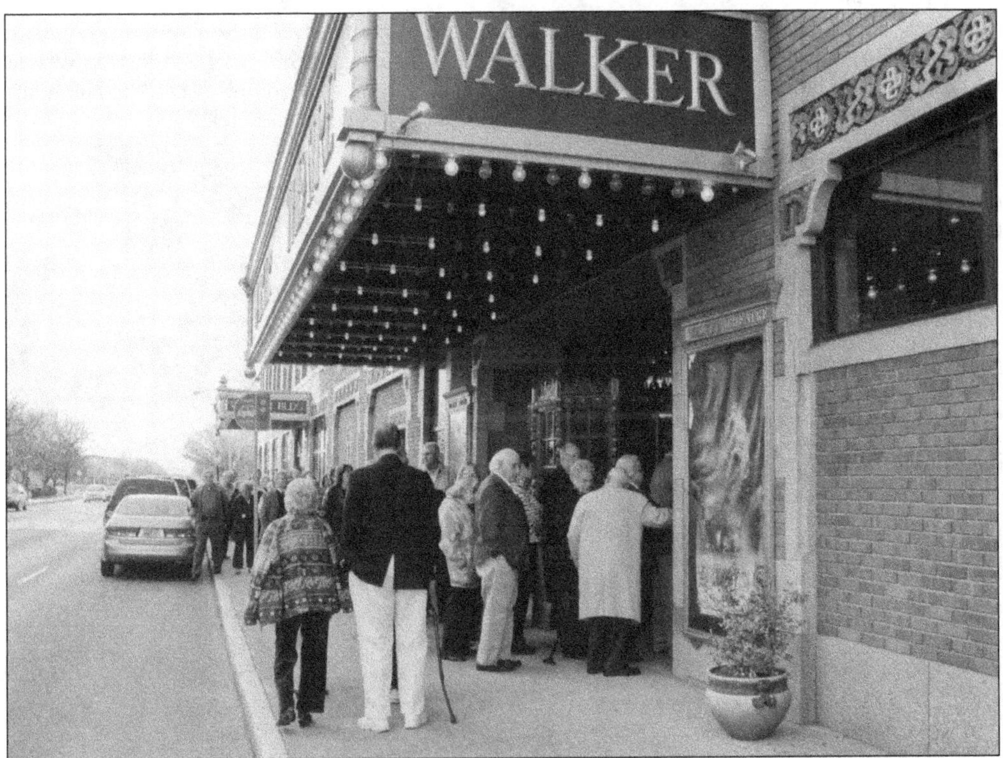

JAZZ ON THE AVENUE. In addition to hosting arts education programs for Indianapolis youth, the Madam Walker Theatre Center continues its role as a showcase for African American performers from jazz musicians and opera singers to dancers and actors while also welcoming a multicultural array of talent. Chinese acrobats, Flamenco guitarists and dancers, Russian ballerinas, and African drummers have appeared on the stage in recent years. (Courtesy of Carl Black.)

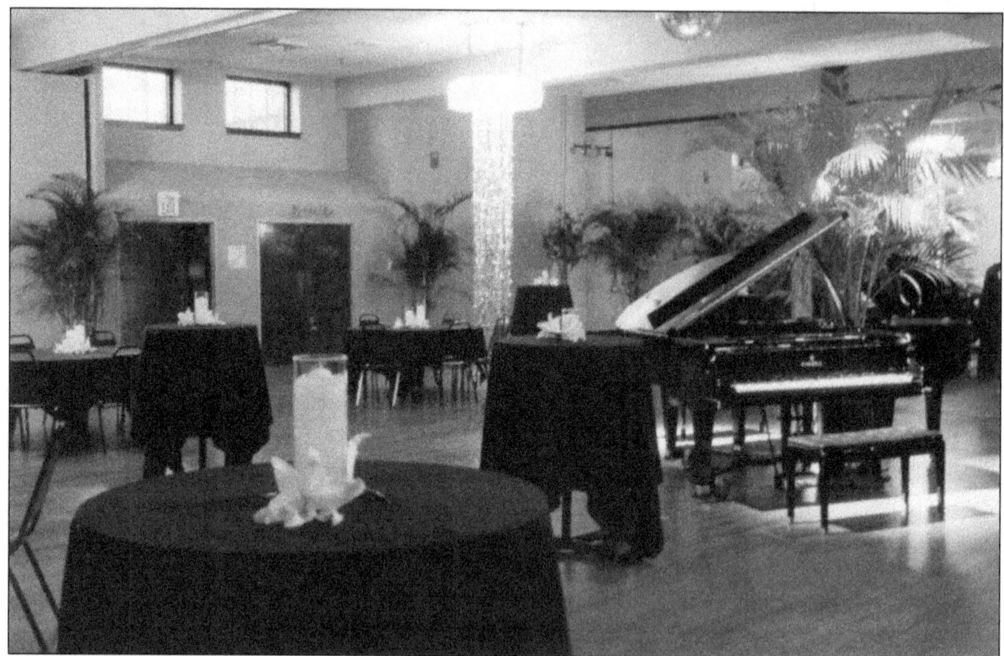

This Joint Is Jumping. The Grand Casino Ballroom is home to Jazz on the Avenue, a monthly concert featuring Indianapolis jazz musicians, whose presence recalls the era when Indiana Avenue nightclubs helped launch the careers of guitarist Wes Montgomery, trumpeter Freddie Hubbard, trombonist J.J. Johnson, and bassist Leroy Vinnegar. (Courtesy of Carl Black.)

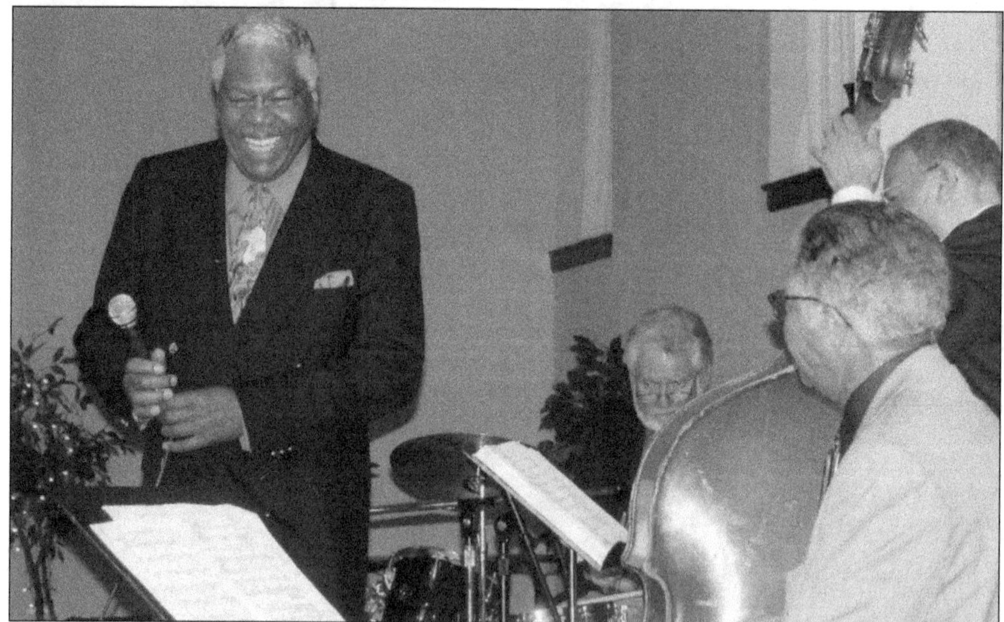

Smooth Croon. Longtime Indianapolis resident Everett Greene is a Jazz-on-the-Avenue favorite. His smooth deep baritone has been compared to the voices of Billy Eckstine and Arthur Prysock "without copying them" by All-Music.com. As a young man, he sang doo-wop but began to enjoy local jazz musicians like Wes Montgomery and Freddie Hubbard after moving to Indianapolis in the mid-1950s. (Courtesy of John Hurst.)

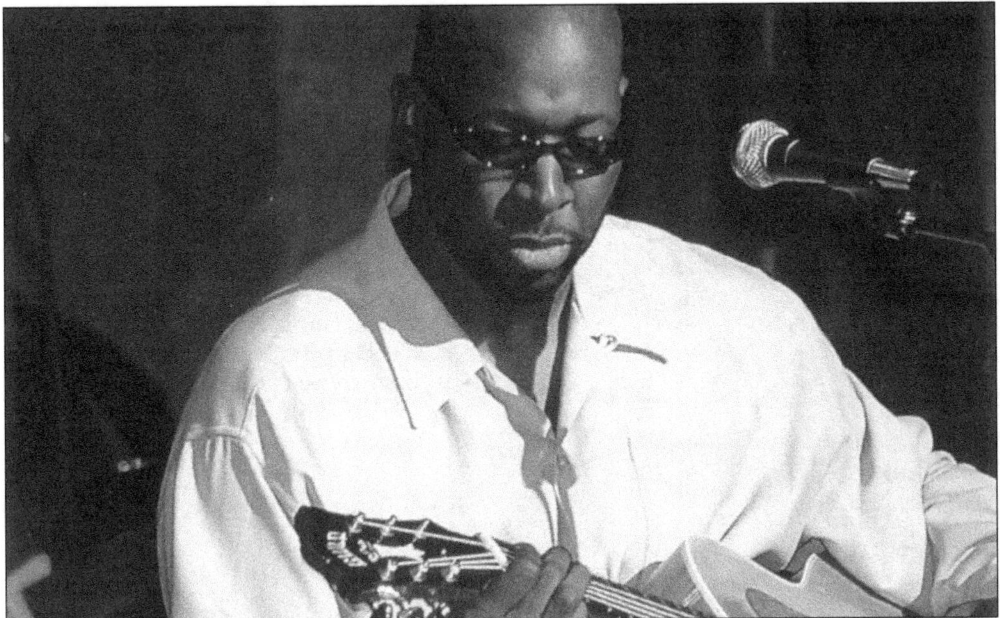

Music Man. Bass guitarist Wayman Tisdale first won the hearts of Hoosiers as an Indiana Pacers center and power forward. After his retirement from professional basketball in 1997, it was his smooth jazz sounds that made Indianapolis fans continue to welcome this Oklahoma native as an adopted favorite son. Before his death in 2009, his appearances at the Walker always were standing room only and standing ovation guaranteed. (Courtesy of John Hurst.)

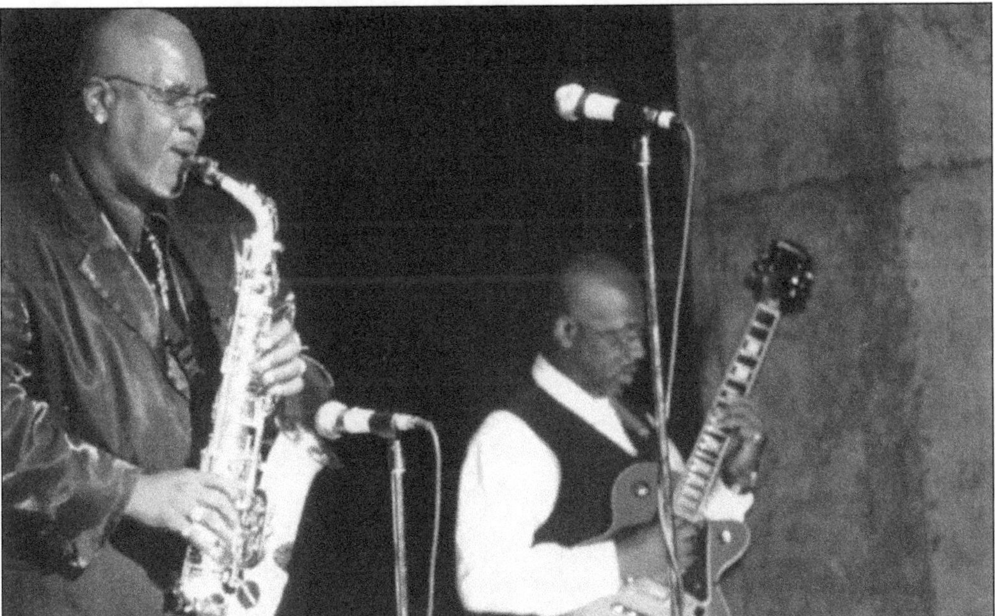

Sizzlin' Sax. Saxophonist Gregg Bacon, an Indianapolis native, taught himself the technique of simultaneously playing three saxophones. This versatile musician has opened for Alex Bugnon, Aretha Franklin, Indianapolis native Kenneth "Babyface" Edmonds, John Mellencamp, and the O'Jays. He also has performed as a featured guest with the Indianapolis Symphony Orchestra. Guitarist James Simmons joins him on the Walker stage. (Courtesy of John Hurst.)

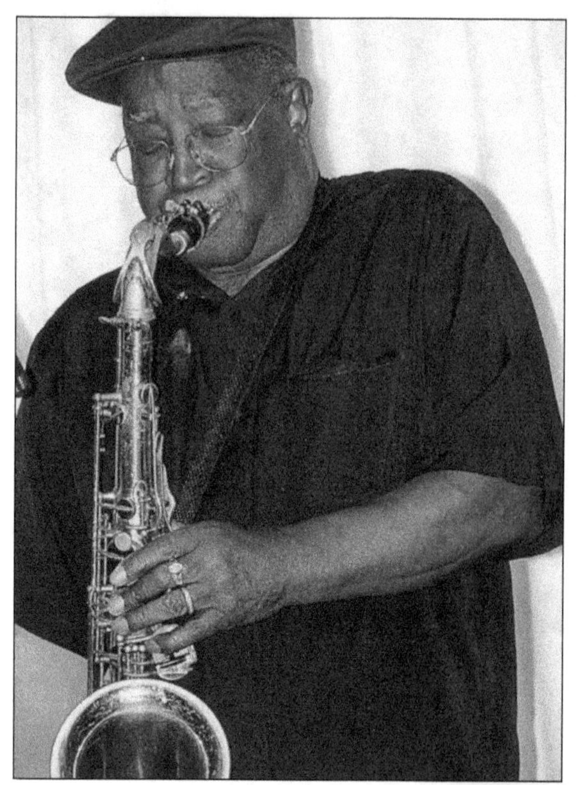

Hometown Favorite. The sounds of Alonzo "Pookie" Johnson's saxophone helped define the Indiana Avenue jazz scene of the 1950s. A graduate of Crispus Attucks High School, he was a member of the US Army Air Force's band during the mid-1940s. Back home in Indianapolis, he played with guitarist Wes Montgomery, appearing on Montgomery's first album, *Fingerpickin'*, with Freddie Hubbard and Montgomery's brothers Buddy and Monk, in 1957. (Courtesy of John Hurst.)

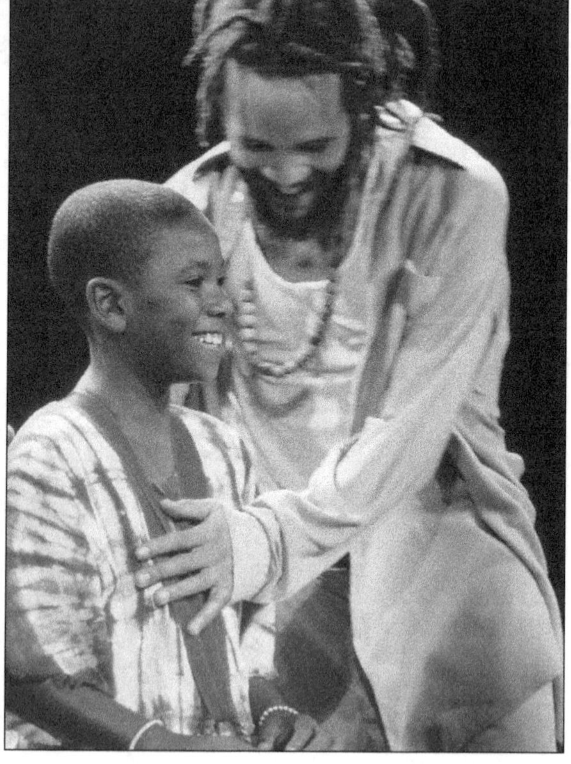

Master and Mentor. Savion Glover, heir to Gregory Hines and the long tradition of master tappers, appeared in "Classical Savion" at the Walker on his 33rd birthday in November 2006. Backed by Otherz, his jazz quartet, and a 10-piece string ensemble, he tapped, contorted, slid, and exploded across the stage to Vivaldi, Bach, and Mendelssohn. In August 2007, he returned to teach a dance intensive for young tappers. (Courtesy of John Hurst.)

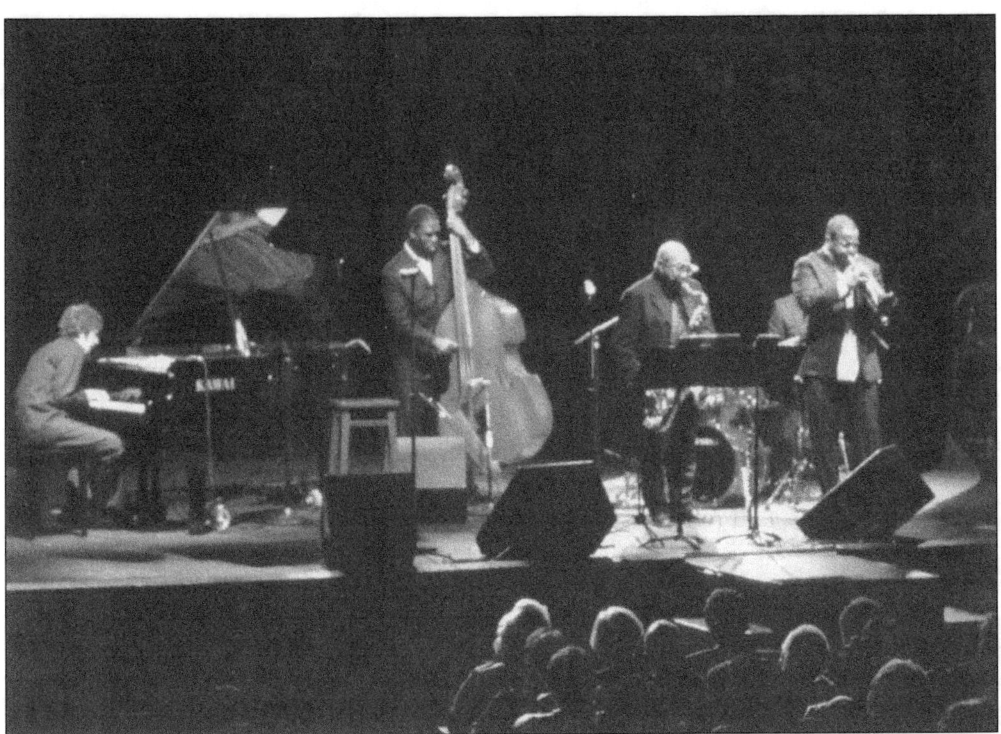

Mellow Mood. The Monterey Jazz Festival's 50th anniversary all-stars, featuring trumpeter Terence Blanchard, saxophonist James Moody, pianist Benny Green, bassist Derrick Hodge, and drummer Kendrick Scott, made a stop at the Walker Theatre in March 2008 as part of a 10-week, 54-city tour. An annual Walker tradition that always draws a sell-out crowd, Monterey Jazz Festival (MJF) returned in March 2013 with vocalist Dee Dee Bridgewater. Photographed here in 2010 during her Walker Theatre debut for Indy Jazz Fest, she was joined in 2013 by bassist Christian McBride, drummer Lewis Nash, trumpeter Ambrose Akinmusire, saxophonist Chris Potter, and a returning Benny Green. (Courtesy of John Hurst and Carl Black.)

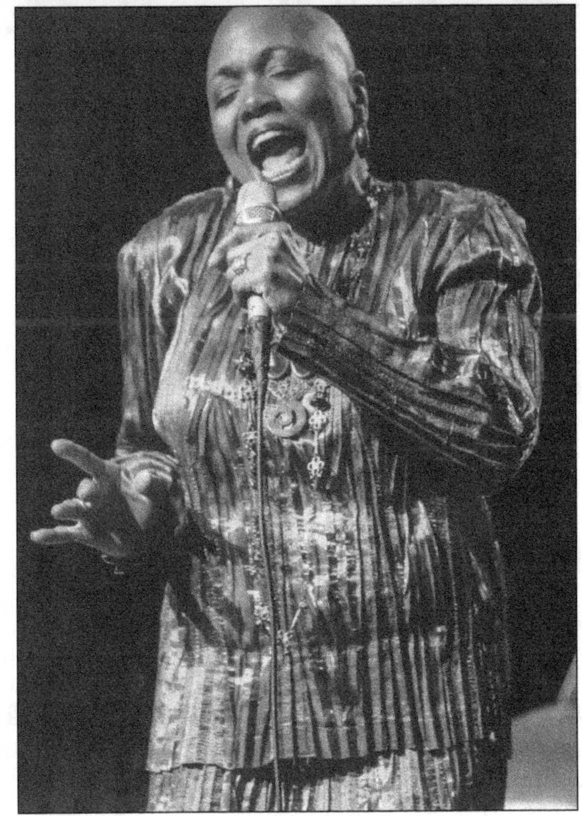

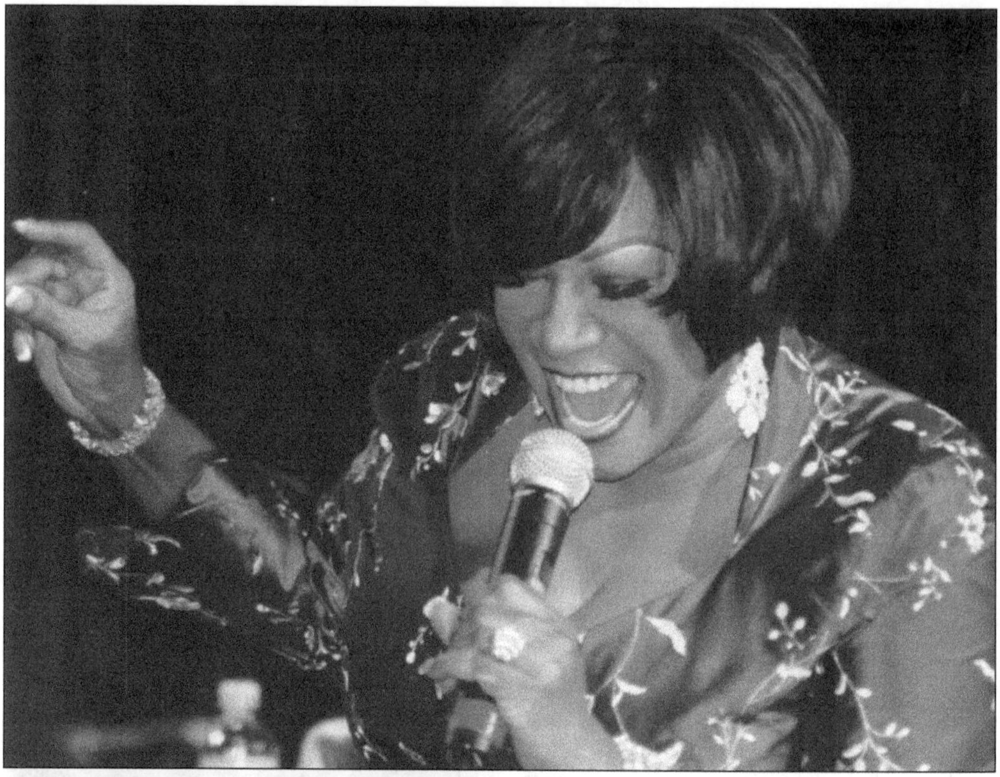

Crowd Pleaser. Grammy Award–winner, actress, and author Patti LaBelle rocked the 943-seat Walker Theatre from the front row to the balcony during the 80th anniversary celebration in November 2007. In the dressing room after the concert, she spoke of her admiration for Madam Walker. (Courtesy of Carl Black.)

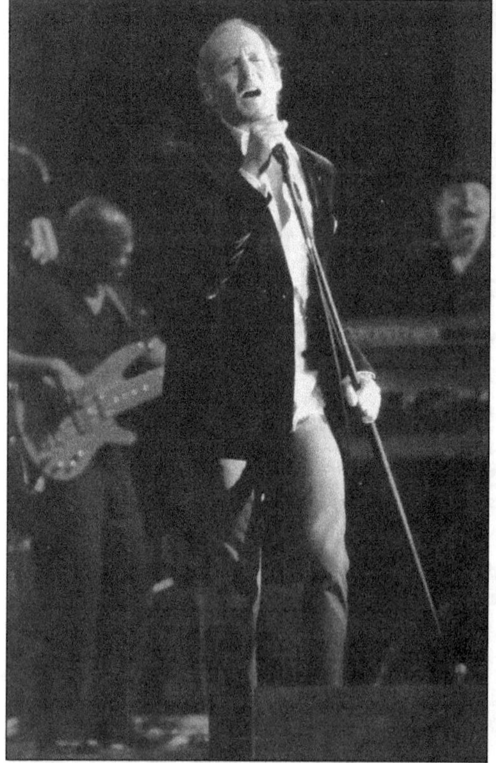

Love Songs and More. Singer-songwriter Michael Bolton—who has sold more than 53 million albums—appeared at the Walker Theatre in December 2008, during a three-year period that saw Ramsey Lewis, Kenneth "Babyface" Edmonds, Kirk Whalum, Smokey Robinson, Will Downing, Wynton Marsalis, Lalah Hathaway, After 7, Gerald Albright, Vesta, and Brian Culbertson take the stage. (Courtesy of Carl Black.)

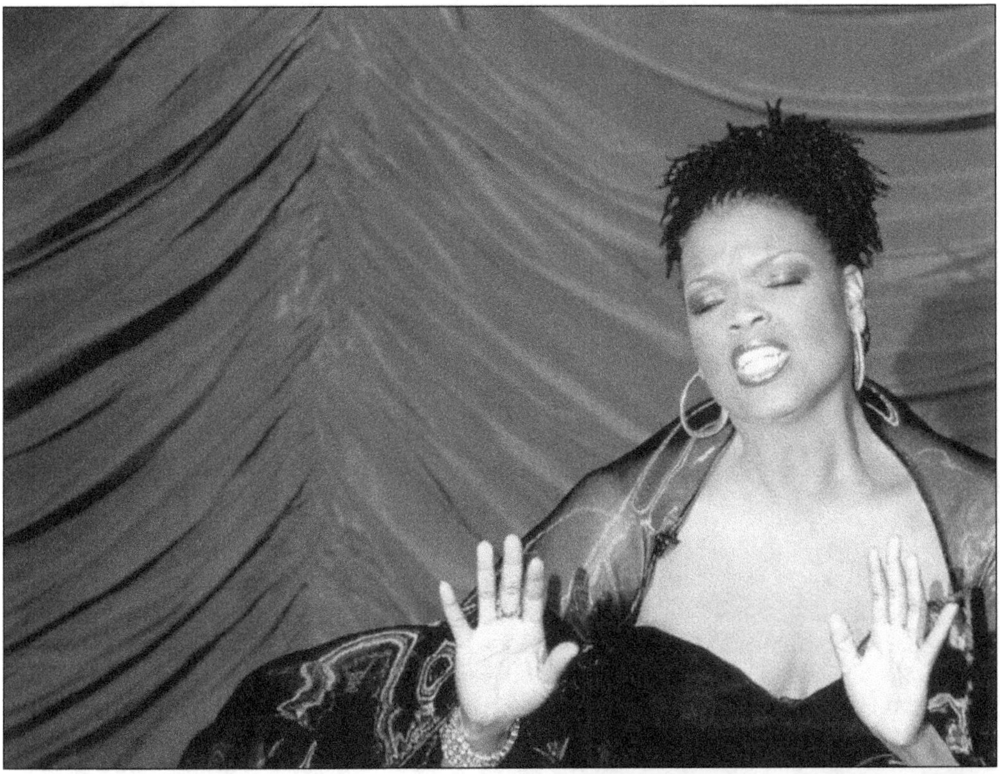

International Star. Dramatic soprano Angela Brown has wowed opera lovers in concert halls from Capetown and Shanghai to Paris and Moscow, but there is no place like home for this Indianapolis native, who always is warmly welcomed when she performs at the Walker Theatre. After her 2004 New York Metropolitan Opera debut in *Aida*, one reviewer gushed, "She combines a potent, dusky lower register with a striking ability to spin out soft high notes of shimmering beauty." A skilled interpreter of African American spirituals, Brown makes the roles she plays accessible to opera neophytes with humorous, down-to-earth commentary in her recital program, *Opera . . . from a Sistah's Point of View.* She chose the Walker Theatre as the setting for these publicity shots. (Both, courtesy of Roni Ely.)

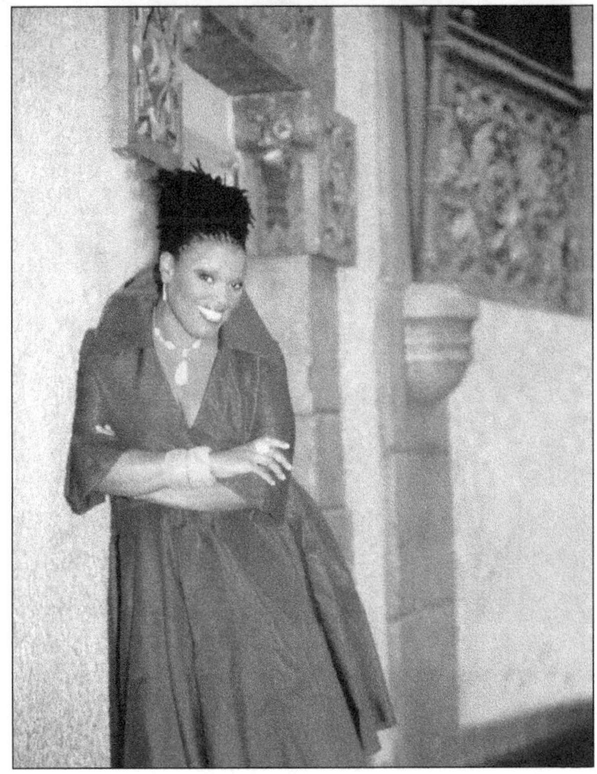

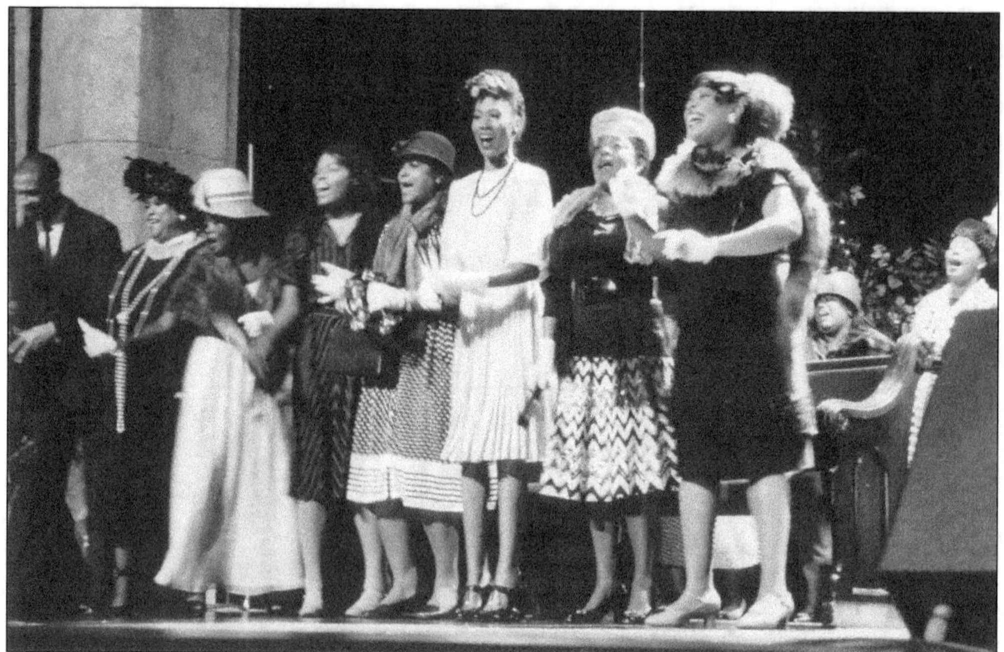

Christmas Classic. The Walker Theatre completed its 2011 season with a 50th anniversary production of *Black Nativity*, Langston Hughes's retelling of the birth of Christ with an all-black gospel-singing cast. Walker staff member Sherri Brown Webster directed the volunteer community theater cast to the delight of three packed houses. (Courtesy of Walker Theatre Center.)

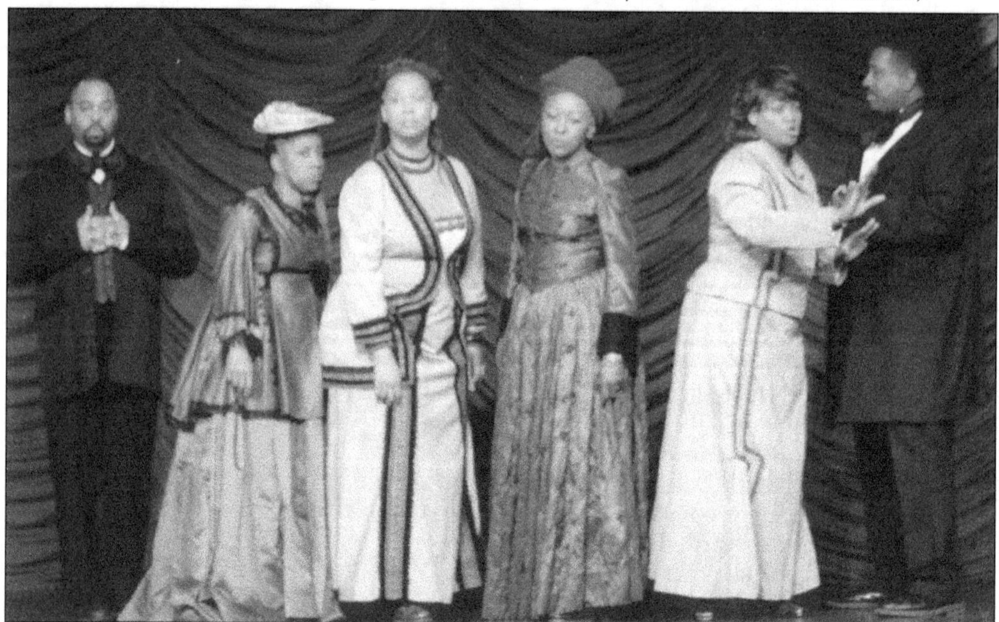

Back in Time. In stirring performances, the Freetown Village Singers interpret the meaning of old Negro spirituals. Based in the Walker Building, Freetown Village—a touring troupe founded by Ophelia Wellington in 1985—is a living history museum that brings to life the experiences of 19th-century African American residents of Indiana through theater, storytelling, and music. (Courtesy of Walker Theatre Center.)

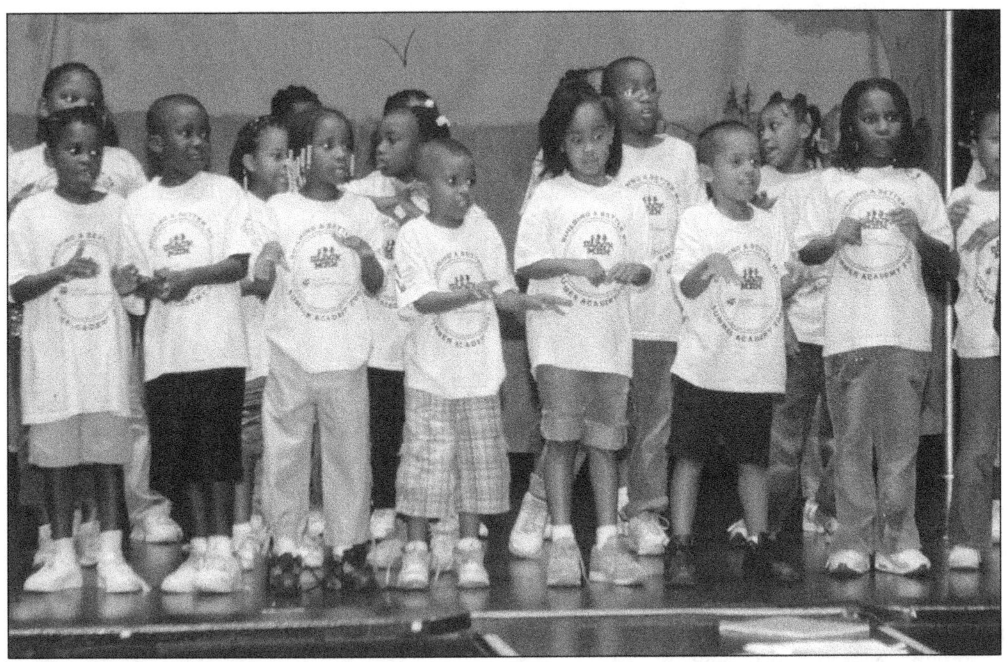

Kamp Kuumba. Since the 1987 launch of its Youth-in-Arts program, the Walker Theatre Center has nurtured arts appreciation in hundreds of Indianapolis children in all-day summer programs by exposing them to dance, theater, visual art, and vocal instruction. Former Walker Theatre president Terry Whitt Bailey founded Kamp Kuumba in 2011. (Courtesy of Carl Black.)

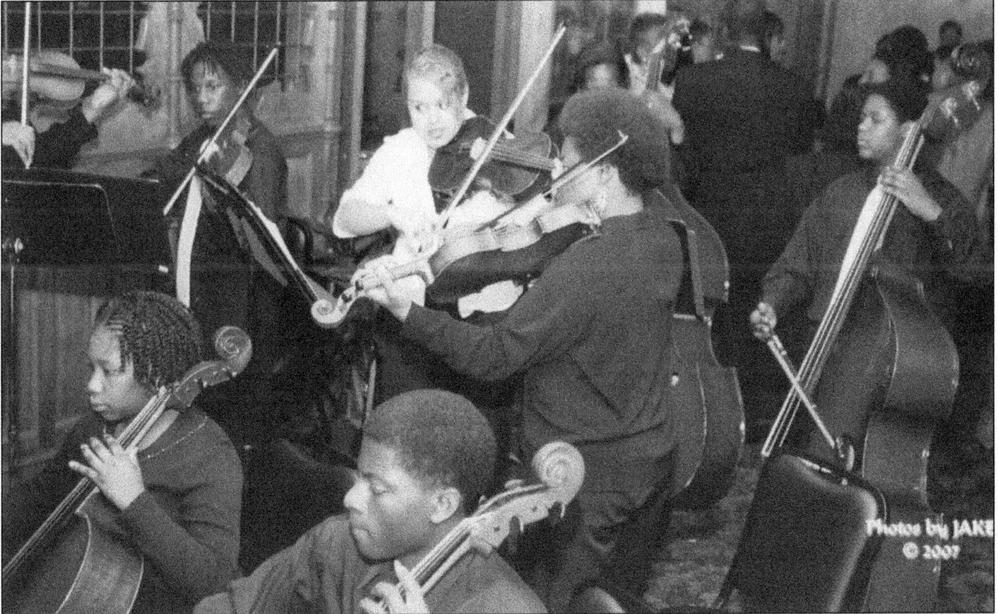

Next Generation. Conducted by Betty Perry, the Metropolitan Youth Orchestra—a youth and family development program of the Indianapolis Symphony Orchestra—has had a long partnership with the Walker Theatre. Since 1995, Perry has nurtured more than 100 students a year with an emphasis on self-confidence and academic excellence as well as music appreciation and skills. (Courtesy of Carl Black.)

Bibliography

Bundles, A'Lelia. *Madam C.J. Walker: Entrepreneur.* New York: Chelsea House/Infobase, 2008.

———. *On Her Own Ground: The Life and Times of Madam C.J. Walker.* New York: Scribner, 2001.

Byrd, Ayana and Lori Tharps. *Hair Story: Untangling the Roots of Black Hair in America.* New York: St. Martin's Press, 2002.

Giddings, Paula. *When and Where I Enter: The Impact of Black Women on Race and Sex in America.* New York: William Morrow, 1984.

Gill, Tiffany. *Beauty Shop Politics: African American Women's Activism in the Beauty Industry.* Champaign, IL: University of Illinois Press, 2010.

Preservationist. "The Walker: Mixing Business with Culture." Historic Landmarks Foundation of Indiana, March–April 1989.

Koehn, Nancy and Martha Lagace. "HBS Cases. Beauty Entrepreneur Madam Walker." *Harvard Business School Working Knowledge*, June 25, 2007.

Mullins, Paul R. and K. Chris Glidden. "Grassroots Politics and Archaeological Engagement along the Color Line." *The African Diaspora Archaeology Network* www.diaspora.uicu.edu/news0308, March 2008.

Bolden, Clyde Nickerson. "Indiana Avenue: Black Entertainment Boulevard" Master's thesis, University of Cincinnati, 1981.

Peiss, Kathy. *Hope in a Jar: The Making of America's Beauty Culture.* Philadelphia: University of Pennsylvania Press, 2011.

Pierce, Richard B. *Polite Protest: The Political Economy of Race in Indianapolis, 1920–1970.* Bloomington, IN: Indiana University Press, 2005.

Rooks, Noliwe. *Hair Raising: Beauty, Culture, and African American Women.* New Brunswick, NJ: Rutgers University Press, 1996.

Thornbrough, Emma Lou. *Indiana Blacks in the Twentieth Century.* Bloomington, IN: Indiana University Press, 2000.

Walker, Susannah. *Style and Status: Selling Beauty to African American Women, 1920–1975.* Lexington, KY: University of Kentucky Press, 2007.

www.aleliabundles.com

www.madamcjwalker.com

www.madamwalkerestate.com

www.walkertheatre.com

About the Madam Walker Theatre Center

Now in its ninth decade, the Madam Walker Theatre Center continues to conjure the magic of a grand past when the Madam C.J. Walker Manufacturing Company was one of America's most successful black businesses and when its stage and ballroom anchored Indiana Avenue's social and entertainment life. A cultural arts center since its restoration in 1988, this National Historic Landmark strives to offer the best of African American performance arts, from jazz and opera to gospel and blues, while also welcoming diverse genres and audiences. Jazz on the Avenue's monthly jam sessions in the Grand Casino Ballroom still attract a loyal following and honor the neighborhood's musical traditions. Nationally known acts from Dee Dee Bridgewater and the Monterey Jazz Festival to the Vienna Boys Choir and the Dance Theatre of Harlem perform in its 943-seat African art deco theater, while talented visual artists display their work in the upstairs gallery.

Kamp Kuumba, the Walker's signature arts education program, welcomes 100 students each summer. For the city's annual Rev. Martin Luther King Jr. Holiday, community leaders, students, families, and elected officials assemble for a symbolic "Freedom Walk" to the Walker Theatre where they are inspired by a program of song, dance, and oration. In keeping with Madam Walker's entrepreneurial and philanthropic spirit, business and professional leaders are honored at an annual corporate luncheon.

Thomas Ridley, the Walker's resident docent, offers a window to the area's heyday with stories about coming of age in the neighborhood during the 1930s, 1940s, and 1950s. Whether he is greeting elementary school students in the theater or guiding international visitors through the small museum, he gives life to Indiana Avenue's rich history.

Beyond the Walker Theatre Center and Indianapolis, Madam Walker's legacy is celebrated in many ways including the ongoing preservation of Villa Lewaro, her Irvington-on-Hudson, New York, home; the Bay Area National Coalition of 100 Black Women's annual Walker luncheon in San Francisco; and the work of the Madam Walker Family Archives in Washington, DC.

www.ingramcontent.com/pod-product-compliance
Lightning Source LLC
LaVergne TN
LVHW081547100826
845153LV00004B/330

* 9 7 8 1 5 3 1 6 6 8 5 9 4 *